S0-AEQ-688

REVIEW OF NATIONAL LITERATURES

SELECTED ESSAYS (1970 – 2001)

ANNE PAOLUCCI

HENRY PAOLUCCI

Copyright © 2006 by Anne Paolucci

Library of Congress Cataloging-in-Publication Data

Selected essays from Review of national literatures, 1970-2001 /
byAnne Paolucci and Henry Paolucci.
   p. cm.
   ISBN 1-932107-20-7
   1. Literature–History and criticism. I. Paolucci, Anne. II.
Paolucci, Henry. III. Review of national literatures

PN501.S45 2006
809– dc22

2006046554

Published for
COUNCIL ON NATIONAL LITERATURES
by
GRIFFON HOUSE PUBLICATIONS
P.O. BOX 98
SMYRNA, DELAWARE 19977
griffonhse@AOL.com

Contents

Introduction

In the fall of 1969, I left the English Department of The City College (one of the best, at the time), where I already had tenure, to join the Presidential staff of St. John's University, New York, as its first University Research Professor — an offer hard to refuse, since it included tenure on appointment and allowed me to carry on independent research and writing without having to teach. I decided from the outset, however, to give time to planning some events and projects that would add to St. John's reputation as the home of a nationally famous basketball team and a highly-competitive law school. These included a series of TV interviews with editors of academic and other journals — *Magazines in Focus* — which ran for two years at prime time on Channel 31 and received "Notable Rating" in the *New York Times* for many weeks; special lectures to community groups; and standing in for the President of the University at fund-raising and other special functions. But perhaps my most important contribution was the launching, in 1970, of *Review of National Literatures*, a series I designed to promote what was then a pioneer effort: the expansion of comparative literary studies into a global context that would include the emergent and neglected literatures of the world.

It was a difficult task for reasons I have explained at length elsewhere, one that provoked many questions and few answers. I had no intention of indulging in or inviting debates about how to expand existing programs into a multicomparative spectrum (it was much too early for that) or how to find the material and human resources to carry out any plan that might surface. My aim was to provide a base that would give comparatists some idea of the many "other" literatures out there, beyond the major European ones that, since the middle of the 20th century and through the efforts of scholars like René Wellek, had been brought together as "comparative literature," or, more properly, "comparative literary studies." My goal was limited to providing basic working materials about some of the "new" or "forgotten" literatures, critical assessments by experts recognized in the field (no actual texts or translations of major works were included) that would eventually help design expanded programs.

There were objections, much speculation, even ironic comments about the use of the plural for "literatures" in the title of the series I proposed. My own commitment was firm, but not without uncertainties about how to proceed. I realized that I was not qualified to prepare such volumes on my own (although at the time I had already ventured into a number of new areas). I recalled that there had been much criticism when "comparative literary studies" first were introduced, dire warnings about the danger of losing the sharp focus and depth of research associated with the study of the individual European literatures (French, German, Italian, Spanish), of having to learn more than one foreign language and culture: the comparatist — many had predicted — would end up skimming the surface. Such fears proved unfounded; I had to make sure my project would also survive. I was optimistic, since the situation had changed drastically in the interim.

By 1970, the mandate for greater global awareness had triggered dramatic changes in all fields of studies. Comparatists soon succumbed to the lure of novelty, but it became evident just as quickly that enthusiasm was not enough to overcome the difficulties inherent in the new agenda. Introducing a large serving of unfamiliar and exciting authors in the familiar menu of "comparative literary studies" livened things up for a while but the result was a large bellyache.

To begin with: the emergent and neglected literatures that had gained interest fell into "clusters" that in many cases did not share the common Western legacy enjoyed by "Comparative Literary Studies"; some alphabets were totally unrelated to anything in the Western tradition (e.g. ideographs, even the more modern scripts of China and Japan), and many of the "new" literatures had very little in common with the priorities and critical language of the literatures in the Western spectrum.

Predictably, the effort to expand along new lines was confused: at best, arbitrary; chaotic at its worst. In many places, courses were designed by eager professors who had developed an esoteric interest in a particular subject or author, but when they moved elsewhere or retired they left a vacuum, since no one else was available to teach that particular course. I remember quite a few examples of this kind of futile effort on the part of colleagues. What was needed were modest but carefully structured pilot programs that could be duplicated, enlarged, and adjusted on a continuing basis, assessed and evaluated periodically. That has not happened. We are still struggling with basic definitions. The enticing new offerings on many campuses are for the most part still quirky, still arbitrary, still isolated.

My own experience produced many questions but few answers. In due course, I came to realize that expanded programs, with access to translations and special lecturers, were possible theoretically but virtually impossible to implement without a concerted and large effort on the part of colleges, universities, and special centers in any one area. I saw New York as an ideal testing ground for a first attempt at expanded programs, with the Middle East Institute at New York University and the center for Japanese and Chinese studies at Columbia contributing experts in those areas and pooling their material resources for such a project.

I had ample opportunity to think about all this, in the thirty-one years in which I planned and edited the *RNL* series; but my original goal remained throughout enough of a challenge to preclude any large effort at consolidation, especially after CNL became an independent self-sustaining operation, and my growing involvement in its activities carried out in the midst of other university and personal commitments.

To allow time to seek out the experts I needed to help me plan each issue, especially those dealing with emergent and neglected literatures (about which I knew very little), and to get the series off the ground without serious obstacles, I planned the first three volumes around subjects I knew fairly well. The first featured Machiavelli. To insure high-quality papers, I held a two-day conference which drew well-known scholars like Leo Strauss, Giuseppe Prezzolini, Gian Roberto Sarolli, and Joseph Mazzeo. Their presentations became the contents of that first volume. The second volume was "Hegel in Comparative Literature," an unusual collection prepared with the help of Dr. Henry Paolucci, who was already known as a thoroughgoing Hegelian, and edited by a younger Hegelian, Frederich G. Weiss. The third featured Iran, an area in which I had access to a number of experts, and knew I could count on their help.

St. John's funded the project for several years, but in 1975 the University was forced to withdraw its support because of the financial crunch. After much debating, I decided to risk "going it alone." I set up an independent non-profit foundation, Council on National Literatures, as the "umbrella" for the series, raised membership fees realistically to insure publishing could continue as an independent, self-sustaining operation, announced that there would be one issue (rather than two) each year, and hoped for the best. Most of our member libraries — by then, *RNL* was in over 40 foreign countries — continued as subscribers, even with the increase in the annual membership fee. Around the same time, I started a companion publication, *CNL/ World Report* — meant to serve as an ongoing dialogue among comparatists about the future of the profession. It first appeared as a single-page quarterly sheet, quickly grew into a semi-annual pamphlet, and in 1985 became an annual volume. Both publications continued until 2001, when I redirected CNL into other areas.

In retrospect, the task was indeed a bold one. The common base and continuity comparatists had grown used to were suddenly threatened with literatures that had totally different alphabets, cultural roots independent of the familiar Greco-Latin tradition, a multiplicity of languages that no one person on earth could even hope to master. A striking example of the cultural and linguistic difficulties encountered (even though our articles were written in English), and aside from the large adjustments required in order to begin to understand, for example, the Japanese and Chinese literary mind-set, was the seemingly impossible demands of the indigenous literatures of Africa. Although some major African authors found ready translators for Englsh-speaking readers (and were therefore assured an international audience), the writings of most African authors often had to be translated into French or English first, then back into the other African languages in order to make them accessible to a wide African readership. A colleague in African studies once told me that there was no one anywhere in the world who knew all the African languages.

In spite of these and other roadblocks, CNL produced two series (about forty volumes) which had a major impact on literary studies here and abroad. When I decided to produce "samplers"of *RNL* essays, I realized that one volume was not enough. I finally resolved on three volumes. The present one contains a selection of essays by me or Dr. Henry Paolucci, or by both of us in collaboration. A second volume will carry selected essays focused on European literatures and authors. A third volume will "sample" essays on emergent and neglected literatures.

I hope these *RNL* "samplers" will help in some way to develop expanded programs, or to serve at least as an introduction to those literatures and authors still waiting for proper recognition in the academic arena.

ANNE PAOLUCCI
NOVEMBER 15, 2006

Multi-Comparative Literary Perspectives

Having watched the development of multi-national comparative literary studies, as an editor, for almost twenty years,[this article was written in 1990] and having participated in many professional discussions on ways and means to enlarge traditional critical disciplines to include cultures and national literatures not in the mainstream, I would like to put down some of my conclusions and tentative recommendations for the future. The present discussion reviews the need for larger more comprehensive studies of literature, discusses the vital call to recognize and support literatures as national voices expressing distinct cultural identities, and presents a plan which could be implemented on the college and university level to provide for a multi-literary approach to the discipline, identifying the vehicles and the materials that can be used for the purpose.

1. The State of the Discipline: Realistic Assessments

The term comparative literature has served for over half a century as a convenient label to describe a discipline which includes the major European literatures that grew out of the Greco-Roman tradition. Comparative study of French, German, Italian, Spanish, and British/English literatures as a meaningful aggregate became popular as the study of

Greek and then Latin began to wane. It was given a solid base with the theoretic formulations of scholars like René Wellek who — while encouraging such study, also warned, very wisely, against deliberate cultivation of an internationalist point of view which has the effect (as he put it) of promoting "an indiscriminate smattering, a vague, sentimental cosmopolitanism" that often mistakes the poverty of a national literature for its wealth. It is a warning that still applies, in my opinion, as we look forward to a restructured comparative literary discipline in which both the emergent literatures and neglected but more sophisticated ones are considered side by side in a systematic and organic world-wide spectrum.

Comparative analyses of individual works and authors will always have an important place in serious literary studies, and the discipline which has come to be known as comparative literature will certainly continue. (I must remark, parenthetically, that there is no such *subject* as comparative literature; there is only the *comparative study* of literatures.) But if vital comparisons between literary works are still a major source of literary critical studies, much has happened in recent decades to convince us that both the principle and the methodology behind such study need to be reassessed. Comparative literature no longer suggests *expanding* interests; on the contrary, it has become a restrictive discipline, well-defined, with its own special content and tradition. In the large multi-cultural reality of our time, comparative literature is a discipline among many. Its role has shifted slowly and subtly in many ways. It can still rightly boast of an unbroken tradition that has furnished it with methodological guidelines and critical principles often lacking in other cultural clusters; but it has, at the same time, tended to settle comfortably in its own assumptions, oblivious of its inner contradiction, particularly as other national literatures and cultures establish claims to "comparative" study.

It is equally clear that, presently, as it is structured, comparative literature cannot really do much in the way of promoting multi-cultural expansion. Its critical assumptions have a long and rich history, making up a tradition that should not be undermined in any way. But that very tradition, stemming back to Aristotle and Plato, makes multicultural communication virtually impossible, at least in the early phases. Where Aristotelian poetics have not had an influence, our Western approach to literature (as well as art and music) will seem arbitrary at best to others in cultures outside the traditional European spectrum. In this age of special area studies, institutes, special organizations and associations and journals dedicated to other cultural areas of the world, comparative literature with its long evolution but narrow European base no longer serves effectively as an incentive for expanding literary studies. Where new interests are introduced into the established format, they tend to appear arbitrary or esoteric and often prove short-lived experiments — in spite of the enthusiastic support of those comparatists who have ventured into new areas.

In the many special institutes throughout the country — on the other hand — emergent and neglected areas of interest are made accessible in vertical structures that cover the full cultural experience of a country or a region, including its history, sociology, art, religion, philosophy, anthropology, psychology, etc. as well as literature. In a self-contained cultural cocoon, Black African studies, oriental studies, Japanese and Chinese studies, Middle East studies, Scandinavian studies, etc. are offered to a relatively small scholarly audience. While comparative literature departments are too often limited to what is available to them within their well-defined area, making use, if needed, of the few scattered comparatists with special or esoteric skills (Dutch literature, Indian, etc.), there are fully-trained experts in institutes throughout our country who could easily be recruited for expanded programs in comparative literary studies. Networking to avail ourselves of what is already in place must be the next step in any kind of pilot experiment in multi-comparative literary studies.

In spite of what seem to many of us to be unnecessary delays in implementing a pilot program in multi-comparative literary approaches, it is also true that the United States has the richest variety of special institutes covering all bands of the cultural spectrum. Columbia University alone has over a dozen (several in the European sector alone, as well as the most prestigious oriental institute and one on Armenian translation); New York University has a fine Middle East Studies institute; The University of Texas at Austin has a world-renowned Black African

Studies institute and publishes one of the best journals in that special area: *Research in African Literatures,* etc. Together, comparative literature specialists and experts in the institutes could easily launch a pilot program for a systematic and carefully structured experiment in multi-cultural and multi-comparative literary studies.

The problems of texts in translation can also be solved easily enough: Professor Marilyn Gaddis Rose's Translation Center at SUNY/Binghamton (Aramaic to Zulu) and her affiliation with national organizations in this field, ALTA and other groups interested in promoting literary translations within the academic world, could furnish translations at cost for the kind of pilot project envisioned here. Commercial publishers, understandably, cannot be expected to provide such works which cannot compete in terms of sales with Nobel-prize-winning authors (often more international than representative of a particular national culture). Besides, commercially-published translations would cost too much for the purpose here outlined. Modest reproductions or computer printouts could do very well for a pilot project of the kind proposed.

In short, the necessary structures and expert-power for an effective networking of the kind here described are in place; the only thing lacking is a master blueprint for a low-cost, effective pilot program, easily expandable and transferable throughout the country.

Not all the expert-power need come from faculty in special institutes and area studies centers; there are in most of our departments of English and Comparative Literature faculty who have special interests and training in "other" literatures. This large and important core of experts has not been tapped effectively. One needs first to find out through a simple computer check what existing departments of English and Comparative Literature (and possibly modern foreign languages and classical languages and literatures) have available. Even a cursory glance at the PMLA listings under 2- and 4-year college and university departments should impress us. The obvious fact is: there is much untapped faculty expert-power at our disposal for implementing programs that include neglected and emergent literatures.

A survey of what is actually in place in our own departments, therefore, is the first order of business. Area specialists in the many institutes would provide the cultural backgrounds and whatever else is needed that cannot be found in place among comparatists. But we must proceed beyond re-aligning faculty and sorting out the materials (especially books and scattered monographs and articles) needed for a pilot project. Publishers too must be made to understand that so-called "world literature anthologies" as presently structured simply will not serve the needs of an expanded program. At a meeting of the Council on National Literatures some years ago, Dave Malone — then Dean of Humanities at the University of Southern California — opened the proceedings with these words:

> One of the ironies of our increased awareness as a nation of the richness and diversity of the different linguistic and cultural traditions throughout the world lies in our failure, to date at least, to reflect that awareness in how we deal with literature in higher education. For almost two decades the best and most widely used anthology for surveys of literature has been the World Materpieces, edited by Maynard Mack and published by W. W. Norton & Company. True, the several volumes are subtitled "Literature of Western Culture through (or since) the Renaissance." But the symbolism of the title implies a chauvinism, which most of us — including Mr. Mack and his co-editors — would deny, as well as the fundamental reluctance of literary scholars to admit into the established canon any literature outside the Western tradition.

Although we cannot rely on commercially-published texts, such as those found in Norton's *World Masterpieces*, for an expanded comparative literature program which includes works not in the familiar European mainstream, we should make publishers aware of our thinking in these matters, urging them to consider from time to time not some isolated translation of a Chinese or Japanese poet or a volume on Australian writing, etc. but a solid anthology of authors and works considered by the experts as the most characteristic of a given literature.

We in the United States have a great deal to reconsider and re-direct in the field of expanded comparative literary studies. But something should be said here, too, about the attitude of colleagues in other countries. In Australia and perhaps to a lesser extent in England also, university programs do not have much in comparative literary studies and as of 1980 few if any degree programs in the area existed. My visits to universities in Australia and my conversations and lectures on matters dealing with comparative literature invariably were received with disbelief and skepticism. Particular literatures should be studied in depth, in the one area, and research should be reserved for topics in that same narrow field. Of course, this approach — the same as the narrow in-depth research required for the traditional Ph.D. — is familiar to all of us. But anyone insisting in this day and age that such intense, narrow research is the only proper approach to scholarship (at the same time that multinational attitudes and world cultural exchanges are being encouraged) is fighting a losing battle. The world is perhaps too much with us, but it is filtering through in every way, including cultural world exchanges. Surely we should face the realities.

In countries like Turkey, comparative literary studies have just begun to be considered seriously. Again, programs as such are scarce; and the attitudes of scholars still are self-centered and ingrained in the old traditions.

Areas like Africa and India, however, provide a natural model for expanded literary studies, Both are made up of independent countries or states or regions, each with its own language, dialects, oral literatures, written texts — some in a highly developed literary context, others still without a formal alphabet. But whereas Africa is a composite of truly distinct countries, each with its own colonial background and history and dual culture, India is a truly integral cultural mosaic, with English as the accepted language throughout and the particular languages and dialects of the various states and regions developing their own literary life. India is indeed an excellent model for the kind of "cultural buttressing" necessary for integrating emergent and neglected literatures into restructured comparative studies programs — about which we shall have more to say in the third part of this paper.

An assessment of the realities of the situation would not be complete without a few words about our professional organizations and associations. They too reflect the apathy that has characterized our "comparative" literary studies over these last few decades. Even the prestigious Modern Language Association — the leader in organizing professionals in our field and promoting high-caliber meetings and publications — has still not addressed the need for new structuring along multi-comparative lines and simply takes on as excrescences the odd esoteric interests of some of its members. Perhaps this is, after all, the natural way to begin. Still, much more could be done by MLA and by the comparative literature associations in our country.

Journals too have an obligation to redesign their format to include — in a structured and organic way — writings about other literatures. Again, special issues exist and some are very fine; but what we sorely need is expanded studies in the particular areas we are all familiar with: — e.g. Shakespeare in a world context, perhaps a constant review of translations throughout the world (the Japanese are in the lead in providing us with such information), studies of productions in various languages, etc. How many Shakespeareans know, for example, that the Bard is read and performed in dozens of languages and dialects in the Soviet Union? And how much do we know about Japanese productions and their adaptations of *Hamlet* and other plays into their own traditional forms?

As editor of *Review of National Literatures* (in its 20th year) and President of the Council on National Literatures (in its 15th year), I have learned that comparatists can do a great deal to establish the critical balance between traditional disciplines and unfamiliar literary conventions outside the Western spectrum. In preparing representative, carefully designed overviews of literatures outside the familiar European core, I would discuss at great length with the special editor of a given issue certain matters, posing questions of interest to me as an informed comparatist *not* familiar with the literature under discussion. These questions followed a certain pattern and were for the most part essentially the same in every case. But what emerged in each instance was dramatically unique. And in the light of the realities that surfaced from such consultations with special editors, the volumes of *RNL* became useful mirrors of literatures and cultures that were to most comparatists inaccessible — partly because of ignorance of language, partly because of the priorities each of us must live by and with. In any case, the editorial questions taught me to be firm in principle, at the same time that flexibility was called for in the practical planning of seven to nine articles that would give us an "overview" and an informed introduction to a literature not in our own familiar mainstream.

The questions asked in the early planning stages of an *RNL* volume have been refined over the years. A sampling might be useful here.

* What historical forces shaped the literature? (In the case of Turkey, the Youth Movement of the early part of the century marks a clear line of demarcation between the old Ottoman traditions and a "new" national literary awareness. With respect to China and Russia — when those issues were being prepared — there was no possibility of cooperation with scholars of Mainland China or Russian writers, so long as editorial control of the volumes was in American hands. In "multi-national" Yugoslavia the big question — but are we not many distinct states and autonomous regions, each with its distinct culture and language? — had to be faced and answered. And so on.

* Who are the major authors? (Quite often the authors recognized within a country as the most important are not necessarily the ones who have established international reputations abroad [Nobel-prize winners, for example].)

* What genre seems to be the most important, historically, in the given literature; and how can this be explained? (Iran has favored poetry for many centuries; Turkey, drama.)

* What authors and works have gained reception outside the given country? (Patrick White, for example, is known abroad, but Australians do not regard him as characteristic of their literary output.)

* What foreign influences and authors have shaped the given literature?

* What critical histories and surveys exist in the literature under discussion? Are there critical surveys in Western languages? Are the native surveys known in the West? Have any of them been translated into Western languages? (This particular line of inquiry has been extremely useful in assessing the critical awareness of other national literatures and cultures. Some are still provincial and isolated from outside influences.)

* What major critical work — within the given literature or outside it — can be cited with profit in this context?

The answers to these questions usually have taken and still take weeks and months to sort out. In the end, each volume emerges according to its own inner laws — but *RNL* does manage to provide a "frame" which usually includes an introductory historical/literary/cultural assessment (basic for any cultural buttressing) and a "Bibliographical Spectrum" which is not a bibliography but an in-depth assessment of the critical surveys and literary histories accessible in our Western languages. Often a "Review Article" follows the "Bibliographical Spectrum," usually calling attention to the major but also often to the most controversial critical work on that literature. The rest of the volume is planned to provide a systematic, organic "overview" of the literature so that comparatists and others interested in literary areas outside the mainstream or beyond their particular areas can quickly learn some basic things about that literature. The volumes of *RNL* are intelligent "introductions" — let me stress once again — not exhaustive treatments of the subjects. I mention this because we have often been taken to task by colleagues who miss certain topics, authors, works, and who criticize us for not extending ourselves beyond our carefully-defined limits. Within those limits, others have recognized in *RNL* an excellent basic model for expanded comparative literary studies. The India volume of *RNL* proved extremely popular as such a model.

Critics have a right to criticize, and to be *negative*, where necessary, in assessing experiments like *RNL* or *CNL/World Report* (the continuing dialogue among comparatists and specialists in other areas on the ways and means of effecting a broader spectrum of comparative literary studies), but they cannot, or at least must not be permitted to call the basic moves. The Turkey volume of *RNL* incensed one colleague who wrote in to complain that the anthology of E. J. W. Gibb, *History of Ottoman Poetry*, should not have been mentioned at all, since it was so old (pub. 1900). I replied that it was still the only massive work available (6 volumes) and therefore of some use—until the writer or some of his colleagues issued a more modern survey. But such strong criticism is rare; on the whole the *RNL* volumes have been well reviewed here and abroad.

The experience with *RNL* and with *CNL/World Report* has convinced me that this multi-track approach — offering a model "overview" of a particular literature (*RNL*) together with the continuing dialogue about aims and

methods, new definitions, problems of translation (with
occasional samplings of poetry and fiction from outside the
mainstream), expanded programs and other aspects of the
important exchange that will determine more flexible principles and a more inclusive format (*CNL/WR*) — is the only
proper way to enlarge comparative literary studies. A third
series should be contemplated in due course: translations
of key works not easily accessible or out of print. I have also
found, over the years, that in working with *RNL* and *CNL/
WR* and in introducing some of the notions here set forth
in a doctoral course entitled "Multinational Literary Perspectives and Literary Approaches" my own views became
clearer and students were infused with new energies and
charged with fresh enthusiasm. Assumptions we had taken
for granted were subjected to close scrutiny and reab-
sorbed in many cases into a larger organic whole. This
pattern of "escape and return" has proved and will surely
continue to prove exciting and rewarding. As one colleague
and contributor phrases the oscillation between the known
and the unfamiliar:

> . . . if one of the objects of comparative literature is to
> identify what is universal to all literature (and so, in a sense,
> to all human nature), then one of its duties must be to set up
> its observation-posts as widely apart as possible — somewhat
> as astronomers fix the exact distance of the heavenly bodies
> by taking their sightings from opposite ends of the earth's
> orbit.

This same colleague — a renowned scholar in classical literatures and a superb translator of Greek and Latin
plays — puts forward a bold argument for the adoption of
classical texts, pointing out 1) the excellence of Greek,
especially, as a means of communication and an artistic
medium both in prose and poetry; 2) the value of Greek
literature as a "primary literature," rising out of its own
experiences and life and not from another literature; 3) the
capacity of Greek literature to formulate universal human
principles clearly and dramatically, shaping the language
for a variety of important functions, and 4) distance —
distance from the time in which we live and from other
cultures in the world.

A bold argument, as I suggested earlier, in an age
when Greek and Latin are almost totally ignored in schools
and colleges. Bottom line: the validity of such comparisons

cannot be ignored. Those cultures and peoples who assert themselves as unique emergent realities and put forward their literature — oral or written — as the expression of their total life must recognize in the ancient Greek experience the same striving for transparent and lucid expression, the same dedication to life, the same evolutionary processes. The argument has special force in our age, when so many emergent nations, whatever their degree of development, insist on asserting their "separate and equal station" within the expanding world community.

2. *Literature as the Key to National Identity*

The Greco-Roman experience can serve us well also as an introduction to this section of the paper. From that rich core, the great national literatures of Europe evolved and traditions were preserved in a unique organic arrangement in which diversity of languages was not an insurmountable obstacle and the common linguistic base served in a most effective way in the "escape and return" which defines the solid roots of the European literatures and their self-conscious emergence in their own image and shape.

The ghost of the Greco-Roman presence lingers on also in the notion of comparative literature as a single body of literatures derived from the classical core; but where new developments have forced a reorientation and new definitions have been attempted so as to include, in the traditional European core, literatures from other parts of the world, such efforts have proved more or less frustrating, and, more often than not, ineffective and abortive.

In this section of the paper I would like to note briefly some of the problems we face in attempting to integrate "other" literatures into the familiar European core, discuss some of the special difficulties in dealing with the literatures of Africa and India — the latter with its self-conscious linguistic diversity — and touch on the situation in Australia and the South Pacific generally.

* *Problems.* At the risk of underscoring the obvious, I must remind all of us that comparative literature, in the best sense of the term, recognized appreciatively the national origins of the major literatures in the European core; and when awareness of such origins began to fade in the effort to create an it "international" bridge between works and authors, when other considerations began to encroach, the

study of comparative literature lost its force and became a simplistic and arbitrary vehicle for studying and comparing works in isolation — and not always those works characteristic of a given literary culture. The strong features of the European literatures suffered erosion and what emerged was a collection of individual authors held together loosely in what may be described as an arbitrary international frame. Writers like Ibsen and Strindberg were easily fitted into such a scheme, since they were considered not as characteristic authors of Norwegian or Swedish literature but as representatives of "world literature." They had, or seemed to have, much more in common with O'Neill and Pirandello than with their fellow dramatists in Norway and Sweden. Noting this trend, René Wellek (who has done more than anyone else among us to promote comparative literature in its early and glorious years) warned, as we earlier noted, that the deliberate cultivation of an internationalist point of view had the effect of encouraging, as he put it, "an indiscriminate smattering, a vague, sentimental cosmopolitanism" that often mistakes the poverty of national literatures for their wealth. "The problem of 'nationality'," he insisted, "of the distinct contributions of the individual nations to this general literary process," will always remain central. And so, my first point is that comparative literature, as it came to define itself in the past half-century, cannot really be used as a model for our time, a blueprint for a larger spectrum. It had begun well, with its focus on national literatures, but then it faded into something else, quite the reverse, building as it were a high-suspension bridge over the assumptions of national political realities and concentrating ultimately on the literary event or on personality as ends in themselves viewed, from a cosmopolitan perspective, in superficial relationships.

A second difficulty is really a logical extension — or paradoxical inversion — of the first: we can learn a great deal from the experience of comparative literature as we turn to "multi-comparative" literary studies. True, the familiar base culture, the common tradition, has given way to so many different national literary voices in so many different phases of development, that a mere catalog of what actually exists may prove to be overwhelming even for the most sanguine of scholars. Like Columbus seeking India and coming smack up against a wall of islands, the new breed of comparatist seeking to enlarge the familiar sphere of comparative literature has discovered that the goal cannot be reached easily by studying the established literary maps. Aristotelian critical theory, Romance or Germanic or Slavic languages as linguistic core groups, general principles and disciplines evolved within comparative literary studies, simply will not work well in a multi-comparative spectrum, where literatures and languages have no vital interconnection in most cases. New untried routes have to be chartered, revised as often as necessary, so as to find a large organic plan that will work for multi-comparative literary studies.

One of the first things that must be done is to redefine and perhaps even discard the term "comparative literature." What the replacement should be is not altogether clear at this point: "other" or "Non-Western" literatures sounds condescending to some; "Non-European" is not much better. More important than an all-inclusive term to describe the larger spectrum, however, is the realization on the part of comparatists that the sophistication and long discipline of the European core literatures cannot be expected in literatures and cultural structures that range from highly-developed Sanskrit in India to Aboriginal and Maori oral legends in Australia and New Zealand. Emergent literatures and neglected literatures must be approached with the same professional interest, whatever their particular state of cultural evolution.

Professional interest will quickly reveal that certain cultural areas are in fact a mosaic of distinct and often unrelated national literatures. In Yugoslavia I learned quickly that there is no such thing as Yugoslav literature. There are states and autonomous regions that not only have their own languages and dialects but their own TV programs as well (often bilingual) — their own authors and cultural priorities and commitments. The tension between the rich mosaic of diverse peoples and traditions and national unity is a reality that cannot be ignored in presenting an "overview" of Yugoslavia's "multinational literature."

* *The African Literary Mosaic: A Challenge to Comparatists.* In the assertive posture of many of the individual nations of Africa we have one of the best self-contained examples of the kinds of difficulties we face in structuring multi-national literary studies. Africa is many languages, some without alphabets; it also has sophisticated writing in French, English, Portuguese — as well as oral works not yet recorded properly. Africa has authors of international stature, many of whom are bilingual and some of whom lecture and teach abroad. Africa has so many languages and dialects that no one expert (I am told by colleagues in the field) knows them all. Major works in one African language or dialect often have to be translated into English or French first and then back into other African languages, The colonial influence and political polarization have intensified the differences.

The colonial experience in Africa lives on in many forms — not the least of which are cultural and literary. For many perceptive writers that experience with all its excesses has now given way, in the inevitable political dialectic, to recognition of internal inefficiency and corruption. In many cases, Africans have themselves become oppressors of other Africans. And, woven through these realities is the large question of Pan-Africanism and its effect on the writers of Africa. Should African writers be marshalled to take up political and social themes as a duty, as a way of realigning forces and educating themselves and clarifying their position for the rest of the world? Or should they write as free agents, following their own creative drive and giving voice to what seems to them vital and important, as individuals?

But what exactly do we mean by African literature or literatures? Black Africa includes Portuguese Blacks as well as Nigerian Blacks. African includes Arab. Black is also Third World and that includes groups and national entities outside Africa.

How exactly does one begin to sift through the particularity of African nations and their literary expression? In Senegal, the French underpinnings are strong, the colonial experience has been assimilated culturally in that country's major authors. A poet like Léopold Senghor — recognized as a major Black literary figure — is accepted outside of Africa as a French writer, a disciple of Paul Claudel, just as much at home in France as in Senegal. How African is Senghor compared to Achebe or Mofolo? Or: how does one deal with the strong Arab strains in both the language and the literary forms which go under the name of Swahili? Writing about Kenya and Tanzania, Lyndon Harries notes that although in those two countries Swahili poetry is fully accepted as an African heritage, the continued Arab presence on the Swahili historical scene makes acceptance of the poetry on a national level somewhat difficult, to say the least. The best Swahili poetry is in dialect, he observes, and it loses much of its original purpose when transplanted to a wider scene, a larger environment. In addition, the relationship of oral literatures to established literary structures is in this instance a complicated phenomenon in which Arab melodic patterns still play a part. Creative writing in Yoruba owes not a small part of its development to the English presence which, as early as 1820, had begun to standardize oral expression and provide the impetus for a written literature. To what extent can Yoruba writing be said to be indigenous? Can the English base be ignored? And, culturally speaking, to what extent has the French or Arab or English influence — political influence — found its way into the life of these different groups? Or, to raise another, more familiar question, as Gerald Moser raises it: "How African is Afro-Portuguese Literature?" That literature is often ignored in assessments of African literatures, or, if not altogether ignored, it is easily dismissed on the grounds that much of it is inaccessible in translation. The very same question has been raised time and again wherever there is political polarization or stratification, as in Canada (to give another dramatic example), where there are two obvious political strains as well as half a dozen or more indigenous fervent national allegiances, racial and tribal voices. Even such a question as "Is There a Canadian Literature?" raises some very serious doubts as to our definitions and our limited political-cultural vocabulary.

Political complexities in Africa are mirrored in a variety of literary efforts toward self- definition. Or, from the opposite direction: literary and linguistic expression reflects national- political postures. These postures tell us a great deal about the difficulties of assessing the African experience as a whole. What Bernth Lindfors says about the literatures of West and East Africa holds, in a general sense, as a pattern, for most of the African nations: a first or assertive phase — illustrated best perhaps by Achebe's now-famous novel *Things Fall Apart* — the early phase of anti- colonialism and the destructive effect of foreign control on the African continent; followed by a second phase, looking to the present, to the immediate problems of Africa, and in which turning back for self-justification is discouraged; and then, these two — what Lindfors calls the Nationalist Phase and the Reformist Phase — give way finally to what he calls in his analysis "Local Colour Literature" which means a settling down to what is characteristic, unique, different, *sui generis*, the particularized experience of a people, that which makes it distinct from all other such experiences and expressions. Yet, even in these obvious dialectical terms of "escape and return," of distance and proximity, the realities are not that easy to grasp. For instance, in each of those phases we must come to terms with the stratification, the fossilization if one prefers, of older superimposed cultures, both African and non-African. In every nation we must raise the question of whether or not self-consciousness has indeed become "identity." And, in the struggle toward that identity — a struggle aptly perceived as the effort to express "local colour" — how much have non-African literatures or multinational Pan-African realities come into play? How "local" can "local colour" be in African nations that have become aware of themselves as a mosaic and of the rest of the world as somehow intimately involved in their own search for freedom, both political and literary?

In many nations the local governments have displayed many of the disturbing tendencies formerly associated with European-colonial oppression. And many African writers have acknowledged this sobering reality, especially in their new literature of local colour. What the Africans have learned in many cases — and the experience of Kenya is perhaps the model of what must happen in the dialectical movement toward self-awareness and true freedom — is that they cannot escape their past without damaging their future; their literature must reflect, in final analysis, both the dualism itself of escape and return and the self-awareness and resolution of that dialectic in terms of a true identity. In Kenya, the first great leader of the people, long imprisoned then freed when the country was given autonomy and independence, did not retain his earlier political posture of aggressive confrontation against the foreign oppressor once he assumed real power. Once established in the responsibility of autonomous government, he began to seek *rapprochement* with the former rulers and for this he was criticized and lost much of his earlier support. What many of the African nations have learned or are in the process of learning is that, at the top, the posture changes as the responsibility takes new shape. The first generation of leaders, the men who remained outside and achieved status politically by infiltrating the established ground, must — by means of a historical sequence that is predictable — give way to a second generation of leaders whose task, in this second phase, is one of solidifying the gains achieved. These leaders are inside looking out; and their image is understandably less dramatic but at the same time perhaps infinitely more important for the future of their countries. The large exception is Gandhi in India. Not only did he grasp the shifting roles he must play; he also adjusted to them with tremendous insight into the changing situation and without sacrificing basic principles and spiritual (as well as social and political) commitments.

* *Gandhi and the Dream of Linguistic Unity.* The figure of Gandhi will always loom large in the history of India's struggle for unity in diversity; a certain basic consistency in his political ideology made him at the same time flexible and true to principle. His is the most interesting canvas for our discussion: Yugoslavia has in a way resisted cultural integration, perhaps because the component nationalities are not many and see one another clearly across common defenses; Africa, on the other hand, is perhaps too large to feel the pressing need for an experiment in cultural diversification supported by political unity. In India, Gandhi's genial efforts to bring all groups into a common core, through language primarily, deserves to be distinguished from all other such experiments.

Gandhi succeeded in deliberately reversing existing attitudes, consciously promoting Hindustani in both the Nagari (Hindi) and Arabic (Urdu) scripts as the language of a newly-independent and potentially unified India, and using that language as the cement for a new India in which the various groups could accept the unity of the whole without giving up any of the separate national and cultural identities. I have adopted and often used the image of the banyan tree as the symbol of that diversity in unity, unity in diversity. It is an image that recurs precisely because it is so

appropriate to the Indian situation, where a kind of paradoxical synthesis seems to have emerged. Under the genius
of Gandhi, India has covered much more ground toward
self-definition — political, linguistic, and literary — and has
coped with many more difficulties in the process. It has
become educated in the subtleties of opposites much more
quickly and with more positive total results than other large
areas with similar problems. Through Gandhi, India has
come very close to a common identity, a sense of national
unity not incompatible with cultural and linguistic diversity.

In India, English cannot be easily uprooted. It is as
basic a force as it is in Singapore; and perhaps much more
lasting. Gandhi, in his ingenious assessment of the situation, did not try to uproot the English language but approached the problem from other quarters. His main concern was to find a common language that would reflect the
democratic principle he had pledged himself to uphold and
implement, an Indian language for all Indians, that indi-
rectly perhaps might at some future date replace English as
a means of general communication and as a native unifying
force. To his great credit, Gandhi moved away from the
elegant and educated language of Bengali, the language of
the literate elite, and in so doing recognized several important historical realities:
1) that most Indians understood, in some measure,
Hindustani, the most widespread of the spoken languages
of India, although not in any sense the most interesting in
a literary context;
2) that although Hindustani was not as pliable, not as
sophisticated a literary tool as Bengali, it could serve very
well to shape a new literature for India (perhaps because
the potential audience, from the outset, would be larger
than any other in the country);
3) that Hindustani represented the logical extension of the
democratic commitment he had assumed and would serve
best to implement democratic principles and help to edu-
cate his people along those lines;
4) that a deliberate assessment of all the languages and
dialects and vernaculars of India (a situation intriguingly
similar to that described by Dante in his work on the
vernaculars of 14th-century Italy) could not justify the
adoption of Bengali or other more developed languages for

the whole of India, that Hindi/Urdu or Hindustani — already widespread — was indeed the best choice since it could be molded and formed according to the democratic principle operating throughout his reasoning. In India, the close association between the political ideology of a great leader (who was both a realist and a committed Indian against great odds) and the changing needs of a multi-faceted people, through its language, is perhaps the most dramatic if not the most successful example of political national literary integration we have viewed thus far. In a sense, Gandhi solved the problem which for the Africans still remains to be defined.

Perhaps it was the presence of the English in India, with their unified administration and long-standing *aparteid*, that established the base for what we have described as Gandhi's success in dramatizing the possibility of Indian unity. Perhaps nothing comparable can ever take place in continental Africa; but whatever difficulties, India's example must inspire our efforts as comparatists struggling for common ground and encourage other countries to work in the same direction — the India-Pakistani-Bangladesh division notwithstanding.

* *Australia and Anti-British Elitism.* In a sense, India and Africa have moved along parallel lines, at different speeds perhaps, but toward the same large objectives. In Australia and countries like Malaysia, the problems take on a different appearance. Who is the underdog in Australia? One might think (with some justification) that the Aborigines of that country are in a position similar to Blacks in African countries. This is only partly true. As in some African countries, oral myths and songs are being collected by others; their language remains to be shaped and recorded; and for many outsiders, their works appear to be simplistic and unselfconscious. But for the most part, the Australian Aborigines have not asserted themselves in the way that many Africans have; and the ethnic mosaic of Turkish, Italian, Greek, Indian, Korean, etc. in Australia is not a realistic social and political force as it is in Africa.

Yet the Australians are in a position not unlike that of the Indians. They have been shaped, of course, by English rule (perhaps more than they care to admit at this point in time); and their rebellion in recent years is simply a deliberate and studious effort to ignore British literature

and concentrate on Commonwealth literature — the literature of the Third World, of India, of the South Pacific — in
which Australia and New Zealand play a major role as
"emergent" cultures.

In Australia we find courses in Commonwealth literature in which British authors and works do not appear at
all: we find former British and American subjects (and
native Australians, who have given up all English or other
European national pretensions or allegiances) turning to
the young cultural heritage of Australia, tracing the lines of
a literature and culture bred from the most unusual circumstances in the history of the world — a convict colony — and
which was bound to be, by its very nature and isolation, a
man-centered culture not very different from our early
American Western myth of isolation and self-sufficiency.

The novelists of Australia, in particular, have given
us the mood and the strange panorama of that country of
outcasts and adventurers, the *outback*, a way of life perhaps
harder than anything that shaped our own "Wild West."
The Australian outback is unique, natural disasters are
almost predictable; a way of life, in fact. The common
theme in the novels of Patrick White and the short stories
of Barbara Baynton and others is *nature against us*, and
nature always wins out. The Australian writer is urbanized
now, and Patrick White is a Nobel Prize winner, internationally known; but the large theme still in Australian
literature is the inhospitable outback, the spirit of adventure, the struggle to evolve human relationships in a hostile
environment, and the tentative effort to speak for the
Aborigines who still cannot speak for themselves in an
effective manner. Australia is the child of Europe in many
ways — not very different from India or Africa in this
respect — but its people are by and large homogeneous in
their provenance and in their language. The present "escape" from British influences — unlike the Indian "escape"
from British rule and British habits — is more an elitist
choice than a politically organic assertion of autonomy.
Still, their attitude is no less genuine than that of the
Indians. They have, as previously suggested, deliberately
assumed Australian priorities, subjects rooted in that continent, stories that trace the development of an indigenous
experience in novels and *novella*, critical essays, the renowned *Bulletin*, and Aboriginal oral accounts. What has

been said of Australia can be said also of New Zealand. There the Maori, like the Aborigines of Australia, are slowly coming into definition but not with the same energetic assertiveness found in Black writings of Africa.

* *Singapore and other South Pacific Cultures.* The political novel in Africa, India, Ceylon, Australia sets up sympathetic chords in our Western historical-minded literary sensibilities; but linguistic definitions and priorities in those countries are so complex, so difficult to sort out for us that many Western comparatists and writers are tempted to ignore the problem altogether. In Malaysia, where English is regarded at best as the language of an immigrant community within the larger national consciousness that recognizes Bhasa Malaysia as dominant and as the true expression of a literary past and present, to write in English means in effect to assume an outsider's posture, making a political statement against the national interest. In Malaysia, English means reactionary, if not counterrevolutionary, at best.

The contrast with Singapore is indeed striking. With its Tamils, Malays, Chinese, its total of 23 languages and dialects reflecting the diversified ethnic and cultural groups living in the place, Singapore recognizes English as the bridge connecting and dominating culturally and economically the kaleldoscopic reality of an international outlook. As a result, English has emerged as the *shaping* medium for literature in Singapore. There is no deep embarrassment, no personal struggle in the Singapore writer who employs English as his medium. Most of the people there accept English as the common language, just as, in many circles and in vital administrative functions, it is accepted in India.

Still, there is for us in the West, a nagging question in all this. How can English be justified (or French, or Dutch, or German, or Portuguese) in countries committed to Third World postures, countries still struggling with their colonial pasts? The paradox is underscored when we see English being used to express Third World struggles: — e.g. Caliban as the spokesman of the Caribs, who uses the language of his master to protest his master's rule. Writers and authors in places like Singapore have been shaped by English sensibilities. As Chandran Nair has written in his *Introduction to Singapore Writing*: "The writer in English seems more concerned, at this moment, with discovering an image of the individual self, of extrapolating human experience. The social milieu of the educated English is a middle class one and they have middle class pretensions."

From our own point of view, the emergence of English as a literary medium in India, Singapore, and — to a lesser extent — Malaysia; the natural re-routing of English in places like Australia and New Zealand (where writers in the mother tongue find their own native subjects and style, reshaping in the process English as we know it); and the important role of English as the cultural intermediary (with French) in Africa must strike us as a fortunate though fortuitous development which can work to good ends in our multi-national comparative literary projections. We have written at some length about the need for translations of characteristic authors from literatures not in the European mainstream, if programs in comparative literary studies are to be expanded organically and intelligently; but the truth is, we have within our grasp excellent texts in English by writers steeped in "other" cultural traditions. A writer like R. K. Narayan (*Waiting for the Mahatma, The Bachelor of Arts*, etc.) is an Indian voice expressing Indian subtleties and sensibilities in English. As Western critics or scholars, we could hardly imagine a more useful cultural gift.

What may have seemed a few years ago esoteric fare — to be tried now and then in the same way that we indulge in exotic foods — has proved substantial and important. In the flush of independence from colonial rule, nations like India, continents like Africa, and many other places about which we have written here, asserted themselves in the "local colour" which is their particularized and independent statement. But that oscillation from one extreme to another is the beginning of a new dialectic, a new set of opposites that are the natural result of growth. In India, writers have begun to realize that a new kind of empire building, from within, now has to be recorded, that history — including the history of dependence — has to be acknowledged and described; that events, especially those that shaped their new identity as a nation, must be sifted and catalogued in many different ways. And, howsoever ironic it may appear, new allegiances must be exploited and implemented with those already in place. The lesson of Greek tragedy is also the lesson of history: we cannot escape what we were or are, and we must take full responsibility, as free agents, of everything we have done or suffered to be done to us. Freedom is wrenched from the master, never given. And in freedom, reversals and paradoxes are no longer contradictory.

The struggle for independence must ultimately become a literary experience (e.g. Narayan in India, Raja Proctor in Ceylon [*Waiting for Surabel*]). "Local colour" must combine with "universality" if the literary product is to survive the historical event. The unassuming genius of Paul Scott must be mentioned, at least, in this context, for his *Raj Quartet* is the model par excellence of history transmuted into unforgettable exquisitely literary inspiration.

3. A Blueprint for Multi-Comparative Literary Perspectives

So far I have understandably stressed the differences and difficulties that must be overcome if a wide spectrum varied pilot program is to be worked out in practical terms. I have stressed the dangers of enthusiastic individual experimentation and arbitrary application of college and university budgets to support experimental programs that "infiltrate" some other literature/author into a core unit or special program already in place. I have personally witnessed excesses of enthusiasm of this kind, and the consequent frustrations, many times; and a good number of my colleagues (scholars who are nationally and internationally known in their respective fields) have shared with me and in the pages of our publications (*Council on National Literatures/World-Report* and *Review of National Literatures*) their disappointments and helplessness in not being given the opportunity to develop new additions to established courses and programs in English and Comparative Literature. Administrators and sponsors — let's be clear about this — will not take on a long-range project without a master blueprint that can account for and insure a *developing* program, not just sporadic experiments here and there.

The obvious large approach, I would say, is in a format of *cluster literatures*, where common tendencies and characteristics help relate a body of literatures to the Western experience. I mentioned earlier literatures in English in such places as India, Malaysia, Singapore, Ceylon, Japan more and more, Australia, New Zealand — literatures which for a variety of reasons (we touched on some) have given their unique stamp and cultural identity to writings in English. Such a body of literary works constitutes a rich storehouse of readings for any course or program in expanded comparative literary studies.

But translations from the indigenous languages can also be had at cost, once the machinery and "expert/people-power" are sorted out and preliminary suggestions are approved by a group of consultants carefully chosen from a number of areas.

A pilot program need not be costly. In fact, a long-range program need not be costly if the proper steps are taken in the first phase to set up a consortium of universities (with supportive colleagues and organizations participating from time to time in panels and meetings to reassess the experiment periodically) where special institutes exist and can provide the "vertical" across-the-cultural spectrum *buttressing* so essential in expanding into unfamiliar literatures. Where departments of English and/or Comparative Literature carry a wide assortment of "experts," those departments should be drawn into the experiment to make the most of the expert power "in place."

A group of consultants can and should be brought together several times during the first year to monitor the tentative program approved for the pilot project. Reading lists must be constantly revised and new translations provided of texts that are deemed essential. Translation centers and national translation resources are available and one or two representatives from such groups should be recruited for the consortium program.

The pilot program should be limited at first to five or six major universities where institutes and "multi-spectrum" comparative literature programs and departments are already in place. In a second phase, the pilot program would be reviewed and scrutinized by those who took part in the first-year project and others recruited from outside centers and institutes. Titles for reading lists should be carefully reviewed at this time, and new texts and other supporting materials suggested and inserted in the program. Translations, of course, are basic; but the value of the expert in history, sociology, etc. recruited from specialized institutes must also be underscored as a kind of essential "translation" of cultural realities. In short, both are needed.

The text in translation, by itself, will not do the entire job, because the teacher with that text may not be qualified to judge it in the original and to place it within the larger cultural whole. For this reason, linguists too must be recruited from time to time — especially in the case of languages from a completely different base, such as Japanese and Chinese. Students must be made aware of the special qualities (and special problems of translation) of such languages and given a realistic appraisal of the possibilities of doing justice to texts from such languages in translation.

Perhaps the trial and error period we have been going through — unwavering enthusiasm on the part of specially-trained colleagues, casual to indifferent responses on the part of administrators — has worked for us in pointing up the difficulties of arbitrary and individualistic approaches to expansion of comparative literary studies. Nothing is ever lost. The experience, howsoever frustrating, will surely guide us in the future as we pave the way toward a more realistic and more lasting experiment. Most important, we have been reminded that — as in the case of Greco-Roman history and Greek and Latin studies — translations will always be the single most important filter through which other cultures can be approached. The situation in our own time is even more dramatic in that respect: the large variety of languages even within one single cultural cluster (e.g. Indian, Yugoslav, African) can frighten away the most dedicated of us. The principle that a large base of linguistic competence is essential before cultural-literary values can be transmitted is entirely false. Dantists are not found among Italian merchants as a rule; very often the person interested in Dante will approach him in translation or through a teacher expounding him in English — and only when the interest has been piqued will that student learn the language and become proficient in it. This has happened among the very best scholars; and I repeat that sound and surely obvious principle here, at a time when much has been put forward to suggest the opposite. Linguistic skills are not necessary for literary studies; they serve well, needless to say, but not as a prerequisite. To insist otherwise is simply to create a mass of semi-literate glorified cultural "tourists."

Perhaps the most important aspect of the first-year

pilot program is an effective testing device among the experts to evaluate the program and to suggest changes for the second and subsequent years. Much will have to be considered — including the "cultural clusters" to be included in the pilot program. Not all can be fitted in all at once. And what is included must have some basis of correspondence that can be justified and easily apprehended by instructor and student alike. Final reports of participating specialists and institutions must be collated and discussed at a general meeting in which all the administrators and instructors, as well as the specialists who have been recruited from the institutes etc., will have a chance to describe their impressions and discuss possible changes for the future. Such a meeting ideally should be attended also by high-ranking Washington administrators, including the Secretary of Education and the directors of national funding agencies that deal with the humanities.

The materials for a multi-comparative literary program are in place and easily accessible in the United States. The only thing that is lacking is the "networking" and that can be achieved along the lines described in this paper. Both the psychological and social conditions are ripe for such a program for the mechanisms are already in hand, as I have shown. What is needed is a re-direction and re-distribution of resources.

A last observation before concluding. There is misunderstanding and often prejudice on the "other," the "nonWestern" side, as well as ours. Re-education must take place on both sides, although in different ways. In some cultures the very notion of "genres" and the entire Aristotelian "codex" of literary laws is looked upon with distaste and misunderstanding. Perhaps there has to be a trimming of sorts; but we need not scrap our own literary heritage, especially the Aristotelian critical tradition, in order to accommodate others. Where Aristotelian principles can be explained we are bound to do so; where they can be inserted and tested within a new body of literature, they ought to be tried out. Many on this side of things, on the other hand, are impatient with "oral literatures" (for example) simply because they feel that in our Western tradition that sort of thing is well behind us. We've had our Homers and our great Nordic sagas, etc. and we have come a long way since. That may be true; it may also be true that

Homer's oral epics were perhaps more culturally rewarding than some of the "oral" modern myths of the Aborigines, for example, or of the tribes in the hills of Turkey or Greece. But if we are to move ahead, we must remember that both Homer and Aboriginal oral literature have a common basic impulse, and in that sense, surely, we can find a common ground for exploration and education. And there should be no resentment because others have taken on the task of sorting out alphabets and myths of cultures not yet ready for any sort of critical apparatus or its applications. The Romans proved to be the best guardians and lovers of the Greek experience. Without their critical insights and sorting processes, our modern literary heritage might have been very different. We can all profit from that experience.

The "purists" on both sides will insist that no translation can possibly do justice to certain concepts or phrases. Again, that may be true; in fact, we have learned to smile about it because it is so self-evident. All translation is betrayal (as the saying goes, and in almost all the European languages). Should that stop us? Did it stop the Roman translators of Homer and Aeschylus and Sophocles and Aristotle and Plato? Or our modern translators of Dante, Petrarch, Boccaccio, Voltaire, Rousseau, Goethe, etc.?

The egocentricity of individual national literatures and cultures is perfectly understandable. Culture has become in our day a function of ethnicity as well as political assertiveness. Psychological/social/political communication may be difficult at first, but it should not stop us. Clearly, each national culture has its own peculiar and unique characteristics. Each also shares with other cultures certain common traits. Once these have been determined and the cultural map of the different national literatures has been laid out in terms that everyone can understand and appreciate, we can move ahead, weaving into the "horizontal" variety of literatures and languages, as they actually exist on our campuses today, the "vertical" cultural mosaic provided by highly focused institutes or special area studies centers as they exist, often side by side, on the same campuses. The comparatist may exult in his gift of tongues, just as the special area scholar may rejoice in the isolation in which he talks to himself, his peers and God — but the confusion of Babel and the eccentricity of the chosen few cannot continue if the changes proposed are to be realized.

And, as in all qualitative change, the result of cooperation between comparatists and area specialists will not be more of the same but a totally new configuration of comparative studies, a synthetic overview of cultural units and their national/political roots.

NOTES

Most of the citations in this paper are to be found in the various issues of *CNL/Report, CNL/Quarterly World Report,* and *CNL/ World Report,* as well as in the various "overviews" represented by the annual series *Review of National Literatures.*

Japanese Initiatives in Comparative Studies: The "Shakespeare Translation Test"

How many ages hence shall this our lofty scene be acted
over in states unborn and accents yet unknown!

Julius Caesar III. i. 111-131[1]

It is necessary for us to translate a foreign drama. In
Germany the Schlegel-Tieck translation advanced her
cultural progress. In our country, however, we have
scarcely any faithful translation except Shōyō's version of
Julius Caesar. We should display our own ability more
fully for such a task.

Mori Ōgai, 1980[2]

Tsubouchi Shōyō (1859-1935) ... made a complete translation of Shakespeare's works which remains the standard one in Japan. He ... sought to find examples in the
earlier Japanese literature of parallels to things which he
praised in European literature, and so to give a native
tradition for writers to follow.

Donald Keene, 1955[3]

Perhaps the most striking Japanese contribution to
the comparative study of literature on a global scale in

modern times has been the founding of *Shakespeare Translation*, a periodical published annually under the auspices
of Seijo University, Tokyo, which has done for Japanese
Shakespeare studies in the late twentieth century what the
founding of *Shakespeare-Jahrbuch* in 1865 did for German
Shakespeare studies in the late nineteenth century.

The first issue of *Shakespeare Translation* appeared in
1974, and, with the exception of 1982, volumes appeared
annually through 1984, for a total of ten, under the original
title. An eleventh volume, bearing a revised title, *Shakespeare
Worldwide: Translation and Adaptation*, was published in
1986. All articles from the beginning have been in English.
But an "Editorial Preface" providing a statement of purpose for the first issue, and reprinted in all subsequent
issues, takes note of the fact that, of all sectors of the field
of Shakespeare studies, those that start with the original
texts of the plays for purposes of translating them and
performing them in foreign lands would seem to hold the
most promise for significant cultivation by foreigners. Im-
plicitly justifying the decision to make the periodical a
Japanese-based English-language publication, its editor-
in-chief Oyama Toshikazu, Professor of English at Seijo
University, began his editorial statement of purpose by
asking:

> Could Shakespeare imagine that his plays would be read and
> performed in many languages other than his own, after
> hundreds of years? Shakespeare wrote for the audience of
> the Globe, but he is even now speaking to his audience, in
> every corner of the world, using a great variety of languages.
> All the people of the world now believe that their Shakespeare
> is the genuine Shakespeare. If so, why are they not given a
> chance of making Shakespeare really global, and to contrib-
> ute to the recent scholarship of the world?

Such a chance, it appears, was to be provided in the pages
of *Shakespeare Translation*, which originated, as Professor
Oyama explained, in a decision taken unanimously in 1971
by the "members of the Investigative Committee on
Shakespeare Translation of the World Shakespeare Congress" which met in Vancouver, Canada, in August of that
year. Recalling the intention of that committee, which he
had chaired, and speaking also as chairman of the editorial
board of the periodical itself, Professor Oyama wrote: "It is
our devotion to Shakespeare and our firm conviction that

Shakespeare is not the sole possession of those whose native tongue is English, that makes us undertake the formidable task of translating Shakespeare and explore the hitherto uncultivated field of Shakespeare studies." Concluding his preface, he expressed the "hope of all the editors that through this publication, we shall be able to contribute to . . . the exploration of a new territory of comparative literature," thereby helping "to make Shakespeare really universal and global." (1, viii)

But behind the decision of contemporary Japanese Shakespeare scholars to take so bold an initiative, there has been a relatively long preparation. That preparation in its earliest phase has been the theme of an article titled "Shakespeare and the Modern Writers in Japan — Translation and Interpretation by Shōyō, Ōgai and Sōseki" that appeared in Volume 7 (1980) of *Shakespeare Translation*, contributed by Kawachi Yoshiko, who, after Oyama Toshikazu's death in 1982, was elected to serve as the new chairman of its editorial board starting with Volume 11.

Tsubouchi Shōyō (1859-1935), Mori Ōgai (1862-1932), and Natsume Sōseki (1867-1916) — each famous enough to be known by his first name — are, as Professor Kawachi makes clear, three of the most important scholars and writers of modern Japan. Elsewhere in these pages, writing about "The Forms of Japanese Fiction," Phillip Tudor Harries stresses the "seminal importance" of Shōyō's *The Essence of the Novel* (1886) for the development of modern Japanese fiction, and then hails Ōgai and Sōseki as "the two giants of the late Meiji period," noting that while the learned Ōgai, who started out as a masterful novelist, eventually applied his narrator's skills "to biographies that seem consciously to eschew the techniques of fiction and take on the air of scholarly research," it was "in Sōseki that modern [Japanese] fiction reached full maturity." Confining herself to Shakespeare's influence on them, Professor Kawachi treats the three writers as if they were Japanese equivalents of the trio of great early German champions of Shakespeare — Lessing, Goethe, and August W. von Schlegel — who had turned England's national poet into *unser* Shakespeare.

Professor Kawachi notes that Shōyō, who is properly "regarded as the father of modern Japanese fiction," managed to make himself Japan's first great Shakespeare scholar

— translating the complete works — without journeying to
the West. She reports his account of the first time he heard
what he called "a theatrical elocution of a foreign play":
one of his English teachers had stood before his class
"grasping a knife with the point downward and recited
the'To be or not to be' soliloquy." In Professor Kawachi's
view, that experience had a great influence on Shōyō's
subsequent career as a writer and translator. As she says:

> While writing plays or translating Shakespeare, he appears
> to have been strongly conscious of the differences in drama-
> turgy between the East and the West. He felt the necessity of
> establishing the methodology of comparative drama in Ja-
> pan, and sometimes he compared Shakespeare with
> Monzaemon Chikamatsu (1653-1724), a representative play-
> wright of *Kabuki* and *Joruri*. He enumerated 18 similarities
> between Chikamatsu and Shakespeare, and wrote an essay
> entitled *Old Chikamatsu Should Be Introduced to the Whole
> World*. Although he went too far in thinking so, he was
> certainly the first to give a serious consideration to what the
> Japanese people could learn from Shakespeare and how the
> Japanese drama could be improved by a study of
> Shakespeare's dramaturgy. He said, "Apart from the English
> or Americans, it is the Japanese, and not the Germans, the
> French, the Italians, or the Russians, who have to learn from
> Shakespeare and to commemorate him." Thus Shōyō viewed
> Shakespeare from the standpoint of a Japanese wishing
> eagerly to improve the drama of his country. (7, 31-32)

Shōyō's eagerness to inspire the Japanese to compete with the continental Europeans as Shakespeareans
reminds one, literally, of what used to be said a hundred
years before, when only France, Italy, and Germany were in
competition. As Wordsworth had put it back in 1815: "At
this day the French Critics have abated nothing of their
aversion to this darling of our Nation. . . . The most
enlightened Italians, though well acquainted with our language, are wholly incompetent to measure the proportions
of Shakespeare. The Germans only, of foreign nations, are
approaching towards a knowledge and a feeling of what he
is. In some respects they have acquired a superiority over
the fellow-countrymen of the Poet.[4]

Shōyō held, with Lafcadio Hearn (who by then had
become a Japanese citizen and university professor with a
legally-adopted Japanese name), that Shakespeare's plays

"should be rendered into colloquial Japanese, . . . that a free translation in the current colloquial language was better than a word-for-word and literary translation." Mori Ōgai, on the contrary, favored the highly literary, German romantic approach to Shakespeare translation, which Shōyō rejected as "too academic and unsuitable for staging." The two scholars early engaged in heated debates on the subject, "which ended in smoke," as Professor Kawachi says, but nevertheless "played an important role in the history of literary criticism in Japan." Ōgai translated only one play of Shakespeare — *Macbeth* — but it won high praise from Shōyō who, in a now much treasured preface for Ōgai's text, said:

> *Macbeth* is one of the shortest plays of Shakespeare, but I was very surprised at the fact that Dr. Mori translated it so fast. To my great surprise, each line of the original text was faithfully rendered into plain and fluent Japanese. I have never seen such a lucid translation of Shakespeare. . . . I believe that it will renew our theatrical world. (7, 33-35)

Turning at last to Natsume Sōseki, Professor Kawachi acknowledges that, unlike Shōyō and Ōgai, Sōseki was at first not interested in drama," as such, not even Shakespeare, which he read and analyzed, it is said, "from the standpoint of a pedantic novelist." For Sōseki, the characters of Shakespeare would always remain alien to his nature, expressing "feelings of joy and anger" that struck him as "extremely unnatural." But their unnaturality, he acknowledged, was the substantive reality of Shakespeare's "poetic world, and only its inhabitants can enjoy and understand it. He is truly a poet, whose active imagiriation conjured up such a world." (7, 38-39)

Sōseki died in 1916. Ōgai lived into the 1920s, Shōyō into the 1930s. Since then Japan has experienced momentous changes in war and peace, all of which have, however, accelerated the process of Westernization. Modern Japan has from the beginning been apparently more determined than any other non-Western nation to accept the achievements of the West (even to vie with it) in many fields, including Shakespeare studies — as Shōyō's words quoted above make clear. In much of the competition, especially with respect to television, computers, electronic communication generally, and the automotive industry, Japan has in fact taken the lead, making the names of its major export

manufactures household words around the world. That its
success is not confined to technology was made clear when
the first World Shakespeare Congress met in 1971, and the
reports of its "investigative committees" — especially those
on international cooperation, bibliography, new research
methods, and translation — began to come in. All those
reports emphasized the need to find ways of dealing "with
the growing complexity of Shakespeare research and theatre activity" on a global scale. Many participated in the
work of those committees; but what their reports clearly
reveal (quite incidentally, to be sure) is that the Japanese
had made good on Shōyō's pledge of a half-century earlier
that they would vie successfully with the Germans, French,
Italians, and Russians in Shakespeare studies.

      In his report on the present state and pressing needs
of coordinating Shakespeare bibliography, for instance,
Harrison Meserole draws heavily on the findings and recommendations of "Professor Takashi Sasayama, who," he
says, "took the lead in this phase of the Investigative
Committee's work.[5] Toshikazu Oyama, it was noted earlier,
chaired the investigative committee on translation; but it
is significant that one of the committee's four other members was also Japanese, namely Oyama Toshiko, the committee chairman's wife, but herself surely also a Shakespeare
scholar and translator of the first rank. The other committee members were French (Pierre Spriet of Bordeaux),
German (Hans W. Gabler of Munich), and Indian (Jagannath
Chakravorty of Calcutta). With Ms. Oyama, each of them
had prepared a preconvention "historical survey of
Shakespeare translation in the country he represented and
delineated briefly the present state of Shakespeare translation." Summarizing their surveys and discussions, Oyama
Toshikazu stressed how the "wide differences" in the linguistic and cultural backgrounds were reflected in their
views on translation; after which he provided an "updating"
of the sort of appraisal Wordsworth had made of
Shakespeare study abroad when it was still confined to the
major Western European nations. In Oyama's words of
1971:

> Germany would be accredited with the oldest history in
> Shakespeare translation, having her own problem, however,
> which is that German translation has tended to become
> stereotyped, as the result of cumulative efforts. French

translations, from the nature of the language, cannot avoid the tendency to become longer than the original. India has also a fairly long history of Shakespeare translation. However, the peoples of India are still in great need of standard translations in various dialects. Japan has no less serious problems. In the case of the Japanese translation, perhaps we might even say that " translation" is not the right word for the kind of work involved and the result thereof, the reason being that, because of the nature of the language, there is such a wide range of choice for the equivalent and the parallel to the original and the entire business is left to the free choice of the translator.[6]

Such problems were to be explored at length in the pages of *Shakespeare Translation*, ten issues of which appeared annually between 1974 and 1984 under the editorship of OyamaToshikazu — the last appearing posthumously after Oyama's death in 1983. The tenth volume included prefatory tributes by leading Shakespeare scholars from around the world, all of which stressed the periodical's achievement as a pioneer project in comparative literary study on a global basis with a single focus — Shakespeare in dozens of languages — which could facilitate, as nothing had before, a sharing of literary insights of the profoundest sorts among peoples of utterly diverse backgrounds.

Professor Fuhara Yoshiaki of Tsukuba University stressed the importance of Oyama's initiatives as contributions to international cooperation in literary scholarship. In his comparative studies, Oyama had not started with Shakespeare. As Professor Fuhara recalls, he and Oyama had read the critical essays of T. S. Eliot together back in 1941, when they were members of a "small circle" of students of English at Tokyo University. Oyama's scholarly specialization in English literature was at first focused mainly on Old and Middle English literature, and only later did it shift to Shakespeare. But from the beginning, Oyama was ever conscious, as Fuhara puts it, "of the international community of Shakespeare study, and it was his desire to bring Shakespeare studies going on in many parts of the world, including Japan, into still closer inter-communication. Actually he was playing a leading part in that activity, his chief editorship of *Shakespeare Translation* being a remarkable aspect of it." (10, xiii) John Lawlor, Secretary General of the International Association of University Pro-

fessors of English, stressed, in his tribute to Oyama at the
time of his death, the importance of his work on that
association's Consultative Committee, where he "served
with distinction for a long period," all the while standing
also as "indeed a tower of strength for English studies in
Japan." (10, xv) But it is the distinguished German
Shakespearean, Werner Habicht, of the University of
Wurzburg, who puts the contribution of Oyama to
Shakespeare studies in truly global perspective:

> Even in the German language area, where for at least two
> centuries there has been no dearth of translations and
> re-translations of Shakespearean drama, recent efforts at a
> systematic study of the problems involved owed a consider-
> able impetus and encouragement to Professor Oyama's ini-
> tiative, by which . . . he created a forum for a comparative
> study and discussion of translation problems and for rechan-
> neling the results and possible solutions into the mainstream
> of criticism in English. The journal *Shakespeare Translation*,
> founded and edited in pursuance of these objectives, has
> indeed established itself . . . also as an excellent example of
> fruitful international and interlingual scholarly coopera-
> tion. (10, xviii)

Professor Habicht's concluding words remind us of the fact
that translation has ever been a most efficacious means of
international education — and indeed an international
education that can be raised to the highest spiritual-cultural
level when the works thus shared by people of diverse
languages are such as Homer's *Iliad*, Dante's *Divine Comedy*, or Shakespeare's plays.

In an earlier contribution to *Shakespeare Translation*,
Professor Habicht had distinguished the two essential sides
of the culture-sharing process involved in serious translation. In the case of Shakespeare, "the translators' activities,
though primarily directed at non-English audiences," are
nevertheless much influenced by the general progress of
Shakespeare criticism and scholarship, with all its developing techniques of research, in English. That is one side of
the culture-sharing process. But there is also a reverse side,
which involves, as Habicht says, a consideration of "the
ways in which the activity of translating and the appreciation of translation in turn generate fresh critical insights
into the fabric of Shakespeare's original plays and into the
conditions of their reception." Reenforcing the point,

Habicht generalizes: "As a translator has to cope with every single detail of the text and is not allowed the privilege of skipping over its cruxes or leaving them undecided, his work constitutes the most complete account of a critical response." (3, xi)

The German writers of the age of Goethe who first made Shakespeare their own were very conscious of the value of translation as a means of developing their own national literary culture. When A. W. von Schlegel's first translations of Shakespeare began to appear, the poet Novalis (Friedrich von Hardenberg) wrote a letter of praise in which he said: "We Germans have been translating for a long time, and the desire to translate appears to be a national characteristic. . . . Except for the Romans we are the only nation which has felt the urge to translate so irrepressibly and whose culture owes so immeasurably much to translation. Hence the many analogies between our literary culture and that of the later Romans." And of Schlegel's particular contribution to the enrichment of German culture in this regard, Novalis did not hesitate to add: "Your Shakespeare is an excellent canon for the scientific observer."[7]

The Germans of Goethe's time were pleased to acknowledge their great indebtedness, through translation especially, to English literature. "Our novels, our plays," Goethe was himself proud to acknowledge in his late years, "from whence have we received them, if not from Goldsmith, Fielding, and Shakespeare?" Pride came into it, for by then the English had come to be powerfully influenced in turn by the great new German authors who were teaching them how to read their own Shakespeare and Byron even as English critics were teaching Germans how to read Schiller and Goethe. Goethe saw in the process the emergence of what he called a *Weltliteratur* or world literature, anticipating which he was prompted to exclaim: "It is splendid that we now, because of the lively interchange among French, English, and Germans, have come to a point where we can correct each other."[8]

It was the high estimate of Shakespeare's genius shared by Samuel Johnson and Lessing, Coleridge and Goethe, Hazlitt and Schlegel that spread like a contagion to the France of Hippolyte Taine and Victor Hugo, the Italy of Alessandro Manzoni and Francesco De Sanctis, and the

Russia of Alexander Pushkin and Vissarion Belinski. And during all those decades of Shakespeare's rapidly mounting and spreading fame in Europe, Anglo-European scholars were carrying forward a momentous effort to make the extra-European cultures of the ancient Indians, Arabs, and Persians, and eventually also the Chinese, their own. The English founded schools for the study of all languages written in the Hindu and Arabic scripts, and in this they were followed by European scholars, with those of Germany taking the lead. Classics of ancient Sanskrit and of Persian Arabic were translated into the European languages, and that opened the way for a new appreciation of the artistic and literary cultures of the Asian peoples of what was then known as the Near East, South Asia, and the Far East.

One consequence of that unprecedented broadening of language study was the development in Europe of a new aesthetics or philosophy of fine art that made possible a sympathetic study of every kind of art that had ever been seriously valued anywhere in the world. The philosopher G. W. F. Hegel, for instance, produced a monumental system of aesthetics that embraced all the kinds of art — architecture, sculpture, painting, music and literature in its narrative, lyric, and dramatic genres — distinguishing symbolic, classical, and romantic stages of development and tracing their development in all lands, Middle Eastern and East Asian, as well as European, and through all times, ancient, medieval, and modern.

In that Hegelian system of aesthetics, a crowning place is accorded the dramatic works of Shakespeare as art of potentially the broadest possible transcultural appeal. In stage performance, dramatic works comprehend in themselves the achievements of all the other arts: sculptured works of art fashioned in flesh and blood instead of marble or bronze, whose action against a colorful set can be masterworks of painting, whose speech can be music at its best, expressed in lines of verse that can be epic, lyrical, and truly dramatic in turn as the poetic perspective shifts. And among the dramatic works of all times, those of Shakespeare, according to Hegel, are the supreme masterpieces, most comprehensive in their artistic embrace, a standard against which to measure the greatness — if not the artistic distinctiveness — of all other art. Although extra-European appreciation of Shakespeare had only just begun in his time, Hegel constantly drew Shakespearean examples to illustrate his meaning in his discussion of the differences between diverse kinds of art and the different genres within each art. And that practice permitted him to observe in 1823: "Shakespeare's tragedies and comedies . . . have been attracting an ever wider public because, despite their very strong national emphasis, the universal human interest in them is incomparably stronger. . . . Shakespeare's works have gained entrance everywhere except where national conventions of art are too narrow and specific."[9]

What the Germans proved to be for the acceptance of Shakespeare throughout Europe during the nineteenth century, the Armenians and the Japanese have proved to be for his acceptance in the Middle East and East Asia during the twentieth century. The Armenians, to be sure, have always considered themselves to be a translating people *par excellence*. They have been able to boast from the beginning of their cultural history that their very alphabet was invented to enable them to read in their own language the holy books of Christianity and related works which they could read previously only in Greek or Syriac. At the close of the nineteenth century, when the Armenians took up the translation of Shakespeare as a means of modernizing their literature, one of their outstanding poet-critics, Hovannes Toumanian, had not hesitated to say: "Shakespeare has become a criterion by which to determine a nation's cultural standards. A people who does not translate Shakespeare is illiterate; those who are unable to understand him are intellectually immature, and the language into which Shakespeare cannot be translated is indeed poor."[10]

The Japanese turned receptively to Shakespeare at about the same time as the Armenians; and they, too, are a people who acknowledge the importance of the role that translation has played from the beginning in their national cultural development. So much of their early culture came to them from China, both directly and via Korea, by means of translation, and the process of translating and borrowing from Chinese texts has continued through the ages. But that the Japanese should have taken so bold an initiative in international Shakespeare studies — taking the lead in promoting international cooperation particularly in the

field of Shakespeare translation — is something altogether
remarkable. The language of the Armenians is, after all, an
Indo-European language, a fact that, at least superficially,
facilitates translation. Japanese, on the contrary, is a thoroughly oriental language, presenting problems for its
Shakespeare translators that have no parallels in Indo-
European languages. Their work in Shakespeare translation has therefore had the effect of overcoming barriers
that might otherwise have continued to appear insuperable.

Still, as in the case of the Armenians and Germans,
it has been Shakespeare's genius that has inspired the
boldest modern efforts of literary translation among the
Japanese. What it is that makes Shakespeare so irresistibly
attractive to translators, enabling him to serve so effectively as a bridge linking peoples of diverse cultures, was
clear enough to Oyama Toshikazu when he founded
Shakespeare Translation, even as it had been clear, on a
smaller scale, to the German, French, Italian, and Russian
critics who first established his "marvelous tyranny" in
Europe.

Shakespeare wrote during England's great age of
discovery, with the results of which he shows a vast and
largely sympathetic acquaintance. His works are full of
representations of the distinctive characters of different
peoples of the world, which fact makes it obvious why his
works seem to mirror so much more of the world's infinite
variety than is reflected in Homer or even in Dante, who are
otherwise his equals in poetic power. Thus, while he remains indeed England's national poet, giving us a very
realistic sense of English nationhood, the mirror of art that
he holds up for us transforms the English experience into
a universal one — an experience with which all the people
of the world can fully identify themselves today as never
before, so that all who read the plays or see them performed in any language can find a national model for
themselves. Translation has been the key to such intimate
national reception of Shakespeare on the part of so many
diverse peoples. And now, as Oyama Toshikazu expressed
it in the words of his original editorial preface previously
cited, "all the people of the world . . . believe that their
Shakespeare is the genuine Shakespeare."

The obvious next step, as Professor Oyama saw it,

was to show that the high-flung bridges raised by Shakespeare translators in all lands need to be perceived as a single global network of such bridges, facilitating cultural passage to and from all the peoples involved. Professor Oyama boldy proposed to establish "distant Japan" — the land of the rising sun, the fabulous *Cipango* that Columbus had sought to reach by sailing westward — as the traffic-control center for such high-level comparative literary study. His immediate aim in establishing *Shakespeare Translation* was, as he said, "to make Shakespeare really universal and global." But by the time its tenth volume had appeared posthumously in 1984, he had indeed moved far also in setting before us all, as comparatists, what Werner Habicht has called an "excellent example of fruitful international and interlingual scholarly cooperation." (1, vii)

NOTES

1. James G. McManaway cites the passage under "Messages from Scholars" in the first issue of *Shakespeare Translation*, Tokyo: Yushodo Shoten, 1974, p. x. Page references to *Shakespeare Translation (ST)* are inserted parenthetically as required, supplying volume and page numbers. See note 2, below.

2. Quoted by Kawachi Yoshiko in *ST*, 1980 (7, 35). For an extended evaluation of the contents and importance of *Shakespeare Translation* (now *Shakespeare Worldwide: Translation and Adaptation*), see Anne and Henry Paolucci, "World Perspective on Shakespeare Translation," *Review of National Literatures, Comparative Literary Theory: New Perspectives* (New York: Council on National Literatures, 1989), pp. 121- 144.

3. Donald Keene, *Japanese Literature: An Introduction for Western Readers* (New York: Grove Press, 1955), pp. 92, 94.

4. Cited in F. E. Hallidav, *Shakespeare and His Critics* (London: Duckworth, rev. ed. 1958), pp. 17-20.

5. Clifford Leech and J. M. R. Margeson, *Shakespeare 1971: Proceedings of the World Shakespeare Congress* (Toronto: U. of Toronto Press, 1972), p. 268.

6. *Ibid.*, p. 276.

7. André Lefevere, *Translating Literature: The German Tradition from Luther to Rosenzweig* (Assen: Van Gorcum, 1977), p. 65.

8. Cited in François Jost, *Introduction to Comparative Literature* (New York: Pegasus, 1974), p. 252.

9. Henry Paolucci, ed. & trans., *Hegel: On the Arts* (New York: Frederick Ungar, 1979), p. 174.

10. Cited in Rouben Zarin, *Shakespeare and the Armenians* (Etchmiadzin: Academy of Sciences, 1969), p. 13; see N. Parlakian, "Shakespeare and the Armenian Theater," in *Council on National Literatures/Quarterly World Report*, Vol. V. No. 4, 1982, pp, 5-10.

The Chinese Enlightenment:
From Polished Ideographs
to Living Words

Whatever else the Chinese may be, they are above all a
literary people. They have cultivated literature as no
other people have done, and they cultivate it still.

H. A. Giles (1902)

Through his collection of ancient songs Confucius provided a strong stimulus to the creation and enjoyment of
poetry . . . . Under his influence poetry became the major
literary achievement of the Chinese people, who find
inward joy and spiritual happiness in a medium which
celebrates the delights of nature and simple pleasures,
and expresses the sentiments of domestic affection and
the edification of cultivated friendships.

Shao Chang Lee (1951)

Satisfied for millenia with a criticism compounded of
learned glosses and polite impressionism, the Chinese
critic today has the happy duty of being the first real
"critic" (in the modern sense) of his nation's oldest
works. How exciting to be in the generation of C. T. Hsia,
James J. Y. Liu, and Joseph S. M. Lau!

Arthur E. Kunst (1971)

Confucius in China, Buddha in India, Zoroaster in

Mesopotamia, the prophets Jeremiah and Ezekiel among the Jews of the Babylonian domination, and Thales at the head of a host of speculative thinkers in ancient Greece are all linked together as products of a wave of enlightenment, or cultural self-awareness, that literally circled the earth in the sixth century, B.C.

Periods of enlightenment hold up a mirror in which cultural consciousness becomes self- conscious. The commandment is in every instance the same: Know thyself. But for each people that undergoes the experience, it is of course its own cultural distinctiveness that comes to be known. Among the Greeks, enlightenment at once became infinitely self-reflective, with one mind after another affirming for itself that a life lived uncritically — an unexamined life — is not worth living. In the Middle East, under the tolerant sway of the Persians, cultural self-awareness among the diverse peoples revealed characteristics markedly different from the Greek character: Egyptians longing for a material continuance of life beyond the grave; Assyrians anxious to seize the day's pleasure before night falls; and faithful Jews awaiting a Messiah yet fearing that he might already have come and gone unnoticed. In the India of Gautama Buddha, enlightenment mirrored a wildly imaginative, self- consuming spirituality; whereas in the China of Confucius it revealed a disciplined, humanistic, infinitely-detailed concern for the proprieties of personal conduct in family, clan, and civic relationships.

Enlightenment gave ancient China a highly polished image of itself in poetry and prose. A veritable priesthood of *literati* rose to treasure, refine, and enrich the legacy. Once defined, the canon of Confucian classics became the permanent basis of education not only for all literate Chinese but also for the millions of Koreans, Japanese, and Southeast Asians who, in a millenial stream, have turned to it for mental discipline even as the peoples of Europe once turned to the literatures of Greece and Rome.

To the extent that it remains representative of Chinese civilization, as the classical civilization of the Far East, the literature of China may still be described as Confucianist. The term hits the truth, wrote Professor Friedrich Hirth of Columbia University back in 1908, "if we look upon it as covering not only the Confucian school, but also anti-Confucian literature and a good deal of what is decidedly neutral." Much has happened in China since 1908; and yet in view of the current anti-Confucianist orientation on the mainland and the heightened acclaim accorded the ancient sage in Taiwan, one may accept as valid today Professor Hirth's conclusion that there is no escaping a Confucian emphasis, pro or con, in Chinese literature. "Certainly the personality of the sage stands in closer relation to the development of Chinese literature," wrote Professor Hirth, "than that of any other individual stands to any other national literature either in Asia or in Europe. In its earliest development Chinese literature was either Confucianist or anti-Confucianist; and even in that conspiracy of silence characteristic of the opposing schools, the one man treated with silence was Confucius."

The West did not begin to become aware of the Confucianist Chinese literary legacy till the seventeenth century. The earliest translations of select classics were the work of missionaries who had spent long years in China. Then came the tide of fascinated appreciation that ranged from the *Novissima Sinica* of Leibnitz and Voltaire's *L'orpheline de la Chine* to Goethe's *Chinesisch-Deutsche Jahres und Tageszeiten*, and beyond.

Under the spell of the "latest news from China," Leibnitz was persuaded that a truly universal language, 'for the intercourse of nations and especially scholars," could be developed by the Western nations on the model of Chinese characters. Small figures could be used, he urged, "which would speak in truth to the eyes," representing "visible things by their lines, and the invisible by the visible that accompany them." Such a mode of writing, facilitated by "having the figures all engraved, ready for printing on paper, and adding thereto afterwards with the pen the marks of flexions or particles," would be very useful, Leibnitz concluded, "in enriching the imagination, and in giving thoughts less surd and verbal than we now have."

Leibnitz's rationalist view of the advantages of Chinese-type writing was widely shared. But there was also a contrary view that emphasized the cultural disadvantages of a written language that "does not present the spoken word to the eye, but represents the ideas themselves by signs." Hegel, for instance, later argued against Leibnitz that, in fact, it was the extended intercourse of nations that "occasioned the need for alphabetical writing and led to its formation. "Hieroglyphic and ideographic language, he noted, has generally characterized autochthonous civilizations which have developed in isolation, resisting foreign influences and restricting as far as possible knowledge of the art of linking written characters for meaningful discourse.

Hegel's insights on how spoken language fails to "mature to distinctness" when there is no attendant effort to define its sounds and words in writing anticipated the views of Abel Rémusat and Wilhelm von Humboldt, summed up in the latter's often-cited conclusion of 1827: "I think that the scholars who have almost let themselves be drawn into forgetting that Chinese is a spoken language have so exaggerated the influence of Chinese writing that they have, so to say, put the writing in place of the language." Such observations gave rise in time to an historically-rooted line of inquiry which is still pursued today, with profound implications for the debate over romanization and the introduction of sound-signs in Japanese as well as Chinese character writing. Without some form of alphabetization and polysyllabic word formation, grammatical definition of parts of speech remains virtually impossible, and with it (so Hegel argued) also the expression of rapidly nuanced thought.

In the light of this Leibnitz-Hegel divergence of views on ideographic writing, Dr. Lin Yutang's new Chinese-English Dictionary is highly instructive. Unlike earlier dictionaries for English-speaking students of Chinese, it assigns parts of speech to the Chinese words it defines and provides on each odd-numbered page a chart of the 33 basic stroke formations of Chinese characters, which the lexicographer refers to as an alphabet. In an almost Hegelian vein, Dr. Lin thus justifies the new approach:

> Today 80 to 90 per cent of all Chinese words are polysyllabic, with single characters simply components of a word. When one accepts this fact, Chinese is no longer esoteric, mysterious and inexplicable, as even many Sinologues have considered it. It becomes as alive and understandable as, say, German. For instance, most linguists have doubted whether Chinese has anything that could be called grammar. Well, one certainly cannot discover grammar until one recognizes and thinks in terms of whole words, which are parts of

speech — nouns, verbs and so on. Then one sees that Chinese grammar exists.

Like the major writing reforms in process on the mainland (reforms that have a long history), Dr. Lin's analytical efforts to integrate the written and spoken languages would seem to support Hegel's view that the pressure of international contacts generates a need for alphabetization. Expressing approval of a mainland directive that Chinese "must move, however gradually, from the one -to -32 -stroke character to romanization based on the Western alphabet," Dr. Lin concluded: "I don't see how we can make written language the property of every Chinese and live in the modern world without adopting phoneticized script."

But these are matters illuminated with expert insight, from diverse perspectives, in several of the essays that follow. Indeed, it is hardly possible to write critically about any aspect of Chinese literature without some reference to the much controverted language question. China's revolutionary transformation in modern times has thrown its entire past into new relief, and the transformational process has had from the beginning a distinctively literary and linguistic focus. It has, of course, been a Westernizing transformation in three main currents: liberal, at one extreme, which means highly individualistic and therefore disruptive of family and clan life; Marxist, at the other extreme, which means communal in an atomistically abstract or supracultural sense; and concurrently, national, which means integratively and self-defensively Chinese. These three have been at odds ideologically, yet each has worked in tandem with the others to complete the break with the past that began in the days of humiliation following the Opium War (1839-42), when the coastal cities of China were forcibly opened to European interests and influences. In self-defense, China broke with a past that seemed to leave it defenseless, not only against the Western powers, but even against rapidly Westernized Japan which, in 1894-95, sent a highly literate army into China to defeat an essentially illiterate Chinese army. The Manchu Imperial Dynasty that suffered such defeats made serious attempts at internal reform, especially of its system of linguistic and literary education; but in the end it was clear that the Imperial Government itself was sustained by the very traditions that most needed reform. In 1911, the two col-

lapsed together, giving way in 1912 to the first Republic
ever established "by a non-Caucasian people."

The revolution that established the Republic of China
was virtually bloodless. But the hope that modernization
might take a relatively peaceful course, as in Japan and in
post-Ottoman Turkey (which were looked to as models),
faded at the close of World War I. The era of violence that
followed, with its clashes between traditional war-lords and
reformers, Marxist ideologues and liberals, Chinese and
invading Japanese, and finally reigning Nationalists and
revolutionary Communists, did not end till 1949, when the
mainland Communist Party forced the Kuomintang
Gorvernment to retreat to Taiwan. At the start of that
troubled period, the linguistic aspect of the struggle was
perhaps best summed up by two prominent literary activ-
ists. Ch'ien Hsüan-t'ing, a leading Marxist who collabo-
rated in founding the Chinese Communist Party, and Hu
Shih, a liberal reformer who, it is generally acknowledged,
set the modern Chinese literary revolution on its permanent course.

Ch'ien Hsüan-t'ing's concern was to shatter completely the past's hold on the revolutionary present — a past
which he deemed to be essentially and pervasively Confucian. "If you want to abolish Confucianism, he wrote, "you
must first abolish the Chinese script." To accomplish that
end, he was prepared to abandon Chinese writing altogether and encourage the development of Esperanto, as
well as the use of English or French in writing, while spoken
Chinese developed itself, through intensive education, into
an effective vernacular, to be reduced to writing only after
all its ties with the old written language were severed. Hu
Shih was hardly less radical about ends, but the means he
proposed showed a profounder insight into the nature of
language. "I think China will have an alphabetic writing in
the future," he said. "But there are too many monosyllables
in the literary language and it would be impossible to
change over to an alphabetic script. So it is first necessary
to replace literary writing with *paihua* writing [representing
the actual spoken usage], and after that to change from
paihua writing to alphabetic writing." Hu Shih's basic
premise was that it is literature itself, "and not any pronouncing alphabet or pronouncing dictionaries, which will
eventually standardize the spoken language."

Professor John De Francis of John Hopkins University has very vividly traced the interwoven developments of Chinese revolutionary politics and language study — especially for the period 1917-1949 — in his *Nationalism and Language Reform in China* (New York, 1950, 1972). About the literature of that period, Professor C. T. Hsia says (in the 1971 edition of his *History of Modern Chinese Fiction*) that while it "is readily distinguishable from the earlier periods by its systematic use of the vernacular and its adoption of Western literary forms and techniques, one cannot apply the same criteria to define its immense difference from the succeeding period of Communist literature, since the more recent writers on the mainland have not departed to an appreciable extent from the linguistic and literary conventions of the immediate past." In C. T. Hsia's view, what fundamentally distinguishes the writing of the tragic 1917-1949 period is its "burdens of contemplation; its obsessive concern with China as a nation afflicted with a spiritual disease and therefore unable to strengthen itself or change its ways of inhumanity." He calls it, finally, a patriotic passion — a longing, in effect, for the actualization of a national ideal worthy of personal sacrifice and of earnest literary expression.

Early in the century, Sun Yat-sen had expressed the same obsessive concern with China by asking "What is the standing of our nation in the world?" and answering with these often-quoted words:

> In comparison with other nations, we have the greatest population and the oldest culture, of four thousand years' duration. We ought to be advancing in line with the nations of Europe and America. But the Chinese people have only family and clan groups; there is no national spirit. Consequently, in spite of four hundred million people gathered together in one China, we are in fact but a sheet of loose sand. We are the poorest and weakest state in the world, occupying the lowest position in international affairs; the rest of mankind is the carving kinfe and the serving dish, while we are the fish and meat. Our position now is extremely perilous; if we do not earnestly promote nationalism and weld together our four hundred millions into a strong nation, we face a tragedy — the loss of our country and the destruction of our race. To ward off this danger, we must espouse nationalism and employ the national spirit to save the country.

Family and clan were precious indeed, but in Dr. Sun's view, without the support of nationalism, they could not conceivably withstand the socially destructive force of Western individualism which had by then penetrated deeply into the Chinese intellectual character. In the West, individualism and sovereign nationhood had initially flourished together, and the force of one had served both to secure and restrain the force of the other. If the "sheet of loose sand" that the Chinese people had become was ever to be reconstituted socially in meaningful patterns, the restraints of national feeling and the strengths of national statecraft would have to be introduced, and quickly. In Dr. Sun's words, the Chinese people "must break down individual liberty and become pressed together into an unyielding body like the firm rock which is formed by the addition of cement to sand."

But with the advance of Marxism in China, a threat to traditional social cohesion was suddenly posed from an opposite extreme. According to the Marxist revolutionary design, it was to be all cement and no sand, on a global scale, in preparation for which all past social and cultural configurations would have to be ground into dust much finer than the sands of unrestrained individualism. Caught between the extremes of Western liberal individualism and Marxist communal internationalism, the disciples of Sun Yat-sen, and particularly those in the Kuomintang Party Government that retreated to Taiwan in 1949, have stressed with candor that, while the Confucian social and cultural legacy remains precious, it needs the actuality of nationhood for its support in the modern world. In recent years, the mainland Communist assault on the Confucian heritage has seemed to be far more radical. But as Lucian W. Pye notes in *China: An Introduction* (1972), for all their vehemence, the latest criticisms have somehow managed to assume an essentially Confucian perspective:

> Under Communism there have been ceaseless attacks on much of Confucianism. Filial piety, respect for ancestors, deference to age, and much else have been condemned. Nevertheless, Mao's revolutionary campaigns contain much of the essence of Confucianism. His moralistic approach and stress on revolutionary behavior are closer to the underlying qualities of Confucianism than to the materialism of Marxism-Leninism. . . . Thus, even though the Chinese Commu-

nists under the leadership of Mao Tse-tung declare that they will rid China of its traditional qualities, they cannot escape reflecting the style and tone of Chinese culture.

Perhaps what Professor Pye identifies as inescapably Chinese, and therefore traditional, in the anti-Confucianism of the mainland Communists is not unrelated to that "continuing obsession with China" that C. T. Hsia defines as the reigning mood of the best writing that has come out of Taiwan since 1949. Western individualism and Marxist communal materialism have provided a dialectic of opposites in modern times not only for the people of China but for most of the rest of the world as well. Perhaps what is in store, after the tension of that dialectic has run its course, is an exemplary national re-formation of the Chinese people as a whole, with sufficient sand and sufficient cement to secure (in a new enlightenment of living words) the entire legacy of their grand past. The essays in this issue on *China's Literary Image* converge on the theme.

[*Editor's note.* In writing this Introduction, I have profited from discussion with Professor Henry Paolucci (*RNL* coordinator), who was in the Republic of China in late 1974, while this issue was being prepared. Especially useful have been his insights on the links between language and politics in the general formation of states — ancient and modern, Asian as well as Western.]

Armenia's Literary Heritage: National Focus and Universal Receptiveness

Shakespeare's tragedies and comedies attract an ever wider public because, despite their very strong national emphasis, the universal human interest in them is incomparably stronger. . . . Shakespeare's works have gained entrance everywhere except where national conventions of art are too narrow and specific.

G. W. F. Hegel, 1823[1]

To say that Armenian writers were intensely fond of Shakespeare would be by far an understatement . . . . Shakespeare was to them a typical example of how a writer, altogether true to the realities of his time, could maintain his force and influence undiminished centuries later. He was confirmation of the great truth which says that to be national is indeed to be universal.

Rouben Zarian, 1965[2]

Most comparative linguists have come to agree, at least since the days of the virtually conclusive studies of Hermann Hübschmann, that Armenian has characteristic qualities that entitle it to a unique place in the Indo-Germanic or Indo-European branch of the great world family of languages. There is first of all general agreement among comparatists qualified to judge that Armenian is in several fundamental respects an "ideal language for translating." The historical evidence leaves little room to doubt that while spoken Armenian developed, like all. other spoken languages, as a means of national self-expression, the same can hardly be said of written Armenian. It would seem, in fact, that, almost uniquely among all national languages, written Armenian came into being rather to permit the Armenians to study and cherish as their own the contents of the best writings in other languages.

Writing came to the Armenian language after it had undergone a very long oral development and after educated Armenians had long been used to reading and writing in other languages, particularly Greek, which they loved, and Syriac, which came with conquerors. In the foreword to the Armenian Text of *The History of the Armenians* of Agathangelos, edited with an English translation, commentary, and notes by R.W. Thomson (Albany, 1976), the translator-editor recalls for us the occasion and consequences of the "invention of a national script" for an already highly-developed spoken Armenian. The conversion of the Armenians to Christianity had started early in the fourth century A.D. But its spread throughout the land, Professor Thomson reminds us, was an understandably slow process, the success of which was often placed in doubt. In his words:

> Enduring success only became possible after the development of a script for Armenian so that religious services and the scriptures could be understood. Until then Greek or Syriac were the languages of the church, though oral preaching was naturally done in the vernacular. The invention of a national script was the work of an indefatigable missionary, Mashtots — also known as Mosrop by later Armenian writers. As soon as the script had been fashioned, c. 400, groups of young men were set to learning it; they were then sent abroad to make translations of the major church fathers and of other texts important for the dissemination of the Christian message. Returning to Armenia with copies of the scriptures, ecclesiastical canons, service books, biblical commentaries, homilies, lives of saints, historical works and other books of Christian interest in Greek or Syriac, these young men not only gave Armenia a vast mass of translated literature within one generation; they in turn became the first original writers in their native tongue. (xiii)

It seems altogether doubtful that spoken Armenian was a primitive language when it acquired its script. On this point, H. Thorossian has summarized scholarly opinion and added several insightful observations of his own in his *Histoire de la Littérature Arménienne* (Paris, 1951). He notes first that universal history offers us no example of a new literature developing so rapidly out of primitive beginnings as Armenian literature developed during the first thirty or forty years after it acquired its script. To be coupled with this as even more conclusive proof is the fact of the great quantity and quality of the translations produced during those years — translations executed, as he says, virtually with "no hesitation, revision, or correction." If the first translation of the Bible was later indeed revised, he clarifies, "the revision was undertaken not on the grounds of any imperfection in style, but simply to guarantee its minute accuracy as a translation." (36-37)

Like the Septuagint translation of the Hebrew Old Testament into Greek made by Hellenistic Jews during the third and second centuries B.C., and the King James English version of both Testaments completed in 1611 A.D., the fifth century A.D. Armenian translation of the Bible, and especially of the New Testament, has received the highest praise. Ara Baliozian echoes the shared judgment of almost all comparatists competent to judge where he writes in his popular book, *The Armenians: Their History and Culture*: "The incandescent beauty, the almost miraculous simplicity of the Armenian translation of the Bible, has led scholars to call it 'the Queen of Translations'." (39)

But translations of Holy Scriptures, expositions of sacred dogmas of revelation, ecclesiastical histories, lives of saints, and manuals of rites were soon enough followed by translations of "other books of Christian interest," including works of Plato and Aristotle, with the commentaries upon them of Jamblicus and Porphory, as well as the books of Euclid, to name but a few. Of these it has been said that the old Armenian translations were so accurate that, if the original Greek versions were lost — which has not infrequently been the case — one could translate them back from Armenian into Greek . . . without losing any of the accuracy of the originals." The accuracy was no doubt due to the intentional faithfulness to the originals, a faithfulness which was almost slavish in the case of some humble or pedestrian undertaking by a lowly monk performing his task in the line of duty; but if the version happened to be the work of a writer of "taste and talent," as the eminent Italian philologist Ubaldo Faldati puts it, "then the translation is likely to rank as a work of art in its own right, and often as one of great merit."[3] There is no denying that the learned H. H. Schaeder had a philologist's professional precision on his side when he insisted that what made Armenian an ideal language for translating was its remarkable syntactical "freedom in the formation of sentences, its preference for participial constructions, and indeed the general fulness of its constructions."[4] But Professor Faldati stresses instead the extraordinary adaptability of Armenian, even beyond its syntactical suppleness, which permits it to penetrate deeply into the "most distinguishing peculiarities and spirit" of the works to be translated; and, to indicate how permanent a capacity of the language that has proved to be, he points to the relatively recent splendid Armenian versions of the celebrated *Oraisons Funèbres* of Bossuet and Ugo Foscolo's romantic masterpiece, *I Sepolcri.*

But the crowning achievement of the sacred art of the Armenian *Sourp Tarkmanichk*[5], or holy translators, as they came to be called — the achievement that reveals the heights and depths of the Armenian literary capacity to sympathize with and possess itself of the highest literary aspirations and attainments of other peoples — is unquestionably its extraordinary success in translating Shakespeare, coupled with the impressive lessons for comparative literary studies that the Armenians themselves have drawn from that success.

What, after all, is a masterful translation, if not an inspired exercise in comparative literary study, aiming to transfuse the spirit of one language into the substance of another? The first significant translations in the Western literary tradition, as is well known, were translations from Greek into Latin; and they were translations made by Greeks, not Romans. Greeks learned Latin in order to be able to teach Romans how to appreciate Greek. To that end they proceeded to translate Greek works into Latin and even to write more or less original works in Latin — all in order to show what an advantage it would be for a Roman with literary aspirations of any kind to learn Greek. That method of teaching proved an immense success. Mighty

Rome in fact succumbed to the power of the manifest perfection of the Greek cultural-literary heritage. The consequence was that Latin, in the hands of its masters of poetry and prose, rapidly became a translators' language *par excellence* — receptive at its most vital center to the precision, charm, and spiritual elevation of Greek.

That reaching out by the Greek teachers of the late Hellenistic period to win the hearts and minds of their Roman students constitutes the real beginning of the Western literary tradition, which would not have become a tradition at all, of course, except for the extraordinarily positive response of the Romans. Plato's *Ion* offers us the image of "a number of pieces of iron and rings suspended from one another so as to form a long chain," all of them deriving their "power of suspension" from an original magnetic stone. That, Plato's Socrates says, is how the Muse of inspired literary composition works. First she herself inspires certain writers; and then, "from these inspired persons a chain of other persons is suspended, who take the inspiration."[6] That image, originally introduced to make the transmission of inspiration from person to person somewhat intelligible, became applicable for the explanation of the formation of great literary traditions across national borders after the experience of the Hellenistic Greek teachers with their Roman pupils.

Armenians have for a long time been fascinated with the problem of international literary receptiveness. And their best speculations on the subject — which we must regard as major contributions to comparative literary study of the trans-national relations of national literatures — have focused increasingly, in recent decades, on their own response as a nation to the national literary genius of Shakespeare. A veritable masterpiece in this regard has been the lecture on "Shakespeare and the Armenians" by Rouben Zarian, delivered in London on May 30, 1965. The original Armenian version was published in Yerevan in 1967, an English version by Haig Voskerchian appeared in 1969, and a French version and possibly other translations into European languages soon followed.

The basic question Rouben Zarian's lecture poses for us as European-American comparatists is this: If it were possible to translate his (or her) greatness, how would a giant of world literature read or sound in the language of a people little known, culturally, to even the best educated classes of a major Western nation? The Armenians have taken great pride in trying to help us to arrive at a satisfactory answer in the case of Shakespeare. The pride derives largely from the fact, as we have already noted, that the Armenian language had been supplied with an alphabet so that it could, from the very beginning, phrase and answer such a question for itself with respect to the Sacred Scriptures of Christianity, and to the writings of the Greek Fathers and other Churchmen immediately inspired by those scriptures.

In the Western literary tradition the comparable question has been, first of all: What would Homer read or sound like had his language been Latin instead of Greek? The question of translating the Bible came much later, and remained limited for centuries to rendering Greek or Aramaic or Hebrew originals into Latin, and then to standardizing a Latin version. Long before there were demands for Bible translations in any of the Western national vernaculars, the basic comparative literary question had become: How would Virgil read or sound had he written in Italian instead of Latin, or in English, Spanish, or French instead of Latin or Italian? Next it was the turn of a Dante or Petrarch to stand in the place of the Greek and Latin masters, as the Western literary tradition continued its transnational development down to the days of Pound and Eliot and Joyce in the English-speaking world and of their counterparts and peers in most of the other major literatures of the West.

But what about the Armenians with their Indo-European language living for millennia on the borders of east and west, and having long since proved themselves masters of the art of inspired translation? Some years before Rouben Zarian delivered his London lecture of 1965, Edward Alexander, who is also of Armenian origin, had published an article in *Shakespeare Quarterly* (IX, 1958, 387-394), titled "Shakespeare's Plays in Armenia," in which he began by pointing out what the staging of Shakespeare's plays in Armenian seems to have meant for the Armenian people in times of communal trial. When non-Armenian rulers of Armenian communities have sought to censor the content, if not the form, of literary works — more or less for the sort of reasons indicated by Plato in the notorious pro-censorship

passages of his *Republic* — the Armenians have had to face
up to an old dilemma: whether to knuckle under to the
censorship completely, or offer open or covert resistence
subtly defying the authorities or remaining silent.

"In the face of this predicament," Edward Alexander
observed, referring to the immediately preceding decades,
the Armenian people living under such pressures and unable to fully comply with the censorship, took to identifying
themselves in their literary aspirations with Western writers generally, and more particularly with English and American writers. "But most of all," Alexander hastened to add,
"the people on all levels seized upon Shakespeare. For one
reason, the English poet dealt in elevated manner with
events removed perhaps chronologically from the Armenian scene but spiritually very much akin. For another,
Shakespeare could be read in a series of translations of the
utmost purity, economy, and beauty of language" — translations into which no "forcibly injected words" of vigilant
censors could enter "with their reminders of the present. "

Edward Alexander was referring to the translations
of Hovhannes Mahseyan, or Massehian, as the name is
spelled in the English version of Rouben Zarian's lecture
on "Shakespeare and the Armenians." To be sure, many
Armenian poets and scholars had tried their hand at translating Shakespeare before Hovhannes Massehian, but, as
Rouben Zarian notes, when Massehian*s translations began to appear, there was at once a sense that the receptive
genius of the Armenian language had at last produced
another of its holy translators.

At the time of the publication of Massehian's first
Shakespeare translation — a version of *Hamlet* — in 1896,
the leading national poet of the day, Hovhannes Toumanian,
introduced his judgment of it with these words: "Shakespeare
has become a criterion by which to determine a nation's
cultural standards. A people who does not translate
Shakespeare is illiterate; those who are unable to understand him are intellectually immature, and the language
into which Shakespeare cannot be translated is indeed
poor." Hailing the appearance of Massehian's *Hamlet*, he
then added: "We can now say that we have indeed made
great progress by way of getting Shakespeare to express
himself in Armenian. . . . This is a great leap forward, a very
great leap."

By the time of his death in 1931, Massehian had published translations of *As You Like It, Romeo and Juliet, The Merchant of Venice, King Lear, Othello,* and *Macbeth,* besides Hamlet. After his death, manuscript translations of *Antony and Cleopatra, Much Ado About Nothing, The Tempest, Julius Caesar,* and *Coriolanus* were found, and publication of several of these soon followed. It is said that he also translated *A Winter's Tale* and *Timon of Athens,* making fourteen plays in all, and perhaps two others. But what we want to underscore are Zarian's views on the comparative literary significance of the art of translating, as exemplified by Massehian. Affirming that Massehian had the power of "coping with Shakespeare and making him ours, making him speak Armenian," Zarian procedes to assert that Massehian brought to his task an "ardent and boundless love," indeed a "passionate enthrallment — no doubt in the sense of the magnetic power in the image of Plato's *Ion* — such as "characterizes great talents," awakening in them "the capacity of making possible what is virtually impossible."

But besides that, says Zarian, Massehian proved himself in those translations to have the technical mastery of a true poet-craftsman. Reading the versified passages of his translations we can hardly fail "to realize that had he chosen, Massehian could have become a poet of the same right as any of our famous poets." And beyond his poetic abilities and passionate enthrallment with his subject, Massehian had also the third indispensable prerequisite for coping with Shakespeare. He was a learned man: a scholar of the first order and a rigorous critic as well, with broad knowledge of the many peoples and affairs of the world. Through all the years he devoted to translating Shakespeare, he was a career diplomat in the service of the Persian government, holding important posts in the capitals and many major cities of dozens of countries, and serving as ambassador in Berlin, London, and Tokyo. He was a master of many languages, including Persian, Arabic, German, Russian, Turkish, and English-and perhaps even, in some measure, of Japanese — as well as of his native Armenian in its classical and popular varieties.

While steeping himself in Shakespeare's English texts, he also studied French and German versions, and, during his service in Tokyo, he may have had an opportunity to speak of the universal relevence of Shakespeare's portrayals of men and women of every variety with Tsubuchi Shuyo, the great Japanese Shakespeare translator. On the matter of Shakespeare's universal relevence, Zarian then says: "Shakespeare is known as the master-creator of the most various human characters. Massehian has been able to retain this variety and, in doing so, has achieved such individuality of speech for each character as has been seldom equalled in the history of translated literature." This Massehian accomplished with the intention of making Shakespeare "the heritage of Armenian literature," so as to give his reader the impression "that what he is reading is not a translation at all, but actually a text originally written in his mother tongue, a text as naturally comprehensive to him as the legends of his native Toumanian or the sonnets of his compatriot Terian."

Zarian could indeed be speaking of the practice of the "holy translators" of the Bible in the fifth century A.D. where he says that "Massehian endeavored — and that was his method — to find out what the Armenian language had to offer by way of equivalents of one or another of the expressions used by Shakespeare and to choose among them the one most appropriate to the given instance and closest to the original text." That gave him an opportunity to reach back through the centuries in order to enrich the present potentials of Armenian. He drew on every available level of Armenian usage, from the elevated style of the early Bible translations, the grammatical perfection of the truly classical writing built upon the style of those inspired translations, and every other variety of style that subsequently asserted itself, especially as a consequence of the century-and-a-half long Mekhitarist classical renaissance that began in 1701 and ended around 1850 when the two major varieties of modern Armenian began to affirm themselves as literary languages.

According to Zarian, Massehian's translations, like those of the fifth century A.D., "spurred on and stimulated the progress of the Armenian literary style." Once again, foreigners were to marvel how the two new varieties of modern Armenian distinguished as Eastern and Western should have suddenly flowered, without notable preparation, into relatively mature literary languages in the years directly following publication of Massehian's translations.

Massehian had of course made modern Armenian flexible and rich enough to cope with Shakespeare, proving — at least for persons competent to judge — that "the language of a small trodden nation" had indeed earned for itself "the right to stand on an equal footing with that of a developed nation."

Zarian ends his lecture by reminding his auditors of what the great Schlegel, who gave Germany a German-speaking Shakespeare, had said of the art and power of translations of literary masterworks. He cites the opinions of Jean Louis Barrault and André Gide (as well as of Peter Brook) on the defects of most French translations of Shakespeare. Of André Gide's efforts to supply the defect with his version of *Hamlet*, Zarian was pleased to note that an edition of Gide's version, with the English text on facing pages, had been published in Boston, and that it had apparently arrested the attention of Shakespeare's countrymen sufficiently to make publication of the bilingual text possible. That, says Zarian, agreeing with what Justin O'Brian had pointed out in a preface to the Boston edition, represented a promising change, since as a rule, "the work of a translator is seldom of any interest to the literature from which it is translated."

But there have been many Armenian translators of Shakespeare before and since Massehian. And the remarkable thing is that editions of Armenian versions of the great plays have been published in cities "as far apart," as Zarian puts it, "as Calcutta, Moscow, Venice, Smyrna, Tiflis, Cairo, Petersburg, Paris, Baku, Constantinople, Vienna, Teheran, Beirut, and Yerevan." Wherever Armenians live, they now have Shakespeare with them. "Could there be any greater proof," Zarian asks, "of the great love the Armenian people — scattered to the four corners of the earth — have for Shakespeare?" Near the close of his paper, Zarian sums up his thesis:

> Shakespeare has been — if you will allow the expression — "naturalized" by the Armenians. I say this not because fifty Armenians or so have attempted to translate Shakespeare. . . . My point is that the Armenian people have found in the person of Shakespeare a dramatist who, better than any other writer, granted them an opportunity for self-expression. Through him they made people at large aware of the sufferings our nation had gone through, of their ardent love

of life and of their humanistic aspirations. And though they performed Shakespeare, they told the world about us, said who we were, where we came from, what tragedies our people had experienced, and what they aspired to — a peaceful spot under the vast blue sky, side by side with other peoples, like other peoples, the right to express what every other people has the right to express, what is theirs and theirs alone, born from their history, and though this is specifically national, it serves, none the less, all humanity."

Every people, in other words, has a right to call Shakespeare its own, once his true power has made itself felt among them. Shakespeare was and is England's national poet, to be sure. But the lesson of his nationalism, for all who make it their own, through the magnetic inspiration of his poetry, is indeed that summed up in the words of Zarian quoted in this paper's caption. Shakespeare has been and always will be confirmation of the great truth which alone can draw the diverse peoples of the world closer together in mutually respected separate and equal stations. It is the truth of highest communal dignity, which says that "to be national is indeed to be universal."

A few summers back, part of the New York Shakespeare Summerfest Festival that ran from June 18 through September 20, 1981, was devoted to a series of weekly presentations titled "Shakespeare and the World." Its purpose was two-fold. Foremostly, the intention was to give experts in Shakespeare studies in foreign lands a chance to show how diverse peoples have responded to the challenge so aptly summed up in the words earlier quoted from the Armenian poet-critic Hovhannes Toumanian: "Shakespeare has become a criterion by which to determine a nation's cultural standards." The series included programs titled "Shakespeare and the Afro-American Community," "Shakespeare in the Hispanic World," "The Greeks Meet the Elizabethan," "Shakespeare's Germany: Plays, Poetry, and Music," "Shakespeare in Japan," "The Hamlet Myth in 19th Century France," "The Many Faces of Love: Shakespeare's Italy," "Shakespeare in Russia: Excerpts from Poetry, Fiction, and Music," "Shakespeare in the Yiddish Theater," "Shakespeare on the Turkish Stage," and, I am pleased to say, also a program on "Shakespeare and the Armenian Theater."[7]

Each of those programs, as one can almost guess

from the titles, provided a distinctive emphasis, often depending, to be sure, on the personality of the director rather than on the nation brought into focus, particularly when the director was not ethnically of that nation. But, to see how differently the Greeks, French, Spanish, Germans, and Russians perceived Shakespeare (and the Shakespearean passages selected for representation often very clearly showed this), proved to be an unexpectedly striking revelation, at least for those who attended all or most of the presentations, each of which, to be sure, drew a rather special audience, by and large. And that leads us to say a word about the second half of the two-fold purpose of the series. For those in the audience whose native language was English, the parallels selected for dramatized recitation made it possible to sense almost instinctively new depths in the universal-national significance of Shakespeare: depths not otherwise easily perceptible. The Greek program, for instance, managed to focus on strikingly Greek characterizations of events and people, even as the Hispanic program — stressing the age-old strain in the cultural relations of Spain and England — managed to draw a powerful, yet altogether poetic lesson for Spanish and European Latin-American relations through readings from *The Tempest.*

In the spirit of Rouben Zarian's lecture, the Armenian program took up without hesitation the challenge of the truly great passages and characterizations of the greatest plays. Before the program was over, the obvious "passionate enthrallment" of the actors and readers with their subject had fully communicated itself to the audience — and particularly to those present who did not understand Armenian. The passages were first read in English and then in Armenian; and the effect was indeed like the generation of a magnetic current. The audience felt at once the capacity of Armenian to "receive" the Shakespearean poetic inspiration and give it a genuinely national re-utterance of its own. What the philologists say about the genius of the language is manifestly true: it has what the creator of its script wished it to have — a protean capacity to receive and give the very best that literary inspiration is capable of.

In the critical essays that follow, the emphasis is on what modern Armenian literature, East and West, has achieved, and is in the process of achieving. The essays cover the whole ground and need no further introduction. All were especially written for this issue, and all are animated with something of the spirit we have attempted to define in this introduction: the spirit of that ancient and complex tradition of universal receptiveness linked inextricably with a national as well as fundamentally religious expressiveness that simply must make itself heard in the world. It is the spirit that gives the papers of diverse perspectives brought together here from lands near and far their common focus.

NOTES

1. *Hegel: On The Arts*, abridged and translated by H. Paolucci (New York, Frederick Ungar, 1979), p. 174, adapted. See also, *Hegel's Aesthetics: Lectures on Fine Art*, translated by T.M. Knox (Oxford, At the Clarendon Press, 1975,) Vol. 11, p. 1176.

2. *Shakespeare and the Armenians*, by Rouben Zarian, translated by Haig Voskerchian (Etchmiadzin, At the Press of the Academy of Sciences 1969), p. 10, adapted. See also, Rouben Zarian, *Shakespeare et les Armeniens*, traduction de N. Haroutounian (Genève, Perret-Gentil, 1974), p. 16.

3. Ubaldo Faldati, "Lingua e letteratura armena," *Enciclopedia italiana* (Roma, Istituto della Enciclopedia Italiana), IV, 430-435.

4. Cited in P. Vardan Hatzuni, *Cenno storico c culturale sulla nazione armena* (Venezia, Prem. Tipografia Armena di S. Lazzaro, 1940), p. 21.

5. A. Baliozian, *The Armenians* (New York, Ararat Press, 1980), p. 47.

6. *The Dialogues of Plato*, translated into English by Benjamin Jowett, 2 Vols (London, Oxford, New York, The Macmillan Co., 1892, Oxford University Press, 1920, Random House, 1937), II, 289.

7. The *Quarterly World Report* of the Council on National Literatures devoted its October 1982 issue (V,4) to this "Shakespeare and the World" program, which had been presented at the American Museum of Natural History in New York, in conjunction with the Folger Shakespeare Library, and funded in part by the National Endowment for the Humanities. The special issue features photographs of most of the presentations listed, and highlights the French and Armenian segments by publishing

Rosette Lamont's introduction to the first and Nishan Parlakian's introduction to the second. An editorial note explains: "One deals with Shakespeare in familiar territory for comparatists . . . the other . . . in a culture not very well-known to most of us."

Hungary's "Neglected" National Literature

The great writers of Hungary are known in Europe only
by name. . . . One of the chief reasons their literature is
practically unknown is the difficulty of the language. The
other European languages are branches of the same tree:
Hungarian stands without relatives among them. . . .
Lyric poetry, the chief asset of Hungarian literature, is
almost untranslatable. This is all the more distressing,
because the composite character of Hungarian literature
found its real expression in a multicolored lyric poetry.

Dezsó Keresztúri, in Stephen Sisa's
The Spirit of Hungary[1990][1]

In the January 1976 *Report* of the Council on National
Literatures (p. 4), Frank J. Warnke carefully distinguished
between "emergent" and "neglected" as used in the Council's
self-identifying statement of purpose: "A Forum to explore
ways of reassessing Comparative Literature, as an academic
discipline and an area of scholarly study, toward the end of
promoting the integration of newer 'emerging,' and older
'neglected' literatures into the traditional spectrum." When
applied to national literatures, Professor Warnke stressed,
emergent and neglected "designate radically different phe-

nomena: the *emergent* literature is clearly felt as such by its creators and its native consumers; the neglected literature is not neglected within its own sphere — it is neglected only by outsiders."

Clarifying the distinction, Professor Warnke added that, as used by Western comparatists, *emergent* literature seems most fittingly applicable to "products of, for example, the sub-Saharan African cultures," whereas *neglected* suggests, rather, "such entities as Persian literature, one of the dominant forces in the great Near Eastern literary community, or Korean literature, an important component of the East Asian community."

Hungarian literature is plainly neither emergent nor neglected in those senses. Despite its Finno-Ugrian ethnic-linguistic origins and its presumedly runic original script (in which nothing literary has survived), the literature of the Magyars as traditionally recorded in Latin script doesn't in any significant respect belong to a community lying "beyond the confines of the West." Unfortunately, even in so prestigious a literary journal as *World Literature Today*, we must still turn to a section headed "Finno-Ugric & Baltic Languages" to find reviews of books about Hungarian literature; yet it remains undeniable that, as Kenneth Katzner has aptly observed: "In the more than a thousand years that have elapsed since [their original settlement in the Danube valley], the Hungarians have become completely Europeanized, with only their language serving to reveal their Asian origins."[2]

1. Europe's Canon of Emergent, Established, and Neglected National Literatures

Besides *emergent* and *neglected*, the broad spectrum of comparative studies necessarily includes a third category of literatures generally ranked as *established*. Established lituratures provide the standard in comparison with which other literatures get to be ranked as emergent or neglected. From a global perspective, the literatures of China, India, and Japan surely qualify today as "established." Yet, as Dr. Warnke stresses, comparative literary study remains an essentially Western phenomenon, even when carried on by Japanese, Chinese, and Indian scholars. To qualify as cornparatists, scholars the world over still find it necessary, it seems, to take as their standard the traditional European "majority linguistic group" made up, as Warnke specifies, of English, French, German, Italian, Spanish, Portuguese, and Russian.

Scholars and critics "rooted" in that majority linguistic group of seven, Warnke notes, have increasingly come "to perceive the desirability of integrating into comparative literary study those literatures which have usually been *terra incognita*" for them. They have therefore tended to look far afield for examples of the emergent and neglected. The result has been, Warnke admonishes, the slighting of a number of Western literatures that still qualify as emergent and often also as neglected, at least "for most members of dominant language societies."

Among the "still emergent" Western literatures, writes Warnke, "might be classified certain national literatures (e.g., Albanian), certain component literatures of multi-national states (e.g., Macedonian in [old] Yugoslavia), and the domestic literatures (e.g., Scots Gaelic, Norwegian Landsmal, Plattdeutsch, Schweizer-deutsch, Basque)." Classed as both emergent and neglected, Warnke elaborates, might be "virtually all European and Arnerican literatures expressed in a language other than one of the seven dominant ones."

Of those dominant seven, four — English, Spanish, Portuguese, and French — have, of course, long functioned as "colonial" languages. Since Columbus's time, they have not only spread in distant places but have also given birth to colonies which have developed into nations on their own. The Italian, German, and Russian languages have never had significant colonial developments. But, for centuries, the colonial English-speakers in the Americas, as well as the Spanish-, Portuguese- and French-speakers, produced literary works that qualified them merely as "branches" of their parent literatures in Europe. American-British English was the first to make a break; and tile break came slowly. As recently as the 1950s, T. S. Eliot could still speak of our American national literature in English as something unique in the world. In his classic address on "American Literature and the American Language," delivered at Washington University in St. Louis in 1953, the long-since "Anglisized" dean of American modernist poets had not hesitated to say, by way of defining the distinctive national identity of American literature: "I believe that we are now justified in speaking of what has never, I think, been found before, two literatures in the same language."[3]

Things have changed radically since 1953. As was noted in *RNL*'s issue on *Australia*, claims of having established two or more national literatures in the same language — in Spanish, Portuguese, Dutch, and French, etc., as well as in English — are now commonplace. The experience of the United States has been and continues to be exemplary. What were once imperial colonies have indeed developed distinctive national literatures of their own, matching and perhaps even surpassing in importance their European parental counterparts.

But Warnke here returns to his primary concern. We are all aware, he writes, of minor Western literatures generally neglected outside their own borders which have nevertheless "from time to time presented the world with masters whose eminence has enforced an entry into the canon of world literaure." As examples, Warnke would have us think "of Ibsen, of Strindberg, of H. C. Andersen, of Kazantzakis or Kavafy." And he might perhaps have added the name of Hungary's Sándor Petofi, of another generation. But his point is:

> There are, however, a vastly greater number of ignored titans, conspicuously, though not exclusively, those whose expression is in verse rather than prose. Vondel, Hooft, and Huygens in Holland; Jens Peter Jacobsen in Denmark; Mickiewicz, Slowacki, and Krasinski in Poland; Endre Ady in Hungary; Mihai Eminescu in Romania; Miroslav KrIeza in Croatian Yugoslavia — these all remain, beyond the border of national culture, known only to the émigré, the specialist, or the eccentric collector of literary esoterica. A question of great importance poses itself. Do we of the West who are confined to a few of the major languages and to the international canon as it exists in translation into these languages suffer from provincialism? Are we missing something, perhaps quite a lot? The revision and expansion of the international canon of great authors may well be one of the most urgent tasks confronting the contemporary comparatist.

A year after he wrote those words, Professor Warnke supplied a "Bibliographical Spectrum" on the subject for our 1977 *RNL* issue (Vol. 8) on *Holland*. Its stated purpose was indeed to illustrate, in the particular case of a currently-neglected European literature, how comparatists might best go about meeting what he had called one of their "most urgent tasks." The reigning view among modern comparatists, he acknowledged at the outset, has long been that "the criteria for identifying a 'national' literature should be primarily linguistic rather than politico-historical." Yet the best of such comparatists — he hastened to add — usually recognize that" political and historical considerations" can indeed radically modify our perception of a literature's national identity which, more often than not, "becomes clearly recognizable only when, taken as a whole, it is compared with other literatures." (p. 180)

2. Linguistic or Cultural Literary History?

But a question at once suggests itself when we speak of comparing one literature, "taken as a whole," with other literatures. What sort of "grasp" must we have of two or more literatures, if they are to be objectively compared as wholes? In a review article titled "Literary Histories or Literary Chronologies?" — published as a companion piece in that same *RNL* issue on *Holland* — Richard C. Clark drew (pp. 195-196) on Sir Philip Sidney for an exemplary answer, which served him also as an answer to a prior question: When does a literature begin?

Dr. Clark had earlier explored aspects of those paired questions in other review articles touching on the diverse approaches of literary historians in dealing with a variety of literatures, whether emergent, established, or neglected. For his piece on Holland, he recalled in passing that one of the pioneer comparatists attempting to treat literatures as wholes had been the distinguished British statesman, diplomat, world traveler, first editor of the prestigious *Westminster Review*, and "extraordinarily versatile linguist," Sir John Bowring (1792-1872). Excited by the great linguistic breakthroughs of British orientalists of the caliber of William Jones (1746-1794) and Henry Thomas Colebrooke (1765-1837), whose labors with Sanskrit, ancient Persian, and Arabic inaugurated the modern era of comparative linguistic studies on a global scale, Bowring devoted decades to studying and translating the poetry of many newly emergent or neglected national literatures, including those of "Russia, Poland, Servia, Hungary, Holland, Spain, etc." The critical approach he assumed for comparative examination of such literatures is well-enough suggested in the extended title for his Hungarian volume: *"Poetry of the Magyars, preceded by a Sketch of the Language and Literature of Hungary and Transylvania* (London: Printed for the Author, 1830)."

Needless to say, Bowring's pioneering work of that kind soon became outdated. He invariably began at the beginning in his historical sketches of the languages and literatures he was sampling in translation; and that was doomed to have a deadening effect, particularly in the case of Hungary, where the linguistic beginnings had only lately been identified as "Finno-Ugric Uralic" — an origin apparently shared by Hungarians with far-off Lapps, and Estonians. The worst thing about starting at the beginning linguistically, according to Professor Clark, is. that it makes literary comparisons with major "established" literatures virtually meaningless. And here is where a lesson can be drawn from the practice of Sir Philip Sidney in his famous comparative "apologie" for poetry, which indeed ranks, in Clark's words, as "the first cursory sketch of a history of English poetry."

Where, then, should a history capable of revealing a nation's literary identity properly begin? "For a true historian," Clark writes, "the answer might well have to be: *in medias res*, rather than at the beginning." The truth is that "Herodotus, Thucyclides, and Polybius (who taught the Romans) all learned to organize histories from Homer or the Greek tragedians"; and their practice was, therefore, "to give the reader, first of all, an arresting sense of the importance of the subject as a whole, so that it was plain at once why the subject merited a history." As Clark explains it:

> For Sidney, writing in 1579, English literature "begins" two centuries earlier with a great master, Chaucer, rather than with some obscure text of a remoter time. Chaucer, Surrey, Spenser: their works, rising above a mass of would-be poets writing in English, justify Sidney's defense of what English poetry has been and promises to be. To account for the literary excellence of such poets, Sidney asks us to look not to English language precedents, but rather to French and Italian authors, and, beyond them, to Roman and Greek masters.

But why not work back to a beginning linguistically?

Why not search with scientific objectivity back through all
the earliest evidences of things written or said in English?
Sidney's reasoning against doing so is thus pursued by
Professor Clark:

> What came before Chaucer in English is, from Sidney's point
> of view, a long linguistic preparation that very gradually
> made English what Sidney called a richly "mingled lan-
> guage"; more various on that account, in its natural rhythms
> and rhymes than French or Spanish; and not, like Italian, "so
> full of vowels that it was ever cumbered with elisions," or,
> like Dutch, so cumbered "with consonants that they cannot
> yield the sweet sliding fit for a verse."

Most of the major developing national literatures of
the west have been similarly treated by their ablest historians. Their best histories begin *in medias res*. A great writer
(like Dante), or several great writers (like Villon and
Rabelais, or Chaucer, Surrey, and Spenser), have given
proof that a genuinely national literature has come into
being. Before such writers appear, all use of the vernacular
is but a preparation for them. And such use only gradually
becomes literary. The earliest specimens of written French
and German, for instance, have come down to us in the
form of paired military oaths sworn by troops and their
commanders at Strasbourg, in 842 AD (just a few decades
before the Hungarians first brought their Magyar tongue
into the Danube valley!).

The commanders at Strasbourg were grandsons of
Charlemagne, engaged in their dark-age labors of dividing
their inherited Holy Roman Empire into the countless
feudal fragments out of which the modern national states
of Europe would begin to take shape several centuries later.
The troops engaged were all Germanic — East-Frankish on
one side, West-Frankish on the other. The difference was
that the West-Franks had merged (as rulers) with the numerous Gallo-Roman population of Gaul, and thus eventually became what we call Frenchmen; while their blood
cousins and brothers-in-law, the East-Franks, never left
their strictly German environment, rarely mingled, and
thus remained German to the core. The paired oaths at
Strasbourg, as the distinguished Harvard historian Ephraim
Emerton long ago impressively explained (after citing the
texts as actually sworn in their *lingua romana* and *lingua
teudisca*), have

an especial value as the earliest specimens of the old romance and the old germanic languages. We see here the former just emerging from the ancient Latin and reminding us of the later French, Spanish and Italian. We see the latter, without any admixture of the Latin, already so like the modern German, English and Dutch that one can read it without much difficulty.

For the earliest specimens of written Italian, on the contrary, one cannot point to beginnings in oaths sworn by kings who divided the world with their contests and disputes. Even so, oaths almost always played a part. As Matthew Pauley has observed, the earliest Italian texts are mostly the "lowly pronouncements of humble witnesses who have been called to testify, on their oaths, that such and such is indeed, to their knowledge, the fact of the matter on trial." As in the case of the Strasbourg oaths, Pauley adds, "such pronouncements usually come to us in reports or annals written in Latin, where the *ipsissima verba* are recorded to stress the fact that they were pronounced under oath."[4]

In all of that, we are far indeed removed from the beginnings of genuine literature. Such materials are historically important, but not for literary histories or even for a history of the emergence of a national literary language. Vernacular poets as founders of new literatures have always learned much more from studying the mature poetry of foreign masters than from digging up their native texts of military or court-recorded oaths. That is the lesson of Sir Philip Sidney's cursory history and defense of poetry: whether one's vantage point is on the Thames or the Arno, the Seine or the Danube: one has to begin in the middle, and look to foreigners for instructive models.

Sidney, of course, addressed himself primarily to English gentlemen and ladies; but the same applies doubly when the historical sketch is intended for comparatists in other countries — which is a point well-made in several of the contributions to this volume. An alternate linguistic approach, stressing the essentially European character of the Hungarian. vernacular *literary* language (as distinct from its *non-literary* counterpart) is suggested in the volume's concluding Review Article.

NOTES

1. Cited in 3tephen, Sisa, ed.,*The Spirit of Hungary: A Panorama of Hungarian History and Culture*, 2nd edition, Morrison, NJ: Vista Books, 1990, p. 344.

2. Kenneth Katzner, *The Languages of the World*, New York: Funk& Wagnalls, 1975, p 93.

3. In T. S. Eliot, *To Criticize the Critic*, New York: Farrar, Staus & Giroux, 1965, p, 51.

4. Matthew Pauley, *I Do Solemnly Swear: The President's Constitutional Oath – What It Means, Why It Matters*, Doctoral Dissertation, Department of Government, Harvard University, Cambridge, MA, 1989, pp. 151-152.

Erasmus, Huizinga, and the Unfinished Business of Dutch Literature

> Erasmus could not have attained to his world-wide celebrity if it had not been for Latin. To make his native tongue a universal language was beyond him.
>
> Johan Huizinga, 1924*[1]

> It is beyond my powers to persuade you to learn Dutch in order to appreciate the poetic efflorescence that has sprung into being during the last half century . . . an efflorescence that is hardly less rich than the flowering of Dutch painting in the seventeenth century.
>
> Annie Romein Verschoor, 1950[2]

> Were Dutch literature as well known as it deserves to be, a number of significant adjustments in our picture of European and World literature would occur. . . . Vondel, Hooft, Huygens, Multatuli, and Vestdijk would take their place among the classic authors [and] a more exact identification of specifically national features would emerge: the cosmopolitan reader would learn to recognize the verbal genre-painting, the homely realism, the peculiar whimsey, the themes of tolerance and community that seem to be constant in the Dutch literary imagination — in the time of Vestdijk as in the time of Erasmus.
>
> Frank J. Warnke, 1976[3]

If translations could reproduce impressions of literary masterworks as faithfully and easily as modern photographic prints reproduce paintings of every sort, would the major writers of the Netherlands be as widely known internationally as its major painters?

"Rembrandt — Vermeer — Hals — these names are recognized by all lovers of art," wrote Professor Henrietta ten Harmsel in the Introduction to her translations of *Jacobus Revius: Dutch Metaphysical Poet*[4]; and then she lamented: "But who knows the name of Revius? Or even the name of Vondel? Although the dark grandeur of a drama by Vondel is comparable to that of a painting by Rembrandt; although the subtle symbolism of a sonnet by Revius is comparable to a scene by Vermeer; still the world has learned to know the painters, not the poets." And the passing centuries seem to have increased rather than diminished the advantage of Dutch painters in this respect. Writing of the Dutch cultural renewal of the past hundred years in all the arts, Frank J. Warnke draws this parallel: "So it is that the names of such painters as Van Gogh and Mondrian . . . are familiar to educated people all over the world; while such literary figures as Multatuli, van Schendel, Boutens, Leopold, and Vestdijk remain virtually unknown." (3, p.4)

Still, it is not simply to decry the relative eclipse of the one by the fame of the other that critics competent in the field more or less inevitably link Dutch literature with Dutch painting — even when making purely literary assessments. In his *Dutch Civilization in the Seventeenth Century*, the eminent historian Johan Huizinga points to an intrinsic link. "Dutch writers," he says . . . are visual in their approach — they see things as the painter sees them. Bredero's comedies are picturesque, and so to all intents and purposes are Vondel's tragedies."[5] One must not assume, however, that the visual approach of the writers derived from or imitated that of the painters; for, in fact, the literature of the Golden Age of Netherlandic culture flowered to maturity a generation before its painting. "It is often said," writes R.P. Meijer, by way of illustrating this point in his *Literature of the Low Countries*, "that several of Bredero's poems are reminiscent of paintings by Adriaan van Ostade, Adriaan Brouwer, and Jan Steen. True, the similarities are often striking, but it is equally true that

Bredero cannot have seen a single painting of any of these three, for when Bredero died, Brouwer was thirteen years old, Van Ostade nine, and seven years were to elapse before the birth of Jan Steen."[6] Similarly, when it is said that a sonnet by Jacobus Revius is comparable to a scene by Vermeer, one must bear in mind that Revius was born in 1586 and Vermeer in 1632.

That the "greater Dutch writers" of the seventeenth century — Huygens, Hooft, and Cats, as well as Bredero, Vondel, and Revius — were "chiefly of an earlier generation than the best painters" is also stressed by J. L. Price in his *Culture and Society in the Dutch Republic During the 17th Century*, but for reasons quite the opposite of those of Professor Meijer. According to Price, Dutch literature would have been better off had it flowered later, so that it might indeed have been influenced by the "native developments in painting," with which — regrettably, in his view — it was "clearly out of touch."[7] Drawing on Gerard Brom's important revisionist study, *Schilderkunst en litteratuur in de 16e en 17e eeuw*,[8] Price argues that, by the time they perfected themselves in their art, the Dutch painters had a "vital indigenous tradition" to build on, and "a well-developed artistic language through which they could articulate this tradition"; the poets and playwrights who preceded them, on the contrary, "were always conscious of the lack of any strong literary tradition in the Republic" and "even lacked confidence in the language which they had to use." Much of what might otherwise have been creative literary energy had to be expended, he says further, in efforts to "make Dutch a language flexible and subtle enough to support a great literature." Especially costly, in his view, were the attempts to follow Italian and French masters in poetry, since "verse forms suited to the romance languages presented almost insuperable obstacles for a poet writing in Dutch." The painters, "by the nature of their art," he concludes, had no comparable difficuly; "in adapting the innovations of foreign contemporaries," they were self-confident enough in their native legacy to "take what they could use fruitfully and reject the rest." (7, pp. 137-8)

Needless to say, such a perception of the advantage enjoyed by painters over poets in a by-gone age has itself the not inconsiderable advantage of hindsight. In sharper historical focus, Huizinga writes: "It is well-known that our

seventeenth century compatriots had little appreciation of
Dutch art and, where they did, they liked it for the wrong
reasons. Poets rather than painters were held in high esteem." And that we today have a reversed preference, he
adds, is by no means all to the good; rather, it is in a way
regrettable "that our ideas about the past are so largely
based on paintings." Though it now "takes second place to
art with most of our people," Dutch literature on the whole,
Huizinga insists, gives us a truer picture, if not of the
depths of Dutch feeling, certainly of the complex actuality
of Dutch cultural life and political aspirations in the seventeenth century. Yet we can hardly help ourselves in prefer-
ring art, he concludes, for the "visible beauty of a painting
casts an irresistible spell over our spirit." (5, pp. 44, 46)

1. What Might Have Been

One needs to admit, however, that when Dutch literature
first flowered in the late sixteenth century and early seventeenth century, it did not in fact try, like Dutch painting, to
make itself an objectively faithful mirror of what is most
intimately and exclusively Dutch. It tried instead to achieve
at once, in the native tongue, the same sort of comprehen-
sion and acceptance in foreign lands that humanists of the
caliber of Erasmus had earlier achieved, as Netherlanders,
by writing in Renaissance Latin.

Certainly of Erasmus himself it can be said that, long
before he died, he had already become what he has since
remained: "by far the most written-about author the country has ever produced."[9] It is known that he pursued
international fame quite deliberately and with great practical skill. He dealt personally with printers in every land
who, when his works began to sell, pressed him for new
manuscripts "before the ink was dry"; and he pressed them,
in turn, with tough negotiations about fees and royalties.
But the manuscripts that passed so rapidly and profitably
from his prolific hand into print were all in Latin — not a
single one in his native Dutch. Why?

Huizinga raises the question in his *Erasmus and the
Age of Reformation*, and it is by no means an idle question.
Dutch literature is the only fully-developed Western literature that has had an Erasmus to reckon with. Hulzinga says
quite pointedly:

It may well puzzle a fellow-countryman of Erasmus to guess

what a talent like his, with his power of observation, his delicacy of expression, his gusto and wealth, might have meant to Dutch literature. Just imagine the *Colloquia* written in the racy Dutch of the sixteenth century! What would he not have produced if, instead of gleaning and commenting upon classic Adagia, he had, for his themes, availed himself of the proverbs of the vernacular? (1, p.43)

Erasmus lived a century before Huygens, Hooft, and Vondel. He applied his Renaissance Latin to every possible use, writing about any and every subject that could conceivably have had a place in his ideal world of "proud Latinity." Had he ventured to use Dutch in the same way, without altogether abandoning Latin, and had he encouraged his Dutch disciples to do the same, would that not have helped to establish a "vital indigenous tradition" in the native tongue on which the Dutch writers of the seventeenth century might have built with confidence? Unfortunately, most Dutch humanists followed Erasmus's example and wrote only in Latin, "with the result that it was some time," as Professor Meijer observes, "before the Humanist ideas began to put their mark on the literature in Dutch." (6, p.77) Thus it became the task of the poets of the proudest era of Dutch national achievement to try to absorb large stores of classical lore into the vernacular for the first time. Boldly and effortfully they did what had to be done, with only the inimitable sophistication of their Italian and French models to guide them and to undermine their literary self-confidence in the process. That would not have been their task had they had a century-old tradition of Erasmian humanism in Dutch behind them. At any rate, the temptation is strong to conclude that, had Erasmus not wholly estranged himself from Dutch, Adriaan Jacob Barnouw, addressing an American audience centuries later, might not still have felt constrained to say apologetically: "The creative genius of the Dutch does not tend toward the literary."[10]

Having himself speculated about what a talent like that of Erasmus might have meant to Dutch literature, Huizinga in his book on Rotterdam's great humanist hastens to admonish that to raise such a question at all "is to reason unhistorically; this was not what the times required and what Erasmus could give." On what Erasmus could personally give, Huizinga the historical psychologist is brief and direct. "Erasmus could only write in Latin," he says, because "in the vernacular everything would have appeared too direct, too personal, too real, for his taste. He could not do without the thin veil of vagueness, of remoteness, in which everything is wrapped when expressed in Latin. His fastidious mind would have shrunk from the pithy coarseness of a Rabelais, or the rustic violence of Luther's German." (1, p.43) As for what the times required, Huizinga is able to show that Erasmus's self-assumed role as a supranational cultural mediator among the Christian peoples accorded exactly with the role that had been prescribed for the Netherlands provinces in the multi-national empire of the reigning Burgundian-Hapsburg dynasty. The Burgundian- Hapsburg chiefs ruled the Netherlands not as a national state but as a loosely coordinated administrative unit which could serve their global interests best in the role of economic and cultural mediator among the great European national monarchies; and that was not a role, Huizinga emphasizes, that could have been effectively played in the early sixteenth century by asserting an emergent Dutch national identity aggressively in the Dutch language.

2. The Mediator's Mission

By the end of the sixteenth century, the Dutch would of course give powerful expression to their emergent national identity; by risking all they had on the tides of maritime warfare and commerce, they would — at least in the Seven Northern Provinces that wrench themselves free from Burgundian-Hapsburg rule — gain a full century of sovereign national glory. Yet, according to Huizinga, the Dutch would not bring themselves then, even as they have not brought themselves since, to abandon their essentially Erasmian role as cultural mediators among the great nations of Europe. Their seventeenth-century poets and playwrights would indeed write in Dutch, not Latin; and their Erasmian classical learning itself would be stored up in great Dutch universities to which foreign professors and students would come, even as Erasmus had gone abroad, to learn and teach. As Huizinga expresses it, "everything that in seventeenth-century Europe went under the name of culture" would suddenly be brought to mature expression in the free Netherlands, with a stamp of Dutch origin and possession upon it. And yet, with only one notable exception, its aim, its purpose, its appeal would remain international or cosmopolitan in the Erasmian sense. Painting alone, writes Huizinga, will take an opposite course; turning inward in its development, after it could no longer grace the church walls and altars of international Catholicism, Dutch painting was to assume an aspect "so intensely national that it became the most profound expression of our character," (5, p.109) even while it was being treated with a "measure of kindly but unmistakable condescension" (5, p.44) by an intellectual class that reasoned and wrote and taught to be understood and appreciated as much by foreigners as by their own more sophisticated fellow Netherlanders.

In Huizinga's view, the unfinished business of Dutch culture, and especially of Dutch literature, is to unite two levels or varieties of cultural expression that ought to have been united in the seventeenth century but unfortunately were not. There might indeed have been an immediate national fusion of all aspects of Dutch life. But instead, under the spell of Erasmian international fame, the literary expression of the spirit of the Netherlands went one way, reaching outward, deliberately, to communicate in an openminded mediative fashion, while its pictorial expression went another, looking inward, not less deliberately, to mirror for the Dutch themselves what is most intimately and exclusively Dutch. Huizinga has made this insight the theme of two brief but important essays — "The Netherlands as Mediator Between Western and Central Europe" (1933) and "The Spirit of the Netherlands" (1935)[11] — where he sharply outlines the pattern of continuity that emerges when the history of the Netherlands, from Erasmus's time to the present, is viewed as a development in which several varieties of Dutch international mediation succeed one another dialectically.

The development in outline has three main periods or phases. The first we have already defined and characterized. It culminates in the career of Erasmus, coincides in duration with the Burgundian- Hapsburg rule of the Netherlands as an administrative unit, and ends when all seventeen provinces rise sporadically in revolt against Charles V's "all-too-Spanish son" Philip II. The mediative role in this first phase is, as already indicated, nationally self-effacing, or cosmopolitan, as the times required. The

second phase is the grand flowering of the Republic of the
United Provinces in the North during the eighty-year
struggle against Spain (1568-1648), in the course of which
the leading Dutch-speaking provinces of the South, Flanders
and Brabant, are economically and culturally crushed,
forcibly separated from Holland and the other Dutch-
speaking provinces, and joined with the Walloon provinces
in total subjection to what will thereafter be despotic
Spanish rule. In this phase, the North will become at once,
as we said, a nationally-aggressive mediator, and indeed,
while its maritime hegemony lasts, a European power of the
first rank. The South, largely through the scholarship of the
ancient university of Louvain, will gradually come to play a
leading role in the Catholic Counter-Reformation; but to
the flowering of Dutch national culture in the North,
"glorious Brabant and fierce Flanders" (as Huizinga characterizes them) "could contribute little more . . . than the
national fervor of the refugees and later, much later, the
fragments of land that the Republic conquered by force of
arms." (5, p.11)

That second phase of mediation ends rather abruptly
in the second half of the seventeenth century. When its
maritime hegemony is challenged by the new navies of
England and France, the Dutch Republic — which had been
from the beginning but a torso, as Huizinga expresses it, of
the Dutch people — is unable to hold its own on the strength
of its own resources, and its role as mediator accordingly
passes into a third phase. Neither self-assertive nor
self-effacing, from a national perspective, this third phase
soon reveals itself to be a stabilized, virtuous mean between
the extremes of the two previous phases; and, without
notable fluctuations, it extends through the eighteenth and
nineteenth centuries toward. the present — with strong
suggestions, however, that a fourth not-yet-clearly self-
defined phase of mediation may have started in the 1880s.

The pattern here outlined permits Huizinga to sketch
brief histories of Dutch commerce, printing, architecture,
classical studies, painting, literature, etc., emphasizing not
chronology but the dialectics of growth, decline, and renewal. Its value as a framework for historical literary analysis is indicated by Annie Romein Verschoor's use of a
version of it in the introduction to her *Silt and Sky: Men and
Movements in Modern Dutch Literature*. The book's purpose

is to persuade foreign readers that a movement of major cultural significance — a literary "renaissance that coincided with a reintegration of the whole economic, social and mental life of Holland" — in fact began in the 1880s. (2, p.15) In her introduction, to place this renaissance in historical context, the author surveys what Dutch cultural life has heretofore been "in the midst of the culture of the surrounding peoples." The Dutch, we learn, have at all times been open-minded mediators, receiving much in painting, music, science, and philosophy, for instance, and giving much in return. In literature, however, because of the language barrier, the flow of cultural influences has been largely in a single direction. In Professor Verschoor's words, the Dutch have had "a literature which, in the Middle Ages, was largely restricted to translations and adaptations from the French, which, in its seventeenth century efflorescence, was still strongly influenced by the French model, and which in the eighteenth century was influenced by England and at the beginning of the nineteenth by Germany." But we fall into gross error, the author warns at this point, if, on these grounds, we are led to regard the Dutch character "as tractable and Dutch literature as mere adaptations and imitations of foreign examples." Nothing, she says, could be further from the truth: "Beneath the silt, the hard subsoil of Dutch literature will soon be struck, for the alluvium is not thick." (2, pp.6-7)

At the hard subsoil level, according to Professor Verschoor, Dutch literature is found to be an authentic expression of the Dutch national spirit. And here lies the paradox that every student of Dutch literature must face. Even the casual visitor to the country becomes aware at once of a unifying character or spirit that manifests itself unmistakably in every aspect and detail of Dutch life. One can easily "visualize" it, as indeed the great Dutch genre-painters did for all the world to marvel at. But to "verbalize" it is far more difficult. For the Dutch language is the language not only of imaginative literature in Dutch, but also of all else that the Dutch do in their mediative capacity. It is the principal vehicle of Dutch open-minded communication with other peoples, and its very capacity to receive foreign impressions sympathetically and faithfully is what makes it most distinctively Dutch.

The Dutch literary imagination is thus paradoxically

most Dutch, in a mediative sense, when it mirrors foreign
impressions — which is to say, in the words of Professor
Verschoor: "The Dutchman's awareness of other countries
is part of his native quality: he is a man whose eyes are fixed
eternally on the horizon, beyond the sea, over the flat
country." The borders of his provinces have never closed
him in. That is the essence of his national spirit. It is most
present — and in literature especially — when it seems to
flaunt itself least. Verschoor will venture to say that it "may
be more original, more specific than any other national
spirit, but it lies deeper." (2, pp.7-10) In all ages, certainly,
it has been the Netherlander's chief defense as well as his
chief delight. His open-mindedness to what is foreign, his
age-old hospitable reception of refugees, his hypersensitiv-
ity to what other people are, to what they value, to what
makes them sell or buy, stand or run, is precisely what
enabled the Netherlander to make himself a nationally
self-effacing redistributor of goods and culture in the sixteenth century, master of world trade and builder of Dutch
national universities during the next one hundred years,
and since then a most practical custodian of what is internationally most valuable in the heritage of Western civilization.

But it appears that a literature imbued with the
mediative spirit doesn't translate well. Foreign readers too
easily find themselves in it and fail to see what the Dutch
literary consciousness has provided that is characteristically its own. Especially in the large national states, the
reader of foreign books has learned to expect writers of the
smaller nations to satisfy his curiosity with distinctively
local color and atmosphere, if at all possible, or with
anguished expression of small-nation exasperated pride.
This, says Professor Verschoor, the Dutch writer cannot
bring himself to do. He has had too long a heritage of
cultural mediation among the great nations for that; much
less can he permit himself to forget that, till yesterday, his
people have been, not an oppressed backward population
awaiting a national liberator, but proud masters themselves
of a far-flung colonial empire. The Dutch generally, writes
Verschoor, "are not flattered when foreigners insist on
regarding them as clogdancing millers or baggy-breeched
fishermen." It is centuries too late — many levels of social
consciousness too late — for that. Indeed, Vorschoor stresses:

> The modern Dutch writer is Dutch because he has no choice, but his conscious purpose is rather to achieve a European level than to express the national spirit. He knows only too well that the conscious expression of the national spirit is the prerogative of the great cultured nations, and that in the smaller nations it too easily degenerates into a hollow chauvinism, for which he has a spirited contempt. But that has led to a one-sided isolation, a literary monologue without an answer. . . . (2, pp. 10-11)

It has been so for the non-Erasmian-minded Dutch writer from the beginning. For a time, during the Great Age, the naval might of the Dutch Republic sufficed to gain an international status even for its native tongue. Yet, for the most part, in that age too, "what was written in Dutch remained Dutch," writes Verschoor, "a fact to be explained only partly by the language barrier." That barrier has indeed for centuries forced small nations "entering international literary life to leave their luggage behind, as it were, so that they have always appeared empty-handed in the European assembly." There has, of course, been a significant change since the turn of the century. Verschoor names half a dozen modern writers since Ibsen's time who have attained European fame despite their small-nation origin; and "others have followed," she says, "but rarely have they been Dutchmen. One cannot ascribe it to lack of talent: "poets such as Gorter, Henriette Roland Holst, Leopold and Marsman, prose writers like Multatuli and Huizinga, are also outstanding Europeans." (2, p.9)

We are still faced, apparently, with Erasmus's dilemma, which he resolved so decisively for himself in his youth. By writing in Latin, Erasmus had in effect chosen to translate himself. How many Europeans were prepared to read Dutch in the late fifteenth century? And yet, as Huizinga has said, if Erasmus and his Latin-writing coadjutors "thought they were really making Latin a vehicle for daily international use, they overrated their power. It was, no doubt, an amusing fancy and a witty exercise to plan, in such an international milieu as the Paris student world, such models of sports and games in Latin as the *Colloquiorum formulae* offered. But can Erasmus have seriously thought that the next generation would play at marbles in Latin?" (1, p.42) Erasmus actually did great service, unintentionally, for the developing national languages by strengthening,

through the schools, their classical legacy. But he altogether mistook what history had in store for his prodigious
flow of writings in an artificially refined Latin that had
neither the reality of ancient Rome nor of his own age to
sustain it from within. Though the great humanist who gave
up his native tongue for a cosmopolitan political and
cultural idea retains his fame as a symbol, "the world," as
Huizinga observes, "no longer reads and enjoys him. Consequently it is impossible to consider his figure altogether
in the classical category. That mind is classical whose
creation — whether poetry, philosophy, or art — in its
details still moves and captivates posterity, strengthening
or irritating as do Aeschylus, Dante, Rembrandt, Pascal.
Not Erasmus."[12]

Professor Verschoor pauses briefly nevertheless to
consider whether the modern Netherlander, eager to reach
a large foreign audience, would do well to follow a modern
equivalent of the Erasmian lead. It is still, after all, "an
ungrateful task," she writes, "to make the literature of a
small country known outside its borders." (2, p.32) Is there
not another course we can follow? "The solution," she
continues, "might seem obvious: to write in French like the
eighteenth-century Dutch philosopher Hemsterhuis, or in
English like the great Irish writers." A temptation in that
direction is apt to be felt by every small-nation writer who
has learned the language of a populous and powerful
country. "But to reject such a solution," Verschoor says at
once, "does not demand adherence to the blood-and-soil
theory." It is simply that what could reasonably be done
elsewhere or at other times would now "mean to the Dutch
the uprooting of their spiritual existence." An Erasmian
recourse to major "cosmopolitan" languages is thus simply
out of the question; the best one can hope and attempt to
do, Professor Verschoor concludes, is "to give an indica-
tion of what the foreigner who makes the effort to penetrate Dutch literature has to gain." (2, p.11)

3. Language and Nationhood

Though his concern is not, like Professor Verschoor's,
exclusively literary, Huizinga too brings his development
of the pattern of Dutch mediation in European cultural life
to focus finally on the problem of foreign appreciation of
Dutch writers in translation as well as in Dutch. Why is it,

he asks, that of all the major writers of the seventeenth century only Jacob Cats — of whom Dutch literary critics are least proud — retained an international reputation after the decline of Dutch maritime power? It was Cats, not Dutch painting, that eclipsed the reputations of Hooft, Bredero, Huygens, and even Vondel, "the greatest of them all by far" (5, p.69) — and not only abroad; for it is a fact that, for two whole centuries, down to the 1880s, Cats was "the poet whose works could be found alongside the Bible in every Dutch house." It has been suggested that "Cats' great and durable popularity remains somewhat of a blot on our national character," Huizinga writes; and yet it is clear that he remained readable all that time because, unlike the writers we so much prefer, he at least gave the Dutch generally "what they understood and liked" and because the "whole nation recognized itself in his often entertaining and always instructive musings and in the utter banality and prosaic sobriety that mirrored their own." (5,pp.65-7) As for his international reputation, we have the assurance of Lord Auchinleck, James Boswell's learned father, that the best reason for studying the Dutch language in 1763 was so as to "divert yourself with Jacob Cats when you come home" — as he explains in a letter to his son, who was then at the University of Utrecht studying Roman civil law.[13]

What a contrast with Vondel! "We Dutchmen know," Huizinga says, "that Vondel must be counted among the finest writers of all time. We also realize, and are resigned to the fact, that the world neither knows him nor is ever likely to do so. Is it simply because he wrote in Dutch? Surely not, for if that were the case, he would have earned world renown in translation, just as Cervantes and other Spanish writers did or, more recently, the Russians and Ibsen. No, he must rather have been lacking certain qualities that make a writer universally admired." Cats apparently had such qualities, in some measure; and the world has found them in Dutch painting. Without seeking to define what those qualities are, Huizinga proceeds to ask and answer for himself a related but less substantive question about Vondel's art and inspiration: "Do we read him often and with pleasure. . . ? I, for my part, freely confess that a play by Vondel — unlike one by Shakespeare — makes great demands upon my patience. . . . How is it that not only Shakespeare but even Racine seems so much closer to us?"

(5,pp.69-71)

Everything that is noblest in the Dutch character is present in Vondel, discernible in all he wrote; there is great music in his lines and great pictorial power; yet, says Huizinga, "we can no longer absorb Vondel through our poetic pores." We know that this man who, at the height of his career became a Catholic in Calvinist Holland, "knew the force of temptation and of inward struggle." But that force is hardly expressed convincingly in his works, where he "rarely if ever deviated from the scriptural or hagiographic pattern." There is missing in him, still in large measure, what Huizinga found to be altogether missing in Erasmus's Latin. Like Erasmus, Vondel worked "with a strictly limited number of . . . stereotypes," of content as well as form. On controversial matters of religious and national feeling, Vondel held back, restricted himself to what the times required, even as Erasmus had done a century before. The past that was permitted to enter his literary consciousness, says Huizinga, "was typical of Holland. Few of his Antwerp antecedents affected his work." (5,p.72) He fascinates us with present things, like the genre-painters; but beyond that, his art is recalcitrant. Certainly a Catholicism coming to him out of the Netherlands past "inspired Vondel with the glorious choruses of his Lucifer," Huizinga writes; but "it could not turn him into the kind of dramatist who, like Shakespeare, makes us tremble with emotion, or like Racine, makes us thrill to the noble sound of his stylized passion." (5,p.99)

Pieter Geyl, who ranks with Huizinga as perhaps the leading Dutch cultural historian of the modern era, makes the question of what is lacking in Vondel — as compared with the chief national authors of England, France, and Spain — the focus of his essay, "Shakespeare as Historian" (1945), major subsections of which are suggestively headed "Hooft's Historical Dramas," "Shakespeare's Aim in the English History Plays," "Shakespeare's Historic Atmospheres, or Backgrounds," and "Vondel's Historical Dramas."[14] Well-known as "both an admirer and severe critic of Huizinga," (5, Foreword) Professor Geyl makes pointedly clear what Huizinga has brought himself merely to hint at in his appraisal of Vondel: namely that, as compared with Shakespeare, Racine, and Cervantes, Vondel in the seventeenth century was heir to a national culture that not only

matured late but that was substantially aborted by the split
that abandoned Flanders and Brabant to perpetual
non-Dutch governance. Geyl's specifically literary treatment of this theme is indeed but a by-product of his life-
long scholarly polemic against all modern Belgian and
Dutch historians who represent the "emergence of the
Southern Netherlands" as "an inevitable development —
nay, a fulfillment,"[15] rather than as what he deems it to have
been: the "violent disruption of a national whole," brought
about by the action of a foreign power, "and its replacement by a different mentality and national outlook in each
of the severed halves." The religious and cultural differences that became so obvious afterward were "not the
cause," Geyl insists, "but the result of the split."[16]

Professor Geyl understands why modern Dutch and
Belgian historians might want to find justification in the
past for the present configurations of the two independent
kingdoms that now divide the old Netherlands between
them; but he thinks it does the cultural maturity of all
modern Netherlanders much more harm than good to
perpetuate, for whatever currently pressing reason, an
essentially false view of the past. For it is false, he insists, to
view the great split that produced the Northern Republic as
a welcome historical necessity, pregnant with good things
for centuries to come, rather than as what the historical
record proves it to have been: a national disaster, a rending
in two of a single people, worthy of the tragic historiography of a Thucydides and the tragic stagecraft of a
Shakespeare.

Geyl reminds his readers that, a century before
Vondel's time, when Erasmus was still cultivating Latin as
a universal tongue, the peoples of England, France, and
Spain had already secured for themselves the basis for
unified national cultures. "The dominance of Latin had
long been weakened," he writes, "and the prestige of literature in the popular language was increasing all the time.
This was only one aspect of a development that sprang, as
it were, automatically from the operation of states embrac-
ing much larger entities and affecting people's lives much
more profoundly, a development of national consciousness
within each particular state. In the episode of Joan of Arc
one sees an early sign of this. How strongly and articulately
does it speak in Shakespeare! And in Holland, a generation

later, in Vondell." (14,p.298) But by Vondel's age, when a national literature supported by political independence could for the first time begin to flower, the Netherlands had been tragically split, and each of the separated parts was already doing its utmost — like the modern Belgian and Dutch historians — to deprive the other of a united cultural past.

Like Shakespeare, Hooft and Vondel made use of the chronicles of their homeland for the matter of many of their plays. But, despite numerous promising details, what was available to the Dutch playwrights proved to be rather "ungrateful and refractory." The trouble is, says Geyl, that in the Netherlands, as contrasted with Shakespeare's England, "there had been too sharp a break with the past. " Besides that, for Hooft and Vondel, the matter of the past could never be the entire Netherlands: it had always to be "Holland, or even Amsterdam, matter. Besides, . . . a continuity was postulated that had no basis in reality. England had not had a similar break; the national kingship went back into the centuries and supplied a natural and closer connection with the older history." (14, p.51) Geyl compares Hooft's *Geraard van Velzen* (which is about the deposition of a thirteenth-century ruler of Holland) with Shakespeare's *Richard II*. Shakespeare disappears behind his characters, making us "live with both sides"; Hooft, on the contrary, is an omnipresent partisan, expounding "constitutional and theological ideas" that distort the past in order to serve the present. (14, pp. 54-5)

Vondel is greater than Hooft. Some of his historical plays, writes Geyl, "are among the glories of Dutch literature." Several of them offer us "dramatized historical events" in full color, set before us most vividly, with a great painter's mastery of detail. In *Gijsbreght van Aemstel* (about the destruction of Amsterdam shortly after the events dramatized in Hooft's *Geraard van Velzen*), for instance, there are moments — says Geyl — "when we seem near to getting scenes such as those through which Shakespeare makes us breathe the historic atmosphere of a play." But Vondel, like Hooft, holds back; whatever his subject matter, he must treat it so as to justify the present in the past, however much, in the depth of his own conscience, the present may trouble him. But it is Vondel's *Batavian Brothers* (about the revolt of the Batavi, headed by Julius Civilis, in early Roman imperial times) that gives Geyl an opportunity to impress upon us how much more heavily the political consequences of the great split weighed upon poets and playwrights than upon painters who were not expected to make the meaning of their representations literally clear. Julius (or, sometimes, Claudius) Civilis is the author and hero of a great revolt. But Vondel's play about him ends before the revolt has taken place. He and his brother are represented as "men of order," consistently loyal to the Romans until Roman rule becomes despotic. Since the play ends before the revolt, its theme is rather one of oppression patiently suffered than of conspiratorial heroism. (14, pp.80-1)

At this point, Geyl introduces a highly instructive comparison: "Just before Vondel wrote his *Batavian Brothers*, Rembrandt had been commissioned to paint the 'Conspiracy of Claudius Civilis' for one of the walls of the Amsterdam town hall. All that is lacking in Vondel's play is to be found in Rembrandt. The barbaric, the savage, the vigorous, the passionate — in the countenances and in the attitudes of the plotters who crowd about the table lighted by the torches in the vast dark room — it has all been grippingly evoked, and the effect is embodied in the mighty one-eyed figure, who, sturdily and fatefully seated, holds his sword aloft, while the others touch it with theirs." Geyl notes that Rembrandt's "blunt presentation of the first Dutch warrior for freedom apparently offended" the burgomasters of Amsterdam, who refused it, expecting perhaps a characterization more like Vondel's. We are in the 1660s; the struggle against Spain had ended in 1648, and already the new English navy had administered a very sobering blow. In 1596, the States of Holland had not hesitated to proclaim, quite in the spirit of Rembrandt's Civilis: "In the command of the sea and in the conduct of the war on the water resides the entire prosperity of the country." (15, p.234) But after the first Anglo-Dutch war — which pitted a "mountain of iron" against what had become a "mountain of gold — the mood of the States of Holland and the burgomasters of Amsterdam had changed fundamentally. Dutch prosperity would thereafter require less heroic virtues for its continued support. Vondel's representation of Civilis reflects the change; Rembrandt's does not. And Geyl concludes: "Modern historic, no less than artistic, awareness will unhesitatingly recognize the veracity of

Rembrandt's fantasy. . . . Rembrandt knew how to render
the primitive and the savage. Everyone can see at once that
his are the authentically desperate conspirators and that
they are moved by very different motives . . . from those the
poet or the painter might have observed around him in the
erudite and decent burghers of Amsterdam, familiar with
the pen and the account book and the law court." (14, pp.
82-3)

Huizinga draws a similar contrast in an often-quoted
passage where he rejects the epithet "golden" to characterize the Republic's great age. He recalls that, in manuscript,
P.L. Muller's classic history, *Our Golden Age* [*Onze gouden
eeuw*],[17] had been titled "The Republic of the United Netherlands in its Heydey." The publisher who ordered the
change said the new title would have greater market appeal.
But Huizinga and others had observed that it was wholly at
odds with the book's approach, since there was "no glitter
at all in the author's matter-of-fact treatment of the state,
the army and navy, the church, trade and industry, ship-
ping, the founding of the colonies, provincial government
and history, social life, literature and art." The *aurea aetas*,
for Huizinga, smacks of the "classical Fools' Paradise, which
annoyed us in Ovid even while we were still in school."
Then he says: "If our great age must perforce be given a
name, let it be that of wood and steel, pitch and tar, color
and ink, pluck and piety, fire and imagination. The term
'golden' applies far better to the eighteenth century, when
our coffers were stuffed with gold-pieces." (5, p.104)

4. The Age of Sobriety

The post-Rembrandtian age, with its gold-filled coffers,
takes us deep into the third phase of Huizinga's pattern of
Dutch mediation in European cultural life. "From 1700,"
he says, "we pass straight to the present day. The rest of the
eighteenth century concerns our problem only inasmuch as
our country lost its dominant position almost as suddenly
as it had gained it, its cultural activity ceasing to be productive and becoming almost entirely receptive." (5, p.152)
But we are warned not to make hasty evaluations, not to
judge an age with which we are out of sympathy according
to alien standards. The Dutch had not risen against Spain
to become warriors forever, in the spirit of Rembrandt's
one-eyed Claudius Civilis. They had faced up to the hard

trial, and when it was over they were generally pleased with the results. They had taken possession of their trade and they had built themselves great universities, fine public buildings, clean and safe streets and squares, and comfortably furnished homes graced almost everywhere with paintings that mirrored back to them in a fascinating way what was dearest to them. The maritime dominance, the literary self-assertion in Dutch? They had been products of a necessary national and heroic exertion, the need for which had now subsided.

Huizinga notes that, while there was undeniably a "general collapse of Dutch culture in the eighteenth century," it was not a collapse that seriously affected the great Dutch universities. Already in the late seventeenth century, he writes, Holland in fact "owed its role as mediator between east and west, north and south, chiefly to its universities. Here people from other countries could meet and exchange books and ideas. . . . The language barrier which today keeps foreign students out of our academies did not then exist — all lectures were delivered in the familiar Latin." (5, p.151) But Professor Geyl reminds us that, in 1585, when Roemer Visscher, Hendrik Laurenszoon Spieghel and their literary friends had first set out to "promote the construction of a sound and many-sided Dutch civilization," they had addressed an impassioned plea to the administrators of the newly-founded University of Leyden urging that all courses be given in Dutch "so that we Hollanders might at last enjoy learning in our own speech, which we must now with great labor cull from unknown tongues." (15, p.286) The plea had been rejected; only in the engineering faculty was an exception made. It was to be the same in each of the several other Dutch universities that sprang into being in quick order — Franeker in 1585, Groningen in 1614, Utrecht in 1636, and Harderwyk in 1648 (Amsterdam's Athenaeum did not become a university until 1877) — as one province after another came to feel that it could afford a study-center of its own.

Geyl notes too that the Dutch language was excluded also from the circles of the numerous learned *émigrés*. Add to this the fact that perhaps half the residents of the great Dutch cities were foreigners living in colonies of their own, speaking their own languages, and it is clear why the triumph of the language of Huygens, Hooft, and

Vondel in the Dutch Republic was anything but complete. Italy's revival of learning, we need to recall, had produced no Erasmus; it had coincided, on the contrary, with the full flowering of her national literature in the poetry and prose of Dante, Petrarch, Boccaccio, Ariosto, and Machiavelli; the proportion of foreign residents in Italy was never great; and while Dutch scholars continued to write learned treatises primarily in Latin, the greatest masterpieces of political science, economics, jurisprudence, history, philosophy, mathematics, medicine, architecture, physics, and astronomy of which Italians were capable were being written in Italian. The use of Latin in the Dutch universities and among many *émigrés*, writes Geyl, "erected a partition between scholarship and the nation." Still, it did not signify in any sense a survival of Erasmian cosmopolitanism; on the contrary, what glory the great scholar gained through classical studies that linked him with learned men abroad was now "reflected quite automatically on the entire nation." (15, p.287) And the glory proved to be great indeed for Dutch scholars in the eighteenth century. In his monumental *History of Classical Scholarship*,[18] J. E. Sandys notes that Dutch classical scholarship at that time, especially in Greek, surpassed that of Italy, France, and Spain, matched that of England on the heights to which Richard Bentley had brought it, and, through the labors of Tiberius Hemsterhuys, prepared the Germans for their great age.

Literary culture in Dutch, meanwhile, began the slow process of receiving into itself the vital prose of Dutch life — the process of compensating for what it had been deprived of first by Erasmus's cosmopolitanism and later by the Latin of the universities and the learned *émigrés*. The seventeenth-century Dutch writers had given the nation an imaginative literature complete in every genre. But, as Huizinga and Geyl emphasize, it was a literature narrowly confined in the scope of its content. Too much had been denied it, of the national past, and of contemporary non-literary culture. That perhaps accounts for the craving of Dutch writers in the eighteenth and nineteenth centuries to know and imitate what foreign writers were doing. "Holland, which had always welcomed foreign cultural influences, opened the doors even wider to them," writes Huizinga, "now that Humanism had ceased to produce a kind of cosmopolitan culture. In its process, the marked

French influence first became diluted and then counter-poised by English and German contributions. This great turning point in the intellectual life of all Europe, *i.e.* the ousting of Romanic influences by predominantly Germanic ones, was nowhere more marked than in Holland." (5, p.153)

That great intellectual turn was, of course, accompanied by a series of political shocks as well as turns. Between 1789 and 1839, in a wave of revolutions, counterrevolutions and great-power settlements, the Northern Republic was overthrown, the whole of the Netherlands was absorbed in the Napoleonic empire, north and south were "restored" temporarily in a united kingdom, and separated, finally, during the 1830s, into the modern kingdoms of Belgium and the Netherlands. In the Netherlands, as elsewhere, the events of this period produced crises of national identity and what has since been called a romantic awakening of the historic sense. The great representative of that awakening in Dutch literature and criticism is Everhardus Johannes Potgieter, an Amsterdam commercial agent, son of a draper, who seemed to embody in himself the spirit of the seventeenth century. While north and south were united, he lived for a time in Antwerp, where he received a powerful impression of the tragic reality of the split that had cut Flanders and Brabant away from the other Dutch provinces.

Back in Amsterdam in 1837, Potgieter helped to found a new magazine, *De Gids* [*The Guide*], which he was to edit for twenty-eight years and which came to be called "The Blue Executioner" because of the severity of its criticism of contemporary authors. He never tired of drawing comparisons between the nineteenth and the seventeenth centuries, in the hope of shaming his contemporaries into "more strenuous activity and emulation of their glorious ancestors."[19] Among his peers, he came to be regarded as "the perfect prose writer, an inexorable yet just critic, and the pure poet." And while it is true that his critical works "have best withstood the passage of time," one needs to recognize, writes Jan Greshoff, that a number of his major poems, "such as *Florence*, and *De Nalatenschap van een Landjonker*," taken together, "form the most monumental body of poetry in Dutch literature." (10, p.273)

Potgieter's most significant critical work, *Het*

Rijksmuseum te Amsterdam (*The National Museum of Amsterdam*, 1844) has been described as a "homage to the 17th century and to the prose style of P.C. Hooft." And it is indeed to Hooft the Dutch prose writer, the Dutch historian, rather than to Hooft the poet and playwright that Potgieter turns. Geyl, too, has a high regard for Hooft's *Historiën* which is imbued he says with a "truly historical spirit . . . and deserves to be numbered among the great achievements of historiography." (14, p.56) But Potgieter knows what is missing in Hooft and Vondel, and he takes his readers directly to it. *Het Rijksmuseum* points to the future in this respect: an "impressive essay" indeed, as R. P. Meijer aptly writes, in which Potgieter "uses the picture collection of the museum as the basis for a glorification of the seventeenth century, all the time urging the Dutch to revive the Golden Age, from the beginning of the essay with its repeated 'there was a time when . . .' to the ending with its exhortation to be inspired by the past." (6, p.213)

The generation following Potgieter would produce two Dutch writers of major importance: one, an expression of the resurgence of Dutch national feeling in Flanders, the poet-priest Guido Gezelle (in Barnouw's view, the "one poet of universal stature Flanders produced in the last century"); the other, Eduard Dekker, son of a merchant-marine captain, whose pseudonym, Multatuli, means "I have suffered much," and who wrote a stinging autobio-graphical novel, *Max Havelaar*, about the realities of Dutch imperial rule in the East Indies. Apart from these two, there was a general leveling down of imaginative literary effort until the last decades of the century. And classical scholar-ship in the universities now for the first time shared in the process of leveling down. Latin ceased to be the acceptable university language it had been in the past. Classical schol-arship became the concern of an ever-narrowing circle of specialists. The mid-century did produce, indeed, the "great-est of the modern Greek scholars of the Netherlands, Carolus Gabriel Cobet," but, as Professor Sandys observes, the quality and emphasis of his scholarship was far removed from that of the great university figures of the seventeenth century — Lipsius, Scaliger, Salmasius, Vossius, and the elder and younger Heinsius — or of the eighteenth, headed by Hemsterhuys, who brought Dutch classical scholarship to its greatest renown. Cobet's great love, says Sandys, was that of editing the texts of great classical authors so as to reduce them "to the dead level of a smooth uniformity." And then he adds:

> Such a tendency may even perhaps be regarded as a national characteristic of the clear-headed and methodical scholars, who dwell in a land of straight canals rather than winding rivers, a land of level plains varied only by a fringe of sand-dunes, a land saved from devastation by dikes that restrain the free waters of the sea. But, as we look back over the three-hundred and thirty-three years which have elapsed since the founding of the first of the universities of the Northern Netherlands, we remember that it was the breaking of those dikes by the orders of William the Silent that brought deliverance to the beleagured city of Leyden, and that the heroism of its inhabitants was then fitly commemorated by the founding of its far-famed university. (18, III,p.291)

5. The Unfinished Business: Art's Unconscious Universality

Has there indeed been, since Sandys wrote those words, a new cultural equivalent of the old breaking of the dikes? We have already cited Professor Verschoor's very positive view; and Professor Barnouw insists even more positively that "Holland's literary movement of the 80s" produced truly revolutionary effects in thought as well as language that remain "clearly apparent more than half a century after the breach occurred." (19, p.231) Huizinga, who is himself a major product of the breach, dwells on language as the key to its significance. Dutch open-mindedness has caused the breach, and the waters that have flooded in are for the most part great new tides of foreign influence — tides that could conceivably sweep away all that has been most characteristically Dutch, for there is certainly no risk-proof way to break dikes. At any rate, today, says Huizinga, "no other country in the world . . . is more open to foreign culture than we are. And precisely this great openness makes us mediators *par excellence* — even if we did little else — for the very absorption, assimilation, and transmission of cultural elements entitles us to that name." (5, p. 154) What is the role of the Dutch language in all this? With the partition that the use of Latin in the universities had erected between scholarship and the nation swept away at last, the Dutch native tongue that Erasmus despised has come finally to possess the entire linguistic-cultural commonwealth. And here Huizinga dwells on an apparent paradox. The Dutch language at once facilitates the influx of foreign influences and secures the Dutch mind against being overwhelmed by such influences. It makes possible the flood but, like a new Sea-Beggars' navy, it rides the flood cross-country to relieve besieged centers of Dutch national culture wherever relief is needed.

"From the nineteenth century onwards, the absorption of English, French and German cultural elements has been accelerated," writes Huizinga, "by fairly widespread and reasonably good knowledge of the languages of our three great neighbors." The Dutch today are not tempted to be as thorough, here, as Erasmus was with his Latin, but still: "We take the training of language teachers very seriously." And if it is true that "most Dutchmen have a somewhat exaggerated idea of their ability to speak German, English, and French," it is not less true, Huizinga insists, "that our own phonetic system makes it far easier for us than for our neighbors to imitate the sound of all three languages." As for the dangers of such openness — one must not exaggerate. For, while it is true that "the educated Dutchman, however patriotic, often has the urge to neglect his own for foreign writers," it is also true that "the foreign influences roughly cancel out — perhaps not in one and the same man but certainly in our nation as a whole. And it is precisely the resulting equilibrium which enables us to play the mediator." (5, pp.154-5) Huizinga rejects the idea that bilingual or trilingual states are better able to sustain such an equilibrium; in his view, the coexistence of two or more languages in the same state invariably represents a cultural cleavage that delays, if it does not altogether foreclose, the kind of integral mediation the Dutch have traditionally provided in Europe.

From a political-cultural perspective, one may say that the Dutch have in their native tongue — "that ancient symbol of their national identity and independence," as Huizinga characterizes it — precisely what Erasmus sought for in vain in his artificially-cultivated Renaissance Latin. "Without a language of their own," he says, the Dutch could not have assimilated foreign influences "evenly and quite freely" and could thus "never have become the great mediators they are." (5, p.156) The modern Dutch mind has a deep "kinship with German thought," close "cultural bonds with France," and ancient "historical links with England" that make it equally receptive "to the influence of all three." Here we have an internationalism far removed from that of Erasmus which made him spurn his native Dutch, chide friends who wrote in it for being "content with Dutch fame," and ignore as well as deplore all that might conceivably be well written in any of the vernacular languages on the grounds that it could only undermine peace by stirring up national feelings, prideful misunderstandings, self interested hatreds, and wars in defiance of the supranational peace-keeping imperial authority. Our traditionally-cultivated receptivity to "positive thought from any quarter," says Huizinga, "does not mean we have become rootless cosmopolitans — far from it." Whereas cosmopolitanism of the Erasmian or modern variety seeks to efface national distinctions in its single-minded pursuit of a spurious global ideal, genuine international mediation seeks instead to comprehend such distinctions and render their co-existence secure. "Our manifold links with different cultures," Huizinga stresses, "have taught us to appreciate the irreplaceable value of each"; and we now recognize with greater clarity than ever before "that better international understanding and greater harmony cannot result either from the premature fusion of disparate elements or from the baseless denial of very real differences. Acknowledge-ment of the alien as such, entering into its spirit and yet maintaining one's own — these are things that all nations will have to learn, no matter how long it takes them to do so."   (5, pp.155-7)

How does one acknowledge the alien as such, appreciate its irreplaceable value, and enter sympathetically into its spirit while maintaining one's own? According to Huizinga, "it is the one thing in which our country may be said to excel. . . . It is a precious luxury that we enjoy — our understanding and response to foreign influences." But it is nothing to boast about, it is not an excellence that the Dutch have consciously sought to achieve. "We are forced into it," says Huizinga, because of our geographic situation; "and we enjoy it because all we ask of anyone is free intercourse — commercial, cultural and spiritual." (5, pp. 116-7) It is for the foreign critic to discover its presence in cultural manifestations of the Dutch national mind and spirit. And here Huizinga's meaning can best be clarified, perhaps, by recalling T.S. Eliot's discussion of the "two characteristics" which in his view "must be found together in any author whom I would single out as one of the landmarks of a national literature."[20] The two characteristics, as Eliot defines them, are precisely what Erasmus sought to avoid by very self-consciously schooling himself in his universal Latin: "strong local flavor combined with unconscious universality." By strong local flavor, Eliot means the opposite of what is only superficially local — like the clog-dancing millers or baggy-breeched fishermen of Holland. That kind of local flavor can satisfy only the most superficial sense of what is local. Genuine local flavor is anything but superficial, and the last person to sense it is apt to be the cosmopolitan traveler who flits from place to place collecting first impressions. In a writer, certainly, such cosmopolitanism is bound to produce more harm than good, for, as Eliot says, "cosmopolitanism can be the enemy of universality — it may dissipate attention in superficial familiarity with the streets, the cafes and some of the local dialect of a number of foreign capitals; whereas universality can never come except through writing about what one knows thoroughly." (20, pp. 54-5) To express what is abidingly local in a thing means, in other words, to express also what is most universal in it.

Huizinga has said that the Dutch excel in doing precisely what Eliot here invites us to do, as critics, when our purpose is to identify landmarks of a national literature. But what about the major landmarks of Dutch literature, past and present? Do they combine strong local flavor with unconscious universality? Huizinga, as we saw, finds that, despite their inherent greatness as writers, Vondel and his peers in the seventeenth century seem to lack (at least for foreigners) the measure of unconscious universality that the genre-painters, for instance, so obviously achieved — for all to recognize today — in works which they offered quite unpretentiously, to satisy a very local demand. What is the secret of the universal appeal of the genre painting, if not its intensely national and local flavor— in Eliot's sense of the term local?

Discussing genre-painting in his *Aesthetics*, Hegel sets it in historical context by noting that modern romantic art, as distinct from classical and neo-classical art, accords poets and painters especially the freedom to take an utterly prosaic subject matter of everyday experience and make something higher and deeper out of it. "And it has been especially the so-called genre painting," he says, "which has not despised such topics and which has been carried by the Dutch to the pitch of perfection." Then he asks: "What has led the Dutch to this *genre*? What is it that is expressed in those little pictures which prove to have the highest power of attraction?"[21] According to Hegel, what really fascinates our attention in such paintings is the artist's manifest absorption in the "pure appearance" of what he has set before us. The industrious Dutch people that bought such paintings no doubt did so in large measure, writes Hegel, because they wished to "enjoy once again in every possible situation the neatness of its cities, houses, furnishings, as well as its domestic peace, its wealth, the respectable dress of wives and children, the brilliance of its civil and political festivals, the boldness of its seamen, the fame of its commerce and the ships that rode the oceans of the world." (21, p.886) That was a content of marketable value that poets of the age, pursuing a more conscious universality, provided far less willingly than painters. But, as distinct from its content, the art of the genre consisted quite obviously in its "heeding with a sharp eye," as Hegel emphasizes, "the momentary and ever changing traits of the present world in the details of its life, which yet harmonizes with the universal laws of aesthetic appearance in faithfully and truly keeping hold of what is most fleeting.... To grasp this most fugitive material, to give it permanence for our contemplation in the fulness of its life, is the hard task of art at this stage.... Here Ostade, Teniers, and Steen are masters. It is a triumph of art over the transitory, a triumph in which the substantial is, as it were, cheated of its power over the contingent and the fleeting." (21, pp.598-9)

Hegel links this triumph over the transitory in art with the contemporary Dutch triumph over the sea in ships of war as well as commerce. "The sea," he says, "invites man to conquest, and to piratical plunder, but also to honest gain and to commerce.... Those who navigate the sea have indeed gain for their object, but the means are in this respect paradoxical, inasmuch as they hazard both property and life to attain it. The means therefore are the very opposite to that which they aim at. This is what exalts their gain and occupation above itself and makes it something brave and noble. Courage must enter into the calculations of commerce on the seas, daring must be fused with prudence."[22] Not that all the Dutch were bold seamen; the majority then and after "consisted of townspeople, burghers active in trade and well-off, who, comfortable in their business, had no high pretensions." In fighting against Spain for their prospering interests, they had put all that they were and cherished, in home and town and trade, on trial. And all that they risked, and would risk again, they came to value with an "utterly living absorption," writes Hegel, which is mirrored most faithfully in the time-arresting "pure appearances" of their profoundly national art. (21, p.885)

What Dutch painting could do in the seventeenth century, the Dutch language, and the literature in that language, can do today, Now a faithful mirror of the Dutch spirit, our language, says Huizinga, "makes it possible for us to absorb foreign cultures without being assimilated by them." It may well now, as in Erasmus's time, "prevent our word from reaching the rest of the world, but it preserves our national identity while enabling us to recognize others. As long as we possess our way of thought, of which our language is the form and expression, and absorb foreign influences in it, there is no need for us to defend ourselves against foreign influences." His final counsel is: "Let us preserve our language in such a way that it remains" — like the genre painting — "good Dutch and becomes"—even as Erasmus might have wished — "as international as possible!" (5, p.117)

NOTES

* After the first full footnote entry for the source cited, further references to it will appear, in parentheses, in the text itself, with the footnote-entry number followed by the page number. (Ft. #, page #)

1. Johan Huizinga, *Erasmus and the Age of Reformation* (New York, 1924), p. 43.

2. Annie Romein Verschoor, *Silt and Sky: Men and Movements in Modern Dutch Literature* (London, 1950), pp. 32-3.

3. Frank J. Warnke, "Neglected Western Literatures: The Example of Dutch," *Council on National Literatures/Report*, Number 5, January 1976 (New York, 1976), p. 4.

4. Henrietta ten Harmsel, *Jacobus Revius. Dutch Metaphysical Poet* (Detroit, 1968), P. 9.

5. Johan Huizinga, *Dutch Civilization in the Seventeenth Century* (New York, 1968), p. 98.

6. R.P. Meijer, *Literature of the Low Countries* (New York, 1971), p. 111.

7. J.L. Price, *Culture and Society in the Dutch Republic During the 17th Century* (New York, 1974), pp. 125-6.

8. Gerard Brom, *Schilderkunst en litteratuur in de 16e en 17e eeuw* (Utrecht-Antwerp, 1957). Cited by Price (see above).

9. See Egbert Krispyn, "Netherlandic Studies in the Seventies," in this volume (pp. 161-2).

10. Bartholomew Landheer, ed., *The Netherlands (Berkeley*, 1946), p. 56.

11. In Huizinga, *Dutch Civilization*: pp. 138-57, 105-37.

12. Johan Huizinga, *Men and Ideas*, trans. by J. S. Holmes and H. van Marle (New York, 1959), pp. 312-3.

13. F.A. Pottle, ed., *Boswell in Holland* (London, 1952), p. 107.

14. Pieter Geyl, *Encounters in History* (New York, 1961), pp. 9-83.

15. Pieter Geyl, *The Revolt of the Netherlands: 1555-1609* (London, 1966), p. 259.

16. Pieter Geyl, *The Netherlands in the Seventeenth Century, Part One, 1609-1646* (New York, 1961), p. 17.

17. P.L. Muller, *Onze gouden eeuw* (Leyden, 1896-8).

18. J,E. Sandys, *History of Classical Scholarship*, 3 vols. (Cambridge, 1908).

19. Horatio Smith, ed., *Columbia Dictionary of Modern European Literature* (New York, 1947), p. 243.

20. T.S. Eliot, *To Criticize the Critic* (New York, 1965), p. 54.

21, G.W.F. Hegel, *Aesthetics: Lectures on Fine Art*, trans. by T.M. Knox, 2 vols. (Oxford, 1975), p. 168.

22. G.W.F. Hegel, *The Philosophy of History*, trans. by J. Sibree (New York, 1956), pp. 90-1 (adapted).

Canada's "Two Solitudes": Foci of a National Ellipse

Canada is not only a nation but a colony in an empire. I have said that culture seems to flourish best in national units, which implies that the empire is too big and the province too small for major literature. . . . The imperial and the regional are both inherently anti-poetic environments, yet they go hand in hand; and together they make up what I call the colonial in Canadian life. This colonial tendency has been sharpened by the French-English split, the English having tended to specialize in the imperial and the French in the regional aspects of it.

Northrop Frye, 1943[1]

Le Canada est audiourd'hui un pays souverain, mais. . . peut-étre à l'heure actuelle trop jeune, trop médiocre, trop incapable de s'analyser pour produire de grandes oeuvres d'art aussi bien en Anglais qu'en Francais. . . . [Au] sein d'un pays bilingue . . . nous somme donc destinés a vivre eternellement ensemble. Cherchons ce que nous avons de commun entre nous dans tous les domaines et en particulier dans les lettres. Cela vaudra mieux que tous les discours académiques de bonne entente.

Jean-Charles Bonenfant, 1956 ([1] 261-64)*

In *O Canada: An American's Notes on Canadian Culture*, Edmund Wilson says that when he first read Hugh MacLennan's *Two Solitudes*[2] about the "antagonism and mutual incomprehension" of Canada's French- and English- speaking populations, he was reminded of Scott's *Ivanhoe*.[3] Since the English Conquest of French Canada in 1760, the "fragments of Europe's most obstinate nationalities," whose lots were then cast together "on the northern margin of habitable North America,"[4] seem indeed to have had a social and cultural history that mirrors in reverse, as Wilson goes on to suggest, the history of Anglo-French relations in Saxon Britain after the Norman Conquest of 1066.

" Four generations had not sufficed," Scott writes in the opening paragraphs of his tale of the times of Richard Coeur de Lion, "to blend the hostile blood of the Normans and Anglo-Saxons, or to unite, by common language and mutual interests, two hostile races, one of which still felt the elation of triumph, while the other groaned under all the consequences of defeat. . . . French was the language of honor, of chivalry, and even of justice, while . . . Ango-Saxon was abandoned to the use of rustics and hinds, who knew no other."[5] And the very little fusion that had already taken place proved to be, according to Scott, even more humiliating than the official stratified isolation of the two languages. A few paragraphs later, we get the once-notorious brief conversation between Wamba the fool and Gurth the swineherd on precisely that theme. Wamba, son of Witless, explains how *swine* and *ox* and *calf* are "good Saxon" while running about "on their four legs. . . . in the charge of a Saxon slave," but become Norman *pork* and *beef* and *veal*, once they have been "flayed, and drawn, and quartered, and hung up by the heels," like traitors, to be cooked and carved and served up for a nobles' feast in the Castle-hall. What is plain English when it requires tendance, Wamba concludes, becomes French when served up for enjoyment. And swineherd Gurth agrees. "By St. Dunstan, thou speakest but sad truths; little is left to us but the air we breathe, and that appears to have been reserved with much hesitation, solely for the purpose of enabling us to endure the tasks they lay upon our shoulders. The finest and the fattest is for their board; the loveliest is for their couch; the best and bravest supply their foreign masters with soldiers, and whiten distant lands with their bones, leaving few here who have either will or the power to protect the unfortunate Saxon." ([5]31-32)

The first scene of MacLennan's *TwoSolitudes* plunges us immediately into a reversal of *Ivanhoe*'s Anglo-French stratified social order. There, as Wilson notes, "after the opening pages of description, it is Pére Beaubien the parish priest and Athanase Tallard the *seigneur*, instead of Gurth the swineherd and Wamba the jester, who take up a good many pages of landscape and social background as a setting for a very brief conversation." But having suggested the parallel, and having acknowledged that MacLennan "sometimes conveys the excitement of Walter Scott," Wilson for some reason suddenly drops it. Ignoring the powerful irony of the reversed roles, he thus chides the author: "It can never have occurred to MacLennan that beginning a book in this way is likely to discourage the modern reader. ([3] 74) For his general assessment, Wilson in fact invokes parallels that have no linguistic-cultural significance. "As a novel, to a reader from the States," he concludes, "*Two Solitudes* rather affects one in the same way as those schematized works of fiction of the period after the Civil War which tried to dramatize the problems of Reconstruction or, in the early years of this century, the relations between capital and labor. Mr. MacLennan, as a social satirist, is amusing when he writes about rich Montrealers entertaining a visiting Englishman, but although he does his honest best with the household, so rustic and antiquated, of Athanase Tallard, the French *seigneur*, one feels that this has not been experienced as imaginative fiction should be." ([3] 70)

In other words, MacLennan's Anglo-French solitudes, unlike Scott's, remain isolated for the novelist as well as for his characters. In this respect, Scott had, of course, the incomparable advantage of looking back upon the Saxons and Normans of medieval England as upon the mixed ancestry of a long-since nationally united people. The ancient antagonism and mutual incomprehension had found its proper solvent, if not in the domestic trials of interclass marriages then certainly on far-off battlefields where shedding one's blood with one's king, whether as conscript or volunteer, could in one day gentle any man's condition, be he ne'er so vile. In 1945, when *Two Solitudes* was originally published (and quickly became a sensation because of the "unprecedented boldness" of its approach to the subject), there were no proper solvents even remotely in sight for Canadian Anglo-French estrangement, and certainly none are suggested in the novel. There, as Robert L. McDougal has aptly observed, "two race legends touch but do not join, and Athanase Tallard, at the point of the novel's real climax, dies an immolation to unappeasable gods. Tallard's son Paul, ostensibly the man in whom the two worlds become one, does *not* rise Phoenix-like from the ashes, and we are to be consoled with the image of oil and alcohol in a bottle which, we are told, 'had not broken yet'."[6]

Can there ever be Anglo-French, oil-and-alcohol fusion in Canada, as there finally was in England? In the midst of the "Quiet Revolution" or "Not-so-Quiet Revolution" generated by the continuing crisis between "the old order and the new" in French Canada, one hardly dares to raise the question. Yet it must be raised, for its cultural and political implications are all-pervasive for Canada's future. In Norman England, the "singular spectacle" of two languages co-existing in close geographical connection, "with little influence of the one upon the other," lasted longer than it has as yet in Canada. Three centuries passed before that original Anglo-French bilingual balance lost political support and broke down. The French of the conquerors had been, after all, not a cherished ancestral tongue but part of the spoils of their earlier conquest of northern France. Their descendants in England nonetheless cherished it as their very own, at least for as long as they aspired to make one kingdom of England and France. When events abroad forced them to give up that aspiration, they gave up their French as well and adopted the "basic English" of their Saxon subjects. In the process of adoption, however, that English was soon overloaded with enough French to make its use comfortable, particularly in the sphere of public law, for a dominant class which, without serious challenge from below, has managed to remain dominant ever since.

When the English conquered French Canada in the eighteenth century, the rule they imposed in fact owed much more to the ancestral language and institutions of MacLennan's Père Beaubien and Athanase Tallard than to those of Scott's Gurth and Wamba. Indeed, one must

venture to say that, stripped of all it owes to the ancestry of
Athanase Tallard, Anglo-Saxon could hardly have functioned in England or anywhere else as a language of effec-
tive governance. How thoroughly French in substance as
well as terminology English law became after the great
Assize of Clarendon, issued in 1166 by King Henry II —"the
French prince who, in addition to England, ruled a good
half of France"[7] — is the theme of an entire chapter of F.W.
Maitland's authoritative *History of English Law*. And there
Maitland makes several observations which help to explain
(if one approaches them by way of Scott's Ivanhoe and
MacLennan's *Two Solitudes*) why there has not yet been and
perhaps never can or need be any significant tendency
toward linguistic fusion in Anglo-French Canada.

1. The "Norman Solitude" in Modern English

Maitland first of all reminds us that, for at least half a
century before the battle of Hastings, the Normans were
indeed Frenchmen in the fullest sense: "French in their
language, French in their law, proud indeed of their past
history, very ready to fight against other 'Frenchmen if
Norman home-rule was endangered, but still Frenchmen,
who regarded Normandy as a member of the state or
congeries of states that owed service, we can hardly say
obedience, to the king at Paris.[8] In France, the Norsemen
had not only "learnt a Romance tongue"; they had also
"adopted the official machinery of Frankish or French
government" which, when they crossed the channel to
become England's "happy few," they proceeded to establish as the operative law of the land. Of the institutional
aspect of the legacy, Maitland writes: "It is enough to say,
at present, that institutions which have now-a-days the most
homely and English appearance may nevertheless be connected, through the customs of Normany, with the system
of government elaborated [in France] in the latter centuries of the Roman Empire." ([8], cii) And of the linguistic
aspect, he writes similarly: "It would hardly be too much to
say that at the present day almost all our words that have a
definite legal import are in a certain sense French." ([8],
80)

The Anglo-Saxon nativist street taunt "Talk white!"
(to which an equally nativist French reply is apt to be, as
Wilson noted, "Tombez mortel" ([3] 245) was probably

already being heard in parts of Canada when, alluding to a more fashionable literary penchant for the Teutonic as against the Romance element in English, Maitland cautioned: "On many a theme an English man of letters may, by way of exploit, write a paragraph or a page and use no word that is not in every sense a genuinely English word; but an English or American lawyer who attempted this puritanical feat would find himself doomed to silence." Scott's Wamba had grudgingly acknowledged and defined the narrowed post-Conquest limits of "basic English" in his particular sphere of competence; and Maitland becomes, in effect, a learned, ironic Wamba, using "we" to mean Anglo Saxon where he writes: "It is true, and it is worthy of remark, that within the sphere of public law we have some old terms which have come down to us from unconquered England. Earl was not displaced by count, sheriff was not displaced by viscount; our king, our queen, our lords, our knights of the shire are English; our aldermen are English if our mayors are French; but our parliament and its statutes, our privy council and its ordinances, our peers, our barons, the commons of the realm, the sovereign, the state, the nation, the people are French; our citizens are French and our burgesses more French than English." ([8] 80-81)

Maitland then totals up the accounts to show the preponderance of French over English elements not only in the vast sphere of land law, where "we should naturally look for many foreign terms," but everywhere else as well, so as to "observe how widely and how deeply the French influence has worked," even where we should not look for it at all. After citing hundreds of instances, he comes at last to the all-important sphere of enforcement, without which all the rest of a legal system, however handsomely elaborated, remains rootless; and there he concludes: "We enter a court of justice: court, justices, judges, jurors, counsel, attorneys, clerks, parties, plaintiff, defendant, action, suit, claim, demand, indictment, count, declaration, pleadings, evidence, verdict, conviction, judgment, sentence, appeal, reprieve, pardon, execution, every one and every thing, save the witnesses, writs and oaths, have French names. In the province of justice and police with its fines, its gaols and its prisons, its constables, its arrests, we must, now that outlawry is a thing of the past, go as far as the gallows if we would find an English institution." ([8] 81)

At the very heart of modern English wherever spoken, there exists, in other words, what one may call in retrospect an impregnable "French solitude — the Norman's revenge, so to speak. To command his tenants, the Norman master, who never cared to share his adopted French with crude Saxons, had had to learn their speech, sacrificing his otherwise closely-guarded cultural isolation or solitude in order to generalize or rationalize theirs. Yet he left his indelible mark, as conqueror and master, where it counted most: conspicuously enough in religion and art, and even more in the spheres of statecraft, war, and law where — for his continued dominance — continuity was indispensabile. And that indelible mark of the French linguistic triumph in English law, says Maitland, is to be counted "among the most momentous and permanent effects" of the Conquest of 1066: "for language is no mere instrument which we can control at will; it controls us." ([8] 87)

Today there is in process, in Canada, a powerful retrospective "search for a nation" (as Janet Marchain's excellent little book on the theme documents)[9] that sifts through the history of "French-English Relations in Canada Since 1759" for its most promising leads, on the assumption that the chief obstacles to genuine national unity are all surely there, in one documentable crisis after another, and need to be studied objectively if serious progress is to be made in the search. Yet may it not be that the old Anglo-French bilingual "Norman connection," in the distant background, provides the point to which the main lines of perspective need to be extended if the historical picture is to be meaningfully complete? The "Norman connection" at once unites the English and the French and assures them of the permanence of their historic cultural separation. Because there was a prior massive "inoculation," dating from a time when Frenchmen ruled Saxons in England, it may be that modern English has been rendered permanently immune, despite close geographical association, to further fusion with French.

Yet it is obvious that neither the French nor the English in Canada, for diverse reasons, much care to remember the Norman connection. The English have understandably preferred to forget a conquest of Saxons that proved to be permanent; for, despite Robin Hood and his merry band, it is a fact that no "Saxon Liberation Front"

(SLF?) ever managed to drive the Normans out. In his seminal "Two Ways of Life: The Primary Antithesis of Canadian History," the eminent English-Canadian historian, A.R.M. Lower, for instance, illustrates without quite intending to do so how deeply the conquered of 1066 have drunk of the waters of Lethe. Urging his readers to try to visualize what life must have been like for the *curés*, *seigneurs*, and *habitants* left behind in Canada when the French imperial administrators were withdrawn in defeat after 1760, Lower admonishes: "It is hard for a people of English speech to enter imaginatively into the feelings of those who must pass under the yoke of conquest, for, except in the Southern States, there is scarcely a memory of it in all their tradition. Conquest is a type of slavery and of that too we have no memory — except as masters." Wamba and Gurth are thus wholly out of mind while an effort is made to "enter imaginatively" into the feelings of MacLennan's Père Beaubien and Athanase Tallard! But Lower is too good an historian to let himself get by with such conveniently "wholesome" forgetfulness. He adds in a footnote: "Yet as late as the nineteenth century an historian like Freeman [E.A. Freeman, author of the monumental *History of the Norman Conquest*, 6 vols., 1867-79] could draw a line between the Saxon people, with whom he identified himself, and their conquerors, the Normans. In his writings the Saxons were always 'we,' and the Normans 'they.' The memory of conquest dies hard!" ([4] 18)

The special irony here lies in the fact that a principal object of Professor Lower's essay was to invite French Canadians to forget the Conquest of 1760! The French ethnic-cultural identity in Canada is secure, he asserts in its final paragraphs, and then he concludes:

> It seems to me, the tensions and troubles of our times... will some day burn out the grosser aspects of our English materialism, giving us a truer and deeper insight into life than what we have now, reforming our society in some such way as society was reshaped at the end of the middle ages and thereby establishing a new set of values in which both races can share. The two communities will never be one, there can be no question of a blood brotherhood, but sooner or later they will take up their respective weights, some kind of equilibrium will be reached, of that I am sure. We have not lived together for nearly two centuries merely to see the

Canadian experiment fail. It will not fail. This country of
high colours and violent contrasts will not fail. One of these
days the two races, forgetting lesser allegiances, will unite in
mutual loyalty to it, and build it into a structure of which our
successors will be proud. ([4] 28)

If there were a clearer English-Canadian recollec-
tion of the triumph of French law in English back in the
days when Saxons passed "under the yoke of conquest," it
might become easier for French-Canadians to accept, among
other things, the current subordination of their Quebec
civil or private law, which is French, to the public law
administered by the federal government in Ottawa, which
is English in the post-Norman sense. The Quebec civil law,
nos lois, together with *nos institutions* and *notre langue*, was
what the leaders of French Canada since the English Conquest had sought to preserve at all costs, as constituting
their very existence as a distinct Canadian people.[10] The
Act of Quebec of 1774, the Act of 1791 which created
Ottawa, and even the Act of Union of 1840 (as qualified in
1848), left Quebec's institutions, language, and civil laws
secure, and the laws were finally codified in 1866, a year
before the British North America Act of 1867, which con-
stituted the modern Canadian confederation. The date of
codification, 1866, co-incidently, falls in line with the two
major dates in the history of the triumph of French law in
Norman England: 1066, of course, which made the triumph
possible; and 1166, the truly "fatal" date, as Maitland
characterizes it, of the Assize of Clarendon, when "the
decree went forth which gave to every man dispossessed of
his freehold a remedy to be sought in a royal court, a
French-speaking court," after which the "ultimate triumph
of French law terms was secure." It is true that almost two
centuries later, in 1362, a statute written in French declared that, for the benefit of a Saxon citizenry little schooled
in the language of the courts, pleas should thereafter be
"pleaded, shown, defended, answered, debated, and judged"
in the English tongue. But by then it was too late. That
benign statute "could not break the Westminster lawyers of
their settled habit of thinking about law and writing about
law in French, and when slowly the French gave way before
English even as the language of law reports and legal
textbooks, the English to which it yielded was an English in
which every cardinal word was of French origin. " ([8]

84-85)

In 1966, the centenary of codification of Quebec's French civil law, a group of French-Canadian scholars issued the first of a series of volumes designed, as the general editor said, to provide *"un inventaire complet des ressources et des faiblesses de la civilisation française du Canada."* The volume was titled *Structure sociales du Canada française: Ètudes de membres de la Section I de la Société Royale du Canada,* and its inventory of the strengths and weaknesses of *les cadres politique* was provided by the eminent French-Canadian man of letters and juridical scholar Jean-Charles Bonenfant, M.S.R.C., *bibliothécaire de la Législature provinciale, Québec.* M. Bonenfant deals specifically with the impact of English on French law in Canada; he recalls very vividly the English Conquest of 1760, which brought on the subordination of French law to English in Canada; but he does not so much as allude, in 1966, to the events of 1066 and 1166 which — as Maitland amply demonstrates — led to the subordination of English to French law in Saxon England. It is a learned, mellowed Wamba-in-reverse, peering out of one solitude into another, who can assert by way of conclusion: first, that *"nos institutions politiques et judiciaires n'ont donc presque rien de français et elles sont même en général d'origine britannique"*; then, that *"les Canadiens français ont su assez bien utiliser les institutions d'origine britannique, mais ils ont aussi créé un système parfois hybride dans lequel ils ne peuvent pas toujours poursuivre leur activité politique et administrative aussi naturellement et aussi spontanement que leurs compatriotes anglo-saxons"*; and finally, that *"il leur a falu en particulier utiliser un language parlementaire et administratif qui, dans sa traduction improvisée, n'a pas toujours respecté les exigences du français tel qu'on le parle a Paris."* ([10] 82) In fourteenth-century England, the *"traduction improvisée"* had to be made from French into English; in twentieth-century French-Canada, it has to be made from English into French — except that, in the latter case, it is an English in which every cardinal word is of French origin.

Yet M. Bonenfant, as a French-Canadian man of letters, no less than as a juridical scholar, believes as firmly as Professor Lower that Canada is and must remain one nation. On the contribution that literature and literary scholarship can make in the common search for a more

perfect Canadian national union, he has in fact been most
eloquent. In his "*L'influence de la litterature canadienne-
anglaise au Canada français*" (*Culture*, XVII, 3, Sept.
1956), addressed to English-Canadian writers and scholars,
Bonenfant quoted with full assent these words of Desmond
Pacey in 1952: "There is still a wide gulf between the
cultures of French and English Canada, and few indeed are
the bridges over it." Pacey had cited a hopeful prediction of
William Kirby in 1877, looking to a future time when the
French and English literary traditions would be "united in
one grand flood stream of Canadian literature," only to
conclude: "That time is not yet; indeed there was more
basis for the hope in 1877 than there is in 1950." ([1] 260)

    M. Bonenfant was prepared to acknowledge that
change was in the air. If there were not yet bridges over that
"obscure and difficult no-man's-land of bicultural relationships," ([I] 247) there had at least been, in recent years, a
series of more or less successful expeditionary ventures,
with English-Canadians, it seemed to him, venturing more
thus far than his own people. Roger Lemelin and Andrè
Langevin were surely better known among English-Canadians, for instance, than Morley Callaghan and David Walker
were among French-Canadians. But Bonenfant hastened to
explain that interest was one-sided for the moment because
"*peut-être, permettez-moi de la dire franchement, offrions-nous
plus d'intérêt pour vous que vous a notre régard. L'existence d'un
groupe français en Amérique anglo-saxonne, un groupe dont la
lutte pour la survivance et dont la transformation sont riches
d'inspiration littèraire, pique la curiosité des anthropologues,
des sociologues et des hommes de lettres. Bien des Canadiens
anglais en sortant du colonialisme et en redoutant 1'écrasement
par les Ètats-Unis voisins ont aussi été heureux de retrouver dans
le jeune littèrature canadienne-française un canadianisme profond
qui s'explique par des raison historiques.*" ([1] 261)

2. Cosmopolitanism: The Big Abstraction

With that observation, M. Bonenfant confirms from a French
Canadian perspective what the leading English-Canadian
literary critics E. K. Brown, Northrop Frye, and John
Sutherland had begun to say in the mid-1940s to correct
the notion then still current that the best way to free
Canadian literature from the divisive, stifling heritage of
colonialism was through deliberate cultivation of some

form of literary cosmopolitanism that would be neither French nor British, nor even American or Canadian-American in any ethnic sense, but manifestly supranational. The chief advocate of decolonialization through cosmopolitanism in the 1920s and 1930s had been A. J. M. Smith, who had launched his crusade against literary bondage to the past while still an undergraduate at McGill University. Rejecting the idea of a deliberately "Canada-conscious" criticism, Smith had argued in 1928 that its cultivation leads almost inevitably to a "mixture of blind optimism and materialistic patriotism, a kind of my mother- drunk-or-sober complex that operates most effectively in the world of affairs and finds its ideal action summarized in the slogan 'Buy Made in Canada Goods'." The result of that kind of "He-man Canadiana," he had concluded, is perhaps "good for business but bad for poetry and, if you happen to think that poetry is more important, you are tempted to ask what is to be done about it." ([1] 31)

Later, in the preface he wrote for *New Provinces* in 1936 — a preface which was, however, for some reason "rejected" before publication — Smith had thus wished to say for himself and the five other poets anthologized with him: "We do not pretend that this volume contains any verse that might not have been written in the United States or in Great Britain. There is nothing specially Canadian about more than one or two poems. Why should there be? Poetry today is written for the most part by people whose emotional and intellectual heritage is not a national one; it is either cosmopolitan or provincial, and, for good or evil, the forces of civilization are rapidly making the latter scarce." ([I] 39-40) Smith hammered on the theme in many other writings, and most strikingly perhaps in his *Book of Canadian Poetry*[11] where, after explicit statement of his thesis in the Introduction, he pressed it into service for the over-all division of the anthology itself. In its design, "The Rise of a Native Tradition" serves to categorize Canada's past efforts in poetry, while "Modern Poetry: The Cosmopolitan Tradition" settles the preferred direction for the present and future.

That same year, E. K. Brown's *On Canadian Poetry* appeared; and while the celebrated essay did not address itself explicitly to Smith's views it contributed much to the kind of replies that other critics would soon be making.

Brown was by no means a champion of Canadian national autonomy of the "He-man Canadiana" variety. "Autonomy," he wrote, "almost always breeds chauvinism, and usually brings as an immediate consequence an unwholesome delight in the local second-rate. Its advent opposes strong obstacles to international currents of art and thought." But having said what needed to be firmly said "against the notion that out of autonomy all good things soon issue," he added: "Still it must be appreciated just as clearly that dependence breeds a state of mind no less unwholesome, a state of mind in which great art is most unlikely to emerge or to be widely recognized if it did. A great art is fostered by artists and audiences possessing in common a passionate and peculiar interest in the kind of life that exists in the country where they live. . . . Canada is a state in which such an interest exists only among a few. I have pointed out how Mr. Callaghan and Miss de la Roche have written as they could not have written if they possessed such interest. And it is the same with Canadian readers." ([6] 40)

Brown stated the case for a national literary environment, as against the appeal of a cosmopolitan (or expatriate) ideal, emphatically enough, saying.: "A great literature is the flowering of a great society, a mature and adequate society." But he will propose no remedies applicable to Canada, he added, "for it is not in the province of a student of letters to say how a society becomes mature and adequate." ([1] 47) Of the Anglo-French division, he wrote: "In French Canada, the sense of cultural nationality is much stronger than in English Canada, but the nationality is French Canadian, not Canadian *tout court*." ([1] 32) Yet, from the French-Canadian point of view, the English Canadians often hardly qualify, dispositionally, as Canadian at all. "The charge that English Canada is colonial in spirit is the most serious of all the many charges," wrote Brown, "that French Canada brings against us." To illustrate the point, he then repeated the story that Louis Saint Laurent, the leading French member of the government, had told in the Canadian House of Commons the year before — about two ex-prime ministers of Canada, one of whom, "on the eve of his departure to live in England," told the other: "I am glad to be going *home*." To which the other reportedly replied: "How I envy you." No wonder the French Canadians are tempted to cry: *Maudits Anglais!* Give us back our

Canada! ([1] 38)

Even worse, in those World War II days, was the imperialistic talk among the English Canadians about the ideal of a "Vaster Britain," with Canada sharing as an equal partner in Britain's global imperial glories. Needless to say, French Canada could never have enjoyed, or wished to enjoy, any share in such glories. As Northrop Frye warned in "Canada and Its Poetry" (*Canadian Forum*, 1943) — reviewing Smith's *Book of Canadian Poetry* — the imperial extreme of the evils of colonialism is as bad, from the literary standpoint, as the provincial or regional extreme. "I know of no poet," Frye wrote, "with the very dubious exception of Virgil, who has made great poetry out of what Shakespeare calls 'the imperial theme': in Kipling, for instance, this theme is largely a praise of machinery, and of the Robot tendencies within the human mind. The province or region, on the other hand, is usually a vestigial curiosity to be written up by some nostalgic tourist. ([1] 89)

But Frye wholly rejected Smith's notion that deliberate cultivation or critical acceptance of a cosmopolitan attitude is an adequate alternative for the extremes of colonialism. "Certainly if a Canadian tries to avoid being a Canadian," he wrote, "he will sound like nothing on earth. For, whatever may be true of painting or music, poetry is not a citizen of the world: it is conditioned by language, and flourishes best within a national unit. 'Humanity' is an abstract idea, not a poetic image." ([1] 88)

Frye nevertheless hailed Smith's anthology as "an important event in Canadian literature." Smith has dealt well, in his view, with the older modern poets, like Campbell and Carman, for instance, tracing the "thin gold vein of real imagination through a rocky mass of what can only be called a gift of metrical gab"; and in judging his younger contemporaries, he has remembered that "a flawed talent is better than a flawless lack of it and that still it is performance and not 'promise' that makes the poet, of whatever age." ([1] 86) Frye especially praised Smith's study of the pre-Confederation poets as the "only one that has been made from anything like a modem point of view." Charles Heavysage, a genuine Canadian Beddoes," Isabella Crawford, "one of the subtlest poets that Canada has produced," the poets of the so-called Maple School, who "sang too much and thought too little," all get their due.

Lampman's supremacy "comes out very clearly," followed by Pratt, who "gets his deserved prominence," while the younger poets "are generously represented." In short, Frye concluded, here in the domain of poetry is "what Canada can do: the reader who does not like this book does not like Canadian poetry, and will not be well advised to read further. Of course, as Mr. Smith says in his Preface, French Canadian poetry is a separate job — still to be done, I should think, for Fourier's *Anthologie des Poètes Canadiens* is, as its editor Asselin frankly admits, more a collection of poets than of poems. But we cannot leave the French out of our poetry any more than we can leave Morrice or Gagnon out of our painting." ([1] 87) Smith would, in fact, make up for the French "deficiency" here in his later anthologies, *The Oxford Book of Canadian Verse* (1960) and his projected revision of the same which turned out to be an altogether new book, *Modern Canadian Verse: In English and French* (1967).

John Sutherland's criticism of Smith's attitude was consistent with the views of Brown and Frye but seemed much more pointed. In their *Making of Modern Poetry in Canada: Essential Articles on Contemporary Canadian Poetry in English*, editors Louis Dudek and Michael Gnarowski allot an entire chapter, titled "The New Poetry: A Manifesto," to Sutherland's Introduction to *Other Canadians: An Anthology of the New Poetry in Canada, 1940-1946* (Montreal, 1947). Characterizing that Introduction as a "buried milestone in our literary history," Dudek and Gnarowski assert that it "has been misunderstood and neglected apparently because critics have been put off by Sutherland's explicit Marxist or socialist position, by his rude polemic against A.J.M. Smith, and perhaps by his later conversion to Catholicism, which seemed to disqualify some of his arguments. Actually, it is a brilliant and prophetic piece of polemical writing, containing a sound core of critical argument, and will no doubt become, with time, a standard reference in Canadian criticism." ([1145)

Sutherland's piece opens with a direct assault on Smith's claim, that "Canadian poetry has been the product of two schools — the native and the cosmopolitan." He cites Smith's words: "One group has attempted to describe whatever is essentially and distinctively Canadian. . . . the other, from the beginning, has made a heroic effort to transcend colonialism by entering into the universal civilizing culture of ideas." ([1] 47) Like E.K. Brown and Northrop Frye, Sutherland holds that Smith does well to reject the crude nativist assumption that "a man who chooses his homeland as his theme" will thereby automatically "make a valuable contribution to Canadian literature." Such an assumption is indeed "colonial" in the worst sense; but Smith's cosmopolitanism is not the answer to it, for cosmopolitanism is simply another variety of colonialism. While representing itself as an escape from colonialism, our contemporary poetry becomes all the more colonial in fact, writes Sutherland, "because it is the product of a cultured English group who are out of touch with the people who long ago began adjusting themselves to life on this continent." ([1] 57) Smith knows, Sutherland argues, though he is reluctant to admit it, that there has been as yet no genuine, discernibly national Canadian poetic tradition; Smith knows that "we could only use the word tradition if we believed that the poetry was so blended with the life of the country that it was able to reach into the present and influence its course." ([1] 50) What Canada has had instead, in this century and the last, are traditions of English poetry which have been transplanted, and which "are native only in the sense of being smaller and more cramped than the home plant." ([I] 54)

Smith's cosmopolitan "tradition" is, according to Sutherland, simply more of the same. It is the current English fashion, and therefore in no sense alters the "colonial basis of our poetry," despite the fact that, by virtue of its being largely Marxist in outlook, it is "committed to a society in which colonies, like colonial attitudes, will cease to exist." ([1] 57) Sutherland then observes that even socialism, for all its supranational or cosmopolitan pretensions, "must take a somewhat different form in every country, and in Canada it cannot be separated from a healthy national point of view." Before significant social change can progress very far in Canada, he says, the colonial ties, which are "well-nigh crippling" in the spiritual sense, must be broken. And breaking them means, for Canada, "that the power of changing our constitution must pass from the hands of a British governing body to the Canadian people; that the economic rights and privileges of the mother country must be abolished; that the middle class with its British sympathies must be changed at its base; and — very important politically — that a fusion of viewpoint must take place between French and English Canada, which is impossible while the allegiance of one is owed to another country." ([1] 58)

Returning to the same theme in 1951 (after having undergone profound changes in his basic attitudes and beliefs), Sutherland recalled that in 1947 he had severely criticized Smith for his "T. S. Eliot" variety of religious emphasis, particularly as projected in interpretations of the tendencies of contemporary Canadian poetry. "Well," wrote Sutherland, "I take it back. I still think Mr. Smith was forcing matters at the time, but the event has shown that he was substantially right. For the new poets have come back, if not always to religion, at least to a soul-searching which has strong religious implications." ([1] 120) Their supra-nationalism, or cosmopolitanism, overshot the mark, even as the crude "He-man Canadiana" tendency undershot it; but that is the way, Sutherland now concluded, national traditions are formed. The religious soul-searching has tended, however unintentionally, to pull the sights down till the target may well be in range at last. The New Poetry is now discernibly part of an emerging national tradition. "I suppose it is sacrilege to speak of it as a Canadian movement," he hastens to add, "when the majority of its members professed a cosmopolitan faith and were opposed to the national idea in any form: yet Canadian in part it obviously was. The phenomenal development of Canada during the last war, relatively greater than that of any country in the same period, gave a marked impetus to poetry as it did to the arts generally. There was an excitement in the air to which no one — least of all the poet — could fail to respond. Even that political point of view, which generally left the national question out of account, was very much influenced in an indirect way by national factors." ([1] 118-19)

Sutherland did not pretend that "soul-searching" had resulted in an outpouring of poetry superior to that of the earlier Marxist-cosmopolitan phase of the New Poetry. On the contrary, "it seems obvious to me," he wrote, "that the recent work of the younger poets is inferior to their work in the early forties, but that, nevertheless, the principles behind this recent work are potentially better principles for poetry." It is generally better for a poet "to be honestly himself than to disguise himself in a big abstraction . . . and it is better for him to use and not oppose the traditions of poetry — and for the Canadian poet not to completely ignore his relation to the tradition of poetry in Canada. These are all admirable tendencies in present-day Canadian poetry: so far they have not been realized fully enough to produce very striking or at least very extensive results." ([1] 121-22)

John Sutherland was thirty-seven when he died in 1956. He had been in his brief years, as Robert Weaver summed it up, "an editor, a critic, occasionally a poet," but also a "kind of literary patron," for his *Northern Review* (like the First Statement Press that issued it) "was able to survive as a forum for writers simply because he and his wife . . . were willing to make continual sacrifices for the magazine." ([1] 80) Judging his labors from the late volume, *John Sutherland: Essays, Controversies, and Poems* (1972), one can agree with its editor, Miriam Waddington, that he was "a critic who tried to define national literature not through political means or core symbols but through the psychological, technical, and historical analysis of contemporary Canadian writing."[12]

3. Toward a Bilingual National Culture

With respect to his labors to "define national literature," it is a pity that John Sutherland did not live to see A. J. M. Smith's anthologies of English and French Canadian poetry that came out in 1960 and 1967. Smith had said in the preface to his 1943 *Book of Canadian Poetry* that "French Canadian poetry is a separate job"; Frye, in his review, had said: "but we cannot leave the French out of our poetry"; and Sutherland, in his *Other Canadians*, had said the same. Yet it was Smith who broke the ground, from a modern perspective. Frye had praised the 1943 volume for the ways in which Smith there gave the variety of poets anthologized their due. Not less deserving of praise is his critical handling of the French poets in the 1960 anthology, ranging from Octave Crémazie and Louis Fréchette, through Albert Lozeau and Emile Nelligan (who "made the most impressive and enduring contribution to Canadian poetry"[13]), to Saint-Denys-Garneau and his cousin Anne Hébert, and beyond. And in the 1967 anthology, which started out as a revision of the 1960 volume but became instead *Modern Canadian Verse: In English and French*, Smith in effect located the beginning of a genuinely bicultural, modern Canadian national literature in the poetry of E.J. Pratt.

In his "Preface to an Uncollected Anthology" (1957), Northrop Frye had not hesitated to say: "It is Pratt who has expressed in *Towards the Last Spike* the central comic theme, and in *Brébeuf*, the central tragic theme, of the Canadian imagination, and it is Pratt who combines the two in *The Truant*, which is in my anthology because it is the greatest poem in Canadian literature." ([6] 190) The first and third of these epic-narrative or *documentary* poems (as Dorothy Livesay prefers to designate the *genre*) celebrate Canadian railroad-building and freedom-defending exploits in a heroic, and sometimes mock-heroic, manner more directly attuned to English than to French Canadian sympathies; and so it falls to the tragic narrative of *Brébeuf and His Brethren* (1940) to carry the burden of a valid beginning, in the epic tradition, for a genuinely Canadian bicultural national literature.

The worst that can be said intelligently about the large poems of E.J. Pratt has been said by Frank Davey (who obviously prefers subjective lyrics) in his "E. J. Pratt: Apostle of Corporate Man" (1970). Summing up his itemized case in a final paragraph, Davey can, however, say no worse than that Pratt's poetic world "is a world where the individual voice, the lyric voice, is obligated to be silent, where gangs, crews, religions, and nations succeed, and private men die. It is a world where ships outlive successive crews, where the [Canadian Pacific Railroad] outlives the individuals who built it, It is a world where it is indeed *dulce et decorum* to die for one's faith, *patria*, ship, or family of whales."[14] Varying the variables, one could say the same for the *Odyssey* and the *Aeneid*. Pratt is no Homer or Virgil. Yet in his sweeping "documentaries" he has given Canada a genuinely epic view of itself; and in *Brébeuf and His Brethren*, particularly, he has provided an epic narrative that is certainly what most critics take it to be: "the most significant [poetic] interpretation of Canada's historical past."[15]

It is noteworthy that Pratt's hero here, the Canadian Jesuit-martyr Jean de Brébeuf (1593-1649) was a Norman. According to the *Biographie Universelle* (Paris, 1843-66), he "belonged to a noble family, from which . . . the English family of Arundel had its descent." Perhaps Pratt saw the "Norman connection." At any rate, as Professor Sandra Djwa aptly notes in her study *E. J. Pratt: The Evolutionary Vision*, the "real problem of the work . . . appears to be the dichotomy between the transcendent seventeenth-century Christianity of Brébeuf, the poem's subject, and the human-centered, turn-of-the-century, new theology of Pratt, the poet. . . . Like T. S. Eliot in *Murder in the Cathedral* (1935), Pratt has invoked a hero from the past whose actions are an example to the troubled present." ([15] 93, 109)

Such an epic "intepretation" of old and new, linking Canada's remote French-Catholic past with its bicultural, secular troubled present, can help, at least, to strengthen the claim of "establishment" Canadian historians that (in W. L. Morton's words) "the history of Canada after 1760 is only a continuation and extension of the history of Canada before 1760," and that there is indeed "but one narrative line in Canadian history." ([6] 48) Yet, in his impressively argued and documented paper on "The British Conquest: Canadian Social Scientists and the Fate of the *Canadiens*," Michel Brunet has shown quite conclusively how much remains to be done in the sphere of historiography before there can begin to be a genuine meeting of minds, much less of hearts, about the facts of the Conquest and its aftermath. English Canadians who have forgotten, or who have never been made aware of the facts about the Norman-French conquest of Anglo-Saxon Britain insist, it seems, on interpreting the English Conquest of French Canada in terms that cannot permit French Canadians to so much as begin to forget it. M. Brunet is particularly severe with the good-intentioned pretense (indulged in, he notes, by even so able a contemporary historian as A. R. M. Lower) that "French liberty" in Canada was somehow "saved" in 1760 precisely by being lost, allegedly because — in Lower's words — "out of conquest came eventually the English institutional apparatus of freedom — popular government and all the guarantees of the common law." M. Brunet will have none of that. Speaking for the Père Beaubiens and Athanase Tallards of conquered French Canada (and thus, in our reverse mirror image, also for the Wambas and Gurths of conquered Anglo-Saxon Britain), he lays it down that "a conquered nation that is unable to drive the invaders [out of] its native land loses its right to self-determination. For it, there is no independence." ([4] 91)

M. Brunet's very legitimate concern is for a true, and liberating because true, account of "the relations which have existed, since the conquest, between *Canadiens* and Canadians." As a shared misunderstanding, however good-intentioned, of reality can serve no fruitful purpose, the "first obligation" of serious Canadian scholars, he concludes, is "to analyze the facts without troubling themselves with the vested interest they will hurt or the unfavorable reactions of the influential people they will scandalize." A fresh approach to "our own historical and social problems," founded upon a determination never to perpetuate old falsehoods as truths and never to exclude from consideration anything that is manifestly true and relevant, will in the long run best serve "the good of Canada, and Atlantic civilization itself." ([4] 97-98)

A liberating pursuit of truth is thus the first requirement, in M. Brunet's view, for genuine Canadian "de-colonialization," on the French side no less than on the English. For the French Canadian, the great need evidently is to be finished with the mood of the flag-bearer in Crémazie's "*Le Drapeau de Carillon.*" In that old poem, memorized by several generations of French-Canadian school-children, the hero journeys to Versailles with his *drapeau*, hoping to move the king to send desperately needed help to the colonists in Canada. Instead he is ignored or laughed at for his provincial loyalty. Back home, he cannot bear to speak of his humiliation. But his *drapeau* is mutely eloquent. Planting it in the frozen ground on the hill above Fort Carillon, where he had bravely and victoriously borne it against the English, the despondent standard-bearer lets himself freeze to death beneath its colors: "*Pour mon drapeau je viens ici mourir.*" ([13] 19) "This poem, for all its old-fashioned rhetoric," wrote Edmund Wilson, in *O Canada*, "I find extremely moving. What differentiates it from most other patriotic ballads is that it tells of tragic defeat and offers no hope of reprisal." ([3] 87)

From M. Brunet's point of view, Crémazie's celebrated poem correctly interprets the facts of the conquest of 1760 and of its aftermath, and English-Canadian historians should not pretend otherwise. At the same time, it is hardly less urgent that the French Canadians in turn put behind them that hardly utterable anguish of their ances-tors, *abandonnés par la France leur mère* ([13]18) as in fact they appear to be doing more and more, especially since the visit of Charles de Gaulle to Quebec in 1967. With that visit, on the centenary of Canadian confederation, it had seemed that Mother France herself had at last returned to Canada to make amends for having so bitterly disappointed Crémazie's flag-bearer. "*Vive le Quebec! Vive le Quebec libre! Vive le Canada français!*" — de Gaulle had cried.[16] And it had seemed for a moment that French Quebec would be more eager to break with the Canadian federation than with French colonial-cultural dependence. But the Montreal *Morning Star* spoke for the reality of the situation when it editorialized that the general had simply "cracked the shell of loneliness which surrounds Quebec on this continent. For once, the few millions of French-Canadians in this sea of English-speaking Americans and Canadians heard glow-ing words in the French language. Confederation may appeal to the head, but the general appealed to the heart. And if confederation is to work, it must appeal to the heart also." ([16] 113- 14)

By a remarkable coincidence, Montreal's mayor at the time was a living *drapeau* — a Jean Drapeau — who, in de Gaulle's presence, reiterated the anguish of "*Le Drapeau de Carillon.*" But for that occasion, charged with so much sentiment, it was fittingly an emotional overflow recol-lected in tranquillity. The mayor recalled that the old *habitants* had been deserted by their imperial administra-tors. And then, directly to de Gaulle he said: "You have saved and renewed France. Our ancestors, our grandpar-ents, our parents, have saved Canada . . . while more cultivated and wealthy people returned to France two cen-turies ago." If we feel "no gratitude toward successive French governments," he went on, it does not mean that we do not treasure "the French language, culture, and civiliza-tion." Reaffirming French-Canada's attachment to France, he nevertheless concluded: "In whatever manner we serve it, if we serve our own country better as Canadians of French origin, then we serve France better and we serve humanity better." ([16]115-16)

The excitement of de Gaulle's visit set off some renewed calls for Quebec's separation from the confedera-tion. Yet what was new in 1967 was not the separatist appeal but the fact that the spell of the colonial past had been broken, and in a way that, as Jean-Charles Bonenfant had anticipated, would profoundly affect English-Canadian feeling. Against the separatist tendencies, but in support of the process of decolonization, Pierre Trudeau had said in his *Federalism and the French Canadians*, which appeared in 1968, shortly after de Gaulle's visit: "The die is cast in Canada: there are two main ethnic and linguistic groups; each is too strong and deeply rooted in the past, too firmly bound to a mother culture, to be able to engulf the other. But if the two will collaborate at the hub of a truly pluralistic state, Canada could become the envied seat of a form of federalism that belongs to tomorrow's world." ([16]79) Four years later, with greater cultural emphasis, he said pointedly: "Whether one is unilingual French or unilingual English, the Canadian lives in a land with a second dimension of immeasurable value." ([16] 239)

        Literature's obligation here is obviously great, as are its opportunities. Bilingualism is the law for the governmental process in federal Canada. But bilingualism must result in writings that compel bicultural interest, or it will amount to nothing more than a cultural straitjacket, a poor exchange for colonialism. Suggesting the power of imaginative literature in this sphere, the American specialist in Canadian history, Mason Wade, thus wrote appreciatively in his Foreword to *Search for a Nation*: "It is absurd to bring up people in watertight cultural compartments, convinced of the righteousness and inevitable superiority of their own tradition, and then expect them to achieve a harmonious *modus vivendi* with others equally devoted to another tradition. Happily, in the years since 1945 there has been much better communication between what Hugh MacLennan justly described as the 'Two Solitudes' of pre-war Canada; and Canadians have become much more conscious of what they have in common, and less given to dwelling on what divides them." ([9], Foreword)

4. Canada's Narrative, Lyric, and Dramatic Voices

Modern Canadian literature still runs in distinctive French and English currents and will no doubt continue to do so for a long time to come. But there is now also a third current into which, one way or another, the best of the other two must overflow, without however losing its French-

or English-Canadian distinctiveness. As that third current swells, it will transform what might have seemed the fixed relationships of the other two in the past. The centuries-old English and French "solitudes" have already come to be seen as linked foci of tension in an epic whole. Since the time of Homer's *Iliad*, enmity and mutual incomprehension between two peoples fated to confront one another, each with its own proud heritage which it justifiably strives to preserve, have again and again excited the literary imagination. Certainly they have done so in Canada, where for most of the population ethnic-cultural tension is a daily experience, either actual or vicarious. One can re-read much of English and French Canadian literature of the past, therefore, as preparation for a truly great epic, whether in poetry or prose. The documentary, long storytelling poems with a theme — which Dorothy Livesay says "may indeed be the most interesting poetically, as well as being deeply representative of the Canadian character" ([6] 269) — and the social novels of the variety studied in Antoine Sirois' *Montréal dans le roman canadien* (1968) — of which *Two Solitudes* remains the masterpiece — have already had a rich modern development, and one senses that the best use of these genres for the epic expression of Canadian national character is yet to come.

Because of its subjective individuality, as the utterance of a poet's innermost self, lyric poetry often seems much too intimately personal and particular to be an expression of national character. In the view of A.J.M. Smith and an entire school of like-minded critics, the better the lyric poetry of Canada became, the less national and the more individualized, in the cosmopolitan sense, did it seem to be. And yet, when one takes the lyric poetry of any country as a whole, there can be no doubt that even the most individualized particulars tend to fit together to form a vast mosaic even more expressive of the unity in diversity of the national character than any one epic poem, however great, could conceivably be. The lyric mosaic of Canadian literature has long since revealed the major contours of its national identity.

Lyric poetry, timeless in its subjectivity, belongs to an eternal present; its seasons come again and again in the course of a national literary history. The epic-narrative genres tend to look to the past, or to project the present back into the past by "documenting" it, for their concern is clearly the beginning of genuine national identity. The future-looking genre, the genre that reaches forward to claim the last word in the expression of nationhood, has traditionally been the drama or theater. Back in 1928, it seemed to Merrill Denison that Canada would never — barring an unforeseeable inner transformation — have a genuinely national theater. In his "Nationalism and Drama," he had observed that, whether or not Canada would ever have a Canadian theater is, fortunately, the concern of only a "very special and narrow group which, for want of a better name, may be called intellectuals." But, having pronounced that cliché, Denison deftly moved for the jugular. "This description is not exact," he wrote, seeming to retreat; and then he hastened to add: "In a country where national intentions are so confused and amorphous as in Canada, the term 'intellectuals' broadens its conventional embrace to include many who simply believe in bigger and better tariffs, and group literature, painting and the drama among the native industries which ought to have protection, whether it will do them any good or not."[17]

Denison specified that staged drama, which is, in its fullest flowering, a synthesis of all the other arts (including "literature" in its epic and lyric voices), is also the most centrifugal: "It flourishes only at the vortex of a culture. Painting, literature, music, sculpture, may conceivably spring into being in the provinces, flower independently of the capital and finally exert an influence on the latter. Such does not seem ever to have been the case with playwriting or the theater. "([17]66) Canada has no national center, and cannot have one — he insisted — until its "national intentions — are greatly clarified." Until then, a play written by a Canadian, set in a Canadian locale, with Canadian characters, will be "Canadian" only in a regional sense, like plays classified as "Mid-Western" or "Southern" in American college drama textbooks. For a Canada that remains colonial in its relations with France and England or the United States, Denison concluded, "the theatre would at best be an artificial graft supported with as great travail of the spirit and the purse as a native orange industry. But there is this to say about a native theatre: in discussion of none other of the arts are the realities of our cultural pretences brought so sharply into focus." ([17] 69)

That was said in 1928. Much has happened in Canada since. All three voices of poetry are coming to be more and more distinctly heard, and in two great languages, which are clearly the *foci* of an emerging national ellipse. It is something new under the sun, perhaps a model for other peoples elsewhere, once it flowers. The flowering comes hard; but, in the words of Jean-Charles Bonenfant (cited bilingually) in *Between Friends/Entre Amis* (1976) — one of Canada's most impressive commemorations of the bicentenary of American independence — "*La plupart des nations ont été formées non pas par des gens qui désiraient intensément vivre ensemble, mais plutôt par des gens qui ne pouvaint vivre séparément./* Most nations have been formed not by people who desired intensely to live together but rather by people who could not live apart."

NOTES

*After the first full footnote entry for the source cited, further references to it will appear, in parentheses, in the text itself, with the footnote-entry number in square brackets, followed by the page. ([Ft. #1] page)

1. Louis Dudek and Michael Gnarowski, eds., *The Making of Modern Poetry in Canada: Essential Articles on Contemporary Canadian Poetry in English* (The Ryerson Press, Toronto, 1967), p. 89.

2. Hugh MacLennan, *Two Solitudes* (Duell Sloan, New York, 1945).

3. Edmund Wilson, *O Canada* (Noonday, New York, 1965), p. 68.

4. W. A. Mackintosh and others, *Approaches to Canadian History* (University of Toronto Press, Toronto, 1967), p. 43.

5. Sir Walter Scott, *Ivanhoe* (Everyman's Library, London, 1967), pp. 26-27.

6. Eli Mandel, ed., *Contexts of Canadian Criticism* (University of Chicago Press, Chicago, 1971), p. 221.

7. Helen M. Cain, ed., *Selected Historical Essays of F. W. Maitland* (Beacon Press, Boston, 1962), pp. 101-02.

8. Sir Frederick Pollock and Frederic William Maitland, *The History of English Law: Before the Time of Edward 1*, Vol. 1, Second Edition (Cambridge University Press, Cambridge, 1968), p. 66.

9. Janet Kerr Morchain, *Search for a Nation: French-English Relations in Canada Since 1759* [J. M. Dent & Sons, Toronto, 1967].

10. Guy Sylvestre, ed., *Structures sociales du Canada français* (University of Toronto Press, Toronto, 1966), p. 4.

11. A. J. M. Smith, *The Book of Canadian Poetry* (W.G. Gage, Toronto, 1943, 1948). The third edition, revised and enlarged (1957) discards "The Cosmopolitan Tradition" to qualify "Modern Poetry."

12. William Toye, ed., *Supplement to the Oxford Companion to Canadian History and Literature* (Oxford University Press, Toronto, etc., 1973), p. 207.

13. A. J. M. Smith, ed., *The Oxford Book of Canadian Verse: In English and French* (Oxford University Press, Toronto, etc., 1968), p. xl.

14. George Woodcock, ed., *Poets and Critics* (Oxford University Press, Toronto, etc., 1974), p. 12.

15. Sandra Diwa, *E. J. Pratt: The Evolutionary Vision* (McGill-Queens University Press, Montreal, 1974), pp. 92-93.

16. D. J. Riseborough, ed., *Canada and the French* (Facts on File, New York, 1975), pp. 110-11.

17. William H. New, *Dramatists in Canada* (University of British Columbia, Vancouver, 1972), p. 65.

The Irreplaceable Work of Justin Winsor (1831-1897)

> The year 1884 was the *annus mirabills* marking the birth of the American Historical Association and the publication of the first volume of Justin Winsor's *Narrative and Critical History of America*, the open-sesame to American historical materials.
>
> Michael Kraus, *History of American History*, 1937

> [My two books] should supplement an irreplaceable work, the first four volumes of Justin Winsor's *Narrative and Critical History of America* (1884-89).
>
> S. E. Morison, *The European Discovery of America*, 1971/74

The major bibliographical studies that make up this issue of *RNL* are drawn from Volume I of the series *Narrative and Critical History of America* (8 vols. Boston and New York: 1884-1889), compiled and edited by Justin Winsor in collaboration with thirty-nine contributing scholars.

That volume, separately titled Aboriginal America, was not the first in the series to be published, however. It actually appeared, together with the eighth and last volume, in 1889, which explains why its critical apparatus includes specific page references to the intervening vol-

umes II- VII. The series had been inaugurated in 1894 with
Volume III, titled *English Explorations and Settlements in
North America, 1497-1689.* As noted above, 1884 is also the
year the American Historical Association was founded; and
one links that founding with Winsor because, even as he
launched his eight-volume series, he had been "chairing"
the new AHA's organizational meeting of September 9-10
at Saratoga, N.Y.

An active membership of 41 — the first *professional*
American historians — was enrolled at that first AHA meeting; and an Executive Council then "selected 120 well-known
American students of history, living in different parts of the
country, to whom invitations to accept active membership"
would shortly be extended by the council's Secretary,
Herbert Baxter Adams of Johns Hopkins University. Eight
years earlier, in 1876, a group of 103 delegates of the
nation's libraries had gathered in Philadelphia, summoned
by Winsor, to "signalize" the nation's "centennial year" by
launching the American Library Association. For ten years
(1876-1885), Winsor served as the ALA's president, and in
1886, he was honored also with the presidency of the
American Historical Association.

By then Winsor's plan for serial publication of his
Narrative and Critical History was well under way. Indeed, in
his "Secretary's Report" for the 1884 inaugural meeting of
the American Historical Association, H. B. Adams had
assessed at length the promise for American scholarship
represented in Volume III of the series, the printer's galleys
for which were already in hand. Its plan, Adams wrote in
1884,

> is, indeed, different from any existing history of large scope,
> inasmuch as the chief aim of the book is to offer a critical and
> bibliographical examination of all the sources of informa-
> tion, and an exposition of the authorities based on original
> material, or presenting in some distinguishable way the
> more common knowledge of the subject. The narrative of
> events is not overlooked, but is given as a condensed sum-
> mary of the best existing knowledge. . . . The writers selected
> represent the principal historical, antiquarian, and archaeo-
> logical societies in the country, and some of those in Europe
> whose field covers American subjects. Eight large volumes
> are so far provided for, and of these the third and fourth,
> pertaining to the English, French, Portuguese (in part), and

the Swedish discoveries and settlements, are already printed, but not yet published. The second volume, covering the early Spanish history of the continent, is now going through the press, and two other volumes are in progress. [*AHAP* 1885:I (1), 33- 341

In 1884 the real first volume of the series — on *Aboriginal America* — was still a long way off. Yet upon its appearance in 1889, it was at once recognized as an exemplar *par excellence* of the genre of "critical and bibliographical examination of all the sources of information" initially projected.

Readers of the *RNL* issue on *Columbus, America, and the World* will recall the praise accorded Winsor by Professors Frank D. Grande and Henry Paolucci (1992, 157-231) in their review article on "American Foundations of Columbus Scholarship." During his long tenure as scholar-librarian at Harvard, Winsor effectively turned that oldest of American universities into one of the world's greatest research centers. But in the process, as the article stresses (pp. 174-176), he did much more. Having single-handedly organized the profession of American scholarly librarians, and having spurred his fellow American historians to professionalize their discipline, Winsor went on to provide a model of the best sort of use American historians could make of American libraries.

1. Winsor's Model for Cooperative Scholarship

Four of the six main chapters in Winsor's *Aboriginal America* were contributed by scholars long celebrated for their narrative skills as historians. They were: William H. Tillingast on "The Geographical Knowledge of the Ancients considered in Relation to the Discovery of America"; Clements R. Markham on "The Inca Civilization in Peru"; George E. Ellis on "The Red Indian of North America in Contact with the French and English," and Henry W. Haynes on "The Prehistoric Archaeology of North America." Winsor himself contributed two narrative chapters: one on "Pre-Columbian Explorations," the other on "Mexico and Central America."

But for all of the primary chapters, including his own, Winsor also provided an extensive two-fold critical apparatus, usually of much greater length than the narratives. That apparatus consisted in each case of a "Critical

Essay" followed by sharply focused bibliographical "Notes."
Such essays and notes serve in each volume to integrate his
work and that of his collaborators on an unprecedentedly
high scholarly level. Their critical sweep and thoroughness
had quickly been recognized, especially by the new school
of scientific historians gathered around H. B. Adams at the
newly-founded Johns Hopkins University.

Professor Adams's chief disciple in those days, C. W.
Bump, published a monograph on "Bibliographies of the
Discovery of America" (1892), introducing his own richly
annotated list with the observation that Winsor's *Narrative
and Critical History of America* "contains in the critical
chapters of the first three volumes, the latest and most
exhaustive bibliographies on all of the subjects mentioned
in this list," not only on Columbus and the Cabots, but also
on the "more or less legendary navigators before the fifteenth century." Of the volume on *Aboriginal America*,
Professor Bump added: "one of the most valuable features
of this connected series of historical monographs edited by
Winsor is the critical examination of the sources at the end
of each chapter. The critical essay in the chapter on
'Pre-Columbian Explorations' is by Mr. Winsor himself,
and is the most complete bibliography of the whole subject
yet published."

Those words of Professor Bump are cited by Grande
and Paolucci (1992, p. 170) in their brief survey of the
record of continued esteem for Winsor's critical labors
down to Morison's frank avowal at the end of his own long
scholarly career that Winsor's first four volumes remained
"'an irreplaceable work." At the well-attended Harvard
memorial service for Winsor's death in 1897, President
Charles W. Eliot had "stressed the importance of the fact
that the University's chief librarian had also been its chief
historian." A few days later, Edward Channing, destined to
dominate historical studies at Harvard during the next
generation, eulogized Winsor for having "made the scientific study of American history possible by making available
its rich mines of material."

In 1937, while Michael Kraus was hailing Winsor's
great work as the open-sesame for new-born American
critical historiography in general, Harry Elmer Barnes was
observing in his *History of Historical Writing* that the "character of the best American historical scholarship in the first

generation of those who imbibed the newer critical methods is to be discovered in the cooperative *Narrative and Critical History of America.*" As Grande and Paolucci point out (pp. 175-76), Barnes also acknowledged Winsor's eight volumes to be an "incomparably more scholarly work" than such earlier series on American materials as those of Jared Sparks or Hubert Howe Bancroft. And, more recently, David D. Van Tassel (1976) has insisted in his article on "American Historiography" for *The Dictionary of American History* that, through the decades since Barnes's judgment, Winsor still stands as the most notable "monument to the work" of the leading modern "organizers of American-focused historical research, teaching, and writing."

But it needs to be noted that before he became a scholar/librarian, Winsor had revealed a powerful appreciation of poetry and drama, as well as a powerful historical imagination. Wayne Cutler and Michael Harris devote a chapter of their *Justin Winsor: Scholar-Librarian* (1980) to what they call his "Literary Novitiate." As an undergraduate at Harvard, they point out, he thoroughly neglected his assigned studies; in their words (p. 17): "His mind resisted preparation for class recitations, and apart from the lure of local dramatic productions, nothing distracted his near total immersion in belles lettres." In fact he went off to Europe before graduating to pursue a career as a poet and literary critic. "It would require," Cutler and Harris conclude, "fifteen years of failure to convince this headstrong youth that his talents lay elsewhere."

Indeed, Winsor was never quite convinced. In 1860, he became "Boston's literary correspondent for Richard Grant White's new daily, the *New York World.*" During the Civil War, he "drafted a lengthy manuscript on the life of David Garrick, whose theatrical career had attracted Winsor's attention as early as 1850." He worked on the project for years, collecting materials and steadily revising and expanding the original manuscript. As the authors put it (p. 18):

> He enlarged the scope of his work, and the final manuscript came to be entitled "The Life and Times of David Garrick: A View of Eighteenth Century England, in its Social, Literary, and Dramatic Relations, and Their Influence upon Continental Life and Letters."

Winsor published much poetry as well critical essays and

theater reviews in New York and Boston newspapers and magazines. He never offered his manuscript on Garrick for publication; but there can be no doubt that his devotion to the theater, and especially to Shakespeare performances, permeated the impression he made as a teacher and scholar-librarian. In his richly-illustrated book on *The First 350 Years of the Harvard University Library* (Cambridge: 1986), Kenneth E. Carpenter begins a short chapter on how "Portraits of Garrick" came to form the "Nucleus of a Great Theatre Collection" at Harvard with these words:

> The Harvard Theatre Collection, the first performing arts research library, marks its beginnings from November 1901 when Professor George Pierce Baker and a group of alumni presented the Library with a collection of portraits of the eighteenth-century actor David Garrick. The gift was in memory of Justin Winsor who had devoted many years to the study of Garrick's life and career. (p. 124)

2. The National Literatures of "Greater America": A Winsor Perspective

In their monograph on Winsor, Grande and Paolucci included a section suggesting how his manifestly dramatic sense of history recalled the model of Thucydides who had drawn on the great Greek tragedians in shaping his account of the fratricidal Peloponnesian War. The arrival of Columbus and the Spaniards had, for Winsor, the promise of heroic poetry: Columbus might have been an Aeneas inaugurating a Rome-like Indo-Spanish America. But, even before Columbus's death in apparent oblivion, that epic moment or opportunity quickly gave way, in Winsor's view, to tragic division. Instead of one Western Indo-European America extending from pole to pole, the New World quickly gave life to what Germán Arciniegas has aptly distinguished as "'four historical areas, four experiences, four styles, four personages in search of an expression, that is, of a culture." The four are, of course, "Indo-Spanish America, Portuguese America (Brazil), English America (the United States), and Anglo-French America (Canada)," each having a comparable geographic size: "3,800,000 square miles, Indo-Spanish America; 3,400,000, Canada; 3,200,000, Brazil; 2,900,000, English America."

Those four areas, experiences, styles, and personages are the subject-matter of the first five volumes of

Winsor's *Narrative and Critical History of America*, through the course of which Winsor, as editor, never permits us to lose sight of the fact that the whole remains for him a *single* America. As Grande and Paolucci (pp. 168-69) summed them up, those first five

> volumes provided narrative and critical accounts of American history from pre-historic times and the years of Columbus's voyages (1492-1504), down through the centuries of exploration, settlement, and struggle of the European nations, in the course of which leadership in the New World passed from Spain to France and, by 1763, to England. The first volume was titled *Aboriginal America*. The second, third, and fourth had parallel titles: *Spanish Explorations and Settlements in America from the Fifteenth to the Seventeenth Century; English Explorations and Settlements in North America, 1497-1689*; and *French Explorations and Settlements in North America and those of the Portuguese, Dutch, and Swedes, 1500-1700*. The fifth volume, *The English and French in North America, 1689-1763*, moved the history to within a decade of the American revolution. Vols. VI and VII, *The United States of North America, Part I*, and *Part II*, alert us in their titles to the fact that American history from 1492 to 1763 had been but a preparation for the emergence of independent New World states, each with a European heritage, to be sure, but each also capable of developing a distinctive national identity.

Through all of that, Winsor never succumbs to a temptation to use the plural *Americas*. It is all one America, and his aim was to provide the scholarly basis for a continuing history of its oneness, despite the emergent distinctive national identities, and statecraft, of its components. As already amply indicated, aboriginal America is in no sense slighted, in no sense subordinated to the histories of the European peoples who invaded and conquered and settled, in their diverse ways. The richness of his survey of the sources — in some nine languages! — is breath-taking in the sweep and detail of its authenticated accuracy. Winsor's contribution to all of that must remind us of the labors of his great European contemporaries who made comparable contributions in other areas of high scholarship: Adolph von Harnack in the history of Christian dogma, Eduard Meyer in the history of the ancient Near East and Greece, Theodor Mommsen in the history of Rome, Erich Caspar in the history of the Papacy, Pierre Duhem in the history and philosophy of science, Friedrich Ueberweg, Wilhelm Windelband, and M. Grabmann in the history of philosophy and theology, F. W. Maitland in early English legal history, and Otto von Gierke in the history of fellowship law (*Genossenschaftsrecht*). Each of these scholars set a permanent criterion for scholarship in a distinctive field. That is the sort of scholarly value Samuel Eliot Morison had in mind when he called the first four volumes of Winsor's history of America "an irreplaceable work."

Certainly it must remain forever an irreplaceable work for all historians of the American national literatures that have developed in the four areas of America distinguished by Germán Arciniegas. One must be prepared to master the bibliographies of Justin Winsor in this regard. Almost half a century before Herbert Eugene Bolton used the phrase "Greater America" as a clarion call in his presidential address to the American Historical Association at its 1933 meeting in Toronto, Winsor had indeed provided a multilingual open sesame for serious research in the cultural and, political-economic history of such an America. As the decades and centuries pass, more and more of the scholarship relevant to the formative years of our Indo-Hispanic-, Portuguese, Anglo-, and French-American literatures will become unusable, unless it is approached through Winsor's work.

But who, in the future, will have the patience to do with that *Narrative and Critical History of America* what Morison acknowledged having done in 1971? Grande and Paolucci have admonished, for instance, that, while both Morison and his disciple Paolo Emilio Taviani certainly qualify as heirs of Winsor, neither of them has come close to matching Wisor's scholarly achievement. Both have, on the surface, adopted Winsor's "method of following each narrative chapter" of their works in the same field with "a section of bibliography and notes." Yet, with no intention to denigrate, Grande and Paolucci (pp. 1845) do not hesitate to conclude, that what the cooperative scholarship of Winsor permitted him "to pack into a single tightly composed page of bibliographical-critical notes is apt to be spread over four or five pages in Morison and ten or more in Taviani — whose pages are therefore proportionately easier to read."

Which takes us to the purpose of this *RNL* volume

covering Justin Winsor's introductory studies on *Native American Antiquities and Linguistics*. With it we begin to realize our intention, indicated previously, to introduce a series of *RNL* issues "focused on the historical foundations of the many nations of the New World that have already developed (or are now developing) independent national literatures of their own in languages shared with their European lands of origin." It has made a difference that those languages have come to flourish anew in America, that millions of speakers and writers of non-European origins have taken them up, and that a pre-Columbian ethnic-cultural legacy now saturates them all.

What our special editors have sought to do is to make Winsor's irreplaceable text on American origins more readable without sacrificing the wealth and accuracy of its bibliographical detail. To get a fair sense of the difficulty, one needs to examine the original volumes. The general title of the series, *Narrative and Critical History of America*, appears on the spine of each volume, with the repeated characterization: "Illustrated." Only the volume numbers, from I to VIII, distinguish them. The same general title dominates each title page, with the volume's particularized title supplied in smaller print in an upper-left hand comer. The editor and publisher are identified, and a publication date is given which bears no sequential correspondence with the volume number. A result has been that the separate volumes have rarely if ever been cited with their specific, distingnishing titles. We must endure being told that a specific narrative chapter or critical essay, with a title of its own, is in Vol. I, IV, or II.

There are worse obstacles to easy reading of these valuable volumes. The narrative chapters are set in fairly large type, compared with which the footnotes at the bottom of the pages are relatively small. But then come the critical essays and bibliographical notes, each in still smaller type, and supported by footnotes of a size that (as H. F. Cary said of the original printing of his first annotated translation of Dante's *Commedia*) readily deterred "a numerous class of readers from perusing it."

To make that Winsor legacy readable on a practical level we have integrated the substance of the small-print footnotes of the original into the body of the text, and have brought together related passages which originally were

widely separated. There has been minor editing to harmonize the sometimes varied materials brought together, and
thereby facilitate reading; but each distiguishable unit of
the whole is clearly marked at the start by superscript
lower-case reference letters ([a, b, c, d,] etc.) with source pages
indicated in the corresponding endnotes. The reference
letter [a] identifies the extended main text of each essay, as
distinct from integrated materials, and it reappears as often
as the main text is resumed, thereby clearly marking where
an inserted passage ends. An exception is made, however,
at the beginning of each article, where the initial "drop
cap" counts as a superscript.[a]

A basic change introduced by the editors has been
the adoption of modern practice in parenthetic references
to sources. Lists of books and articles cited and acronyms
of periodicals and learned societies etc., cover the range of
references in all the published studies, so that bibliographical repetition is kept to a minimum. Extended titles of
books, articles, and periodicals are supplied in the text only
where they are themselves the focus of discussion.

A model of economy for such typographical editing
was long ago supplied by Henry Smith Williams in his
monumental *Historians' History of the World*, published in
27 volumes by The Encyclopædia Britannica Co. (London
& New York: 1904-1926). Williams greatly admired the
cooperatively authored major works of Winsor — his 4-vol-
ume *Memorial History of Boston* (1880-81) as well as his
8-volume history of America — and reprinted dozens of the
specialized monographs collected by Winsor in his own
cooperative history. And one can hardly doubt that he
approached his editorial task from Winsor's bibliographical vantage point.

Williams had earlier written an important prefatory
essay on "The Influence of Modem Research on the Scope
of World History" for the *Encyclopedia Britannica*, 10th ed.,
and a 4-volume *History of the Art of Writing* (London & New
York, 1902), and was therefore well prepared critically to
undertake the difficult task of integrating a multi-faceted,
many-volumed product of cooperative research. As he explained in an editor's note for the comprehensive "Bibliographical Index" that completes his *Historians' History*, his
adoption of the plan of "superior-letter" references "gave a
flexibility to the use of authorities which would not other-

wise have been possible." The aim was to integrate materials collected from many sources, giving essential continuity to the whole — something that would prove impossible if extended references were repeatedly interpolated. "Even were such references given as footnotes," he observes, "the pages would be disastrously cumbered, and (since an author may be quoted many times in a given chapter) the loss of space involved in repeated footnotes would be, in the aggregate, enormous." Williams then concludes:

> The reader who has become familiar with our use of superior-letter references in the text finds it a perfectly simple matter, with the aid of the Brief Reference Lists, to keep himself informed as to the author quoted. . . . Using those lists he will find specific reference, in the case of all important quotations, to the precise edition of each work that we have used, and to the volume and page where the original citation may be found. The alphabetical arrangement here employed makes such reference as easy as could be desired, and the reader who keeps the index volume at hand will be able to trace any given quotation to its source with all the accuracy that the most exacting scholarship could demand. (vol. 27, pp. 567-68)

Rigorous application of such a system of scholarly integration of texts and notes has enabled us to complete this readable transcription of Winsor's irreplaceable work on Native American *Antiquities and Linguistics.* Five Winsor studies make up the core of this volume — the first surveying the major contributions to American studies before 1890, the next three covering the traditional and scientific approaches to the still controversial question of the "origin of man" in America, and the fifth laying bibliographical foundations for all further serious study of the origins of all the American national literatures. In addition, we offer a review-article titled "Winsor's *Aboriginal America*: The Perils of Empirical Archaology," in which Richard C. Clark and Henry Paolucci recall Winsor's admonitions on the importance of language study for deepened understanding of native American contributions to the broad mosaic of our New World cultural history.

This issue of *RNL* will be followed by comparably-edited issues on *Cultures of the Ancient Aztecs, Mayas, and Incas* and *Early Spanish, French, and English Encounters with the American Indians*, made up of studies by Clements R.

Markham and George E. Ellis, as well as Winsor, drawn from both Volumes I and II of his cooperative *History*. These three "Winsor" issues taken together will provide an indispensible scholarly support for later issues of *RNL* devoted to the many established, emergent, and neglected national literatures of our "Greater America."

Modern archeological views and new theories and methodologies cannot ever replace the intelligent and detailed analysis by Winsor and his scholar-collaborators. The careful amassing of data, the conclusions reached, the historical continuity stressed, and the sharp critical focus remain a sure guide and a solid base for all future study.

Winsor on the Emergence of a New World of National Literatures

The glory of the first successful, as of the first well-intentioned, colonization belongs to the French. . . . The French and Indians in general lived very amicably together, and intermarriage was the common thing. . . . Yet by the irony of history, French institutions have had far less influence in the New World than either English, or Spanish, or even Dutch.

H. S. Williams Historians' History of the World, 1904

While a fraction of the autochthonous populations were mercifully spared, the cultural contempt of the literate conquerors for the illiterate natives . . . effectively prevented their idioms from being reduced to writing, and, consequently, from developing a modern type of literature [C]olonization . . . represented a potentially enormous extension of European language writing: English and to a lesser extent French north of the Rio Grande, Spanish to the South with the Portuguese enclave in Brazil, and a patchwork of Western languages in the Caribbean.

Albert Gérard Contexts of African Literature, 1990

The bibliographies in the two previous volumes of our *RNL* "Winsor series" confined themselves essentially to pre-Columbian matters — *Native Anicrican Antiquities and Linguistics* and *Cultures of the Aztecs, Mayas, and Incas* — reviewing studies that ranged in dates from 1494 to 1889. This third volume of selections from Winsor's *Narrative and Critical History of America* (vols. I & II) takes us out of pre-Columbian times, to focus on the early encounters of Europeans and "native Americans" that prompted the emergence of new national literary identities on the mainlands and islands of the Western Hemisphere.

1. Naming America

As originally published in the 1880s the first two studies printed here made up the critical, supporting apparatus for a narrative biographical chapter titled "Amerigo Vespucci," supplied by Sydney Howard Gay, a popular author and journalist, editor of the Chicago *Tribune* and later of the New York *Evening Post*. Winsor's title for them was simply "Notes on Vespucius and the Naming of America." We have separated them into two parts to stress their inherent division of labor. Part I presents a survey of the bibliography on the controversial subject of the alleged "Four Voyages of Amerigo Vespucci"; part II reviews, bibliographically, the "high drama" of how Columbus's glory as a discoverer came to be eclipsed by the small-press mapmakers of St.-Dié — an otherwise insignificant little town in the department of Vosges, France, patronized in those days by the dukes of Lorraine.

Discussing how the newly encountered continents of the Western Hemisphere came to be named as they are, Winsor suggests that there is a sense in which "America" — adapted to accord with the old feminine continental names of Europe, Asia, and Africa — is the first genuinely "'literary expression" of the New World. Winsor, indeed, hails that naming as the "most striking and significant of all the literary movements which grew out of the new oceanic developments." (Winsor 1892, p. 538.)

"Age of Discovery" scholars have generally made the naming of America a central focus of study. Those of them who, in our time, get to read what Winsor has supplied on the subject will appreciate at once why his bibliographical studies must continue to rank as an irreplaceable contribu-

tion. Scholars who ignore Winsor's work today are doomed
to waste much effort in repeating researches that have long
since been more than adequately accomplished.

2. Red Indians of North America: Crushed Between the French and English

The next two bibliographical studies in this volume focus
on the initial European-New World encounters that shaped
the linguistic-literary future of North America. The two
re-edited selections originally provided the critical apparatus for narrative chapters on "The Red Indian of North
America in Contact with the French and English" and "Las
Casas and the Relations of the Spaniards to the Indians."
For both chapters, Winsor had drawn on the expertise of
George E. Ellis, a Unitarian clergyman, who was professor
of systematic theology in Harvard Divinity School, as well
as Vice-President of the Massachusetts Historical Society.

In those narrative chapters, Professor Ellis supplied
model studies that mark the extremes of complexity embraced in the breadth of his subject. Treating things chronologically, he would, of course, have had to start with the
earlier Indian-Spanish encounters. But he treats the experience of the Red Indians with the French and English first
because it presented a truly simple pattern of development,
anticipated in the earlier experience of the Central and
South American Indians also, to be sure, but not easily
isolatable there because of the richness of the pre-Columbian
culture and the length of the period when the Spanish
exercised their sway among them without a European rival.

Ellis's precisely-narrowed focus in his narrative chapter on the experience of the Red Indians permitted him to
define at once a relatively simple underlying pattern. He
observes at the outset that the "relations into which the first
Europeans entered with the aborigines in North America
were very largely influenced, if not wholly decided, by the
relations which they found to exist among the tribes on
their arrival here." Simply stated, those relations were
"fiercely hostile." Indeed, he insists, "in every instance and
in every crisis," the newcomers to the "northerly parts of
the continent found

> their opportunity and their impunity in the feuds existing
> among the tribes already in conflict with each other. This
> state of things, while it gave the whites enemies, also fur-

nished them with allies. So far as the whites could learn in their earliest inquiries, internicine strife had been waging here among the natives from an indefinite past.

RUINS OF MAGAZINE AT FORT CHARTRES

Fort Chartres, built by the French in 1720, was in its time the strongest fortress in America. . . . The veteran soldiers to whom the fort was surrendered in 1765 were the "first English troops who ever set foot on the Illinois country."

That's the starting point. And from there, Ellis undertakes to "trace the development of our subject through five periods."

As a result of empirical historical study, the first period defined by Ellis reveals itself to have been very brief — "marked by the presence of a single European nationality": the French. The French, Ellis writes, might have sustained a friendly alliance "with one tribe"; but it happened that that tribe was feuding with other tribes, compelling the French in due course to "espouse" its long- standing enmities. A second period began with the appearance of a second European nationality, namely the English, who renewed in the New World their inherited Old World animosities toward the French. As a result, says Ellis, the Indians soon found themselves "ground between two mill-stones."

A third period in the pattern of development is marked by the extinction of French power" on the North American continent. That is where Ellis's narrative chapter actually ends; though, in his introductory paragraphs, he goes on to define a fourth period when the English colonies in North America and their mother country across the Atlantic come to play the parts of mill-stones for the hapless Indians caught between them. A fifth and continuing period is defined, in which the United States government takes less and less account of Indian tribal interests and conflicts.

That pattern underlies Indian relations with all the independent New World governments as they emerge during the course of the nineteenth and twentieth centuries. But the bearing of it on the distinctive development or collapse of emergent national literary identities is well illustrated in the closing pages of Ellis's narrative, which dwell on the Conspiracy (1763-1766) of the Indian Chief Pontiac in the course of which Fort Chartres, the "citadel of Illinois," surrendered to the English — a surrender represented by the lowering of what proved to be the last French flag flying on our North American territory. "In that act,"' Francis Parkman had written with a literary flourish, "was consummated the double triumph of British power in America. England had crushed her hereditary foe, and France, in her fall, had left to irretrievable ruin the savage tribes to whom her policy and self interest had lent a transient support." [XXIII, 227]

Here it is worth calling attention to how the English and French approaches to the Red Indians of North America differed. Basically, the English tended to wipe out the natives in their way, as they colonized; the French, who did less colonizing, more or less left the Indians on their own, when they were not aligned with foes of one tribe against another. But in his critical *History*, Winsor includes the views on the subject of many distinguished scholars and public officials. Notable is Andrew M. Davis's chapter on "Canada and Louisiana," which ends with a citation of the words of a French colonial statesman, contrasting French and English colonization in North America:

> Before leaving the colony in 1754, the Marquis Duquesne summoned the Iroquois to a council, In the course of an address which he then delivered he said: "Are you ignorant

of the difference between the King of England and the King of France? Go, see the forts that our King has established, and you will see that you can still hunt under their very walk They have been placed for your advantage in places where you frequent. The English, on the contrary, are no sooner in possession of a place than the game is driven away. The forest falls before them as they advance, and the soil is laid bare so that you can scarce find the wherewithal to erect a shelter for the night." No more powerful contrast of the results in North America of the two methods of colonization could be drawn than is presented in the words of the French Governor. [v. 62-3]

3. Early Spanish/Indian Relations and the Scholarly Burden of the Leyenda Negra

When we pass from Professor Ellis's account of Red Indian relations with the French and English in North America to his treatment of "the Relations of the Spaniards to the Indians," we are struck at once by the marked contrast. Presenting the actions of the French and English, Ellis does his best to proceed empirically, to be objective. He neither offers nor looks for an established "authority" on the subject. Viewpoints and opinions are many. One can classify many secondary as well as primary " sources" as pro-French, or pro-English, or pro-Indian; but there are not wanting major authors whose objectivity is beyond question. Partisan views counterbalance one another. Serious disputes about rights and. wrongs end up being settled not in scholarly papers but on fields of battle; and even then the spirit of *noblesse oblige* surfaces; and we are reminded of why the ancient Greek and Roman epic poets so often depicted the foes of their own peoples as morally in the right, especially in defeat.

Ellis's title makes things plain. He offers us an authority on the subject: Bartholomé de Las Casas. All during the years and decades when the Spanish had no European rivals to contend with in the New World, there was ever the judgmental voice of the "Apostle to the Indians" to be heard on every side. Spain was at pains both to preserve the polemical writings of Las Casas and to prevent their circulation. When European rivals for Spanish hegemony in the New World were not yet physically involved, they were already arming themselves with "the witness" of

Las Casas against the Spanish.

On the broad circulation of the accusations of Las Casas against the treatment of the native peoples by the Spanish conquerors in New Spain, we quote this observation of Ellis, with notes by Winsor (1884-89, II., 340f):

> The number of versions of all or of part of the series of the 1552 tracts [of Las Casas] into other languages strikingly indicates the interest they created and the effect which they produced throughout Europe. None of the nations showed more eagerness to make public these accusations against the Spaniards by one of their own number, than the Flemings and the Dutch. The earliest of all the translations, and one of the rarest of these publications, is the version of the first tract, with parts of others, which appeared in the dialect of Brabant, in 1578 — the precursor of a long series of such testimonies, used to incite the Netherlanders against the Spanish rule.

It has been a continuing phenomenon. International literary comparatists have long been familiar with its history and effects. In the Preface to his updated *Short History of Spanish Literature,* James R. Stamm, for example, reminds his English-speaking readers that the "diffusion of Spanish culture has been considerably inhibited by the operation of the *leyenda negra*, the 'black legend,' a phrase which expresses, perhaps exaggeratedly, the low opinion in which Spanish culture has been held by other European nations since the beginning of the Reformation" (Stamm 1979).

Certainly Spanish literary scholarship has had for centuries to labor under the burden of the *leyenda*. At its heart is an abiding conviction of many that the early Spanish encounters with the American Indians must be viewed as part of a long-lasting inquisitional religious oppression — most oppressive, allegedly, precisely when its purpose was conversion and the priestly pasture of souls. Ellis's historical narrative in fact treats Las Casas as if he were a great enemy of the Spanish as a nation; and he agrees with Winsor that Las Casas provides in himself, with his criticism of Spanish Catholic leaders, the equivalent of anti-nationalist, or anti-Hispanic archives bolstering the *leyenda negra.*

4. Literary and Linguistic Aspects of the Indian Encounters with the European Maritime Powers

As the titles of the Ellis narratives on early Indian contacts
with the French and English in North America and with the
Spanish in Central and South America make clear, the
focus of interest remains throughout the basic historical
evidence of the actual encounters. The purely linguistic
approach to the study of the same materials was largely
covered in the earlier volume of *RNL* on *Native American
Antiquities and Linguistics*. Materials on the subject in that
volume were drawn from the introduction and several of
the six bibliographical studies by Winsor that make up the
appendix to vol. I of his *History*. Especially relevant was a
composite study titled "American Linguistics: Its Scholarly
Foundations," with major subdivisions on" Languages of
the North," "Central and South American Languages and
Literatures," and a"Summary/Update on North, Central,
and Southern American Literary-Linguistic Studies." The
purely linguistic approach as there presented in Winsor's
bibliographic surveys showed exhaustive, indeed, over-
whelmingly detailed scholarship, pursued through some
seven modern languages as well as revived scholarly Latin.
This current issue of *RNL* includes two other such bibliographical articles, covering pre-Columbian American myths
and completing Winsor's inventory of major scholarly treatises, learned societies, and periodicals.

In the core of this issue of *RNL*, the focus and
emphasis is not linguistic but ethnic and national. Ellis and
Winsor both stress the fact that it takes more than linguistic
materials to produce national literatures. Even so, in the
bibliographic notes coauthored by Winsor and Ellis we are
constantly reminded that in the earliest colonial-American
contacts — whether the Europeans were Spanish, Dutch,
English, French, or Portuguese — learning the languages of
the natives by the Europeans, or of the Europeans by the
natives, had a strictly utilitarian end. The apparent exception was when the ultimate aim was religious conversion,
There was little doubt that where a religious intent of that
kind was officially proclaimed, the European "Propagan-
dists of the Faith" engaged in serious linguistic study of the
autochthonous Amerindian tongues. That was, of course,
especially true of the pioneer Spanish missionaries; but it
was true also of the Dutch, French, English, and Portuguese
missionaries and preachers.

Spanish missionaries engaged in linguistic studies,

producing bilingual dictionaries, grammars, and religious
ceremonial works in the native Indian languages, transliter-
ating them into letters and syllables of the Latin alphabet.
The Portuguese and French Catholics engaged in comparable labors, as did also the French Protestant Huguenots,
though to a lesser degree than the French Catholics.

Where the English took up the study of native
Amerindian tongues, we had the exceptional cases of Apostle
John Eliot with his rendering of the Bible for the Massachusetts Indians and his *Grammar of the Massachusetts Indian
Language,* and of John Cotton's *Vocabulary of the Massachusetts Indian Language* (see Winsor 1884-89, I. 423, and cf. m.
355):

> the conversion of the natives was the one object set forth in
> the Massachusetts charter; Roger Williams had, while a
> resident of Massachusetts and Plymouth, taken deep interest
> in them, and in 1643 . . . he drew up *A Key unto the Language
> of America.*

Winsor adds a note here explaining that, for a thorough account of Williams's *Key* and its history, and "much
relating to the embodiment of the Indian speech in literary
form," his readers should turn to "Dr. J. H. Trumbull's
chapter on 'The Indian Tongue and the Literature fashioned by Eliot and others,' in the *Memorial History of Boston*
(Winsor 1880-81, I. 465). Even so, it is fair to say that, for
the most part, the English in America early subordinated
their proselytizing Indian language-studies to other interests. But we want to comment briefly here on the contrast
presented by the Hispanic experience.

5. Lifting the Burden of the Leyenda Negra: The Examples of Ureña, Gingerich, and Bierhorst

As already noted, the emphasis to this day among
non-Hispanic critics of Spanish culture, especially of colonial times, continues to be on representing it as a systematic
suppression of all native Indian literary achievements. But,
in fact, what survived that so-called suppression proved to
be all that has remained vital of the native literary linguistic
culture down to our own times. It has been on the wealth of
Spanish literary transliteration of the oral tradition that
modem scholarship now labors to make sense of and give
value to the pre-Columbian heritage, even when its aim is to
present that legacy not as a primitive stage of a Western

European-like pattern of development, but as an alternative achievement on a par of excellence with the major European and Asian literatures.

For a broad, critical perspective on recent efforts to exorcise the infectious vitality of the legend, we can still best be guided by the views of Pedro Henriquez Ureña (1884-1946). A Dominican literary critic and historian, Ureña still ranks as "one of Latin America's most eminent men of letters." We cite his widely influential *Siete ensayos en busca de nuestra expressión* (Buenos Aires, 1928), a translated section of which (pp. 18-35) is included in Benjamin Keen, ed. 1955, *Readings in Latin- American Civilization, 1492 to the Present* (1955).

In the selection reprinted by Professor Keen (pp. 440-441), Ureña notes that the "problem of expression" is far more complex in literature than in all the other arts. In music, by contrast, it is readily possible to renounce completely the tonal languages of Europe. And that has been done, he says, in the Indian musical culture of Peru and Bolivia. It is so also in the plastic arts, as exemplified in the "Mexican system of Adolfo Best, conducted on the basis of the seven lineal elements of Aztec drawing, with frank acceptance of its limitations."

Even so, it is true that, in music and the plastic arts, the "parting of the ways" is dear: the choices are "either the European or the Indian way, or at any rate the creole way." [440] Yet, "strange or familiar, the tonal language and the plastic language of the native stock are intelligible." But, what about literature? Can we return

> to the Indian languages? The educated person generally does not know them, and the difficult task of studying them and writing in them would finally lead to his being understood by very few, and to the immediate reduction of his reading public. Verse and prose in the Indian language were composed after the Conquest and are still being composed today, because there yet exist enormous and widely diffused native populations that speak a hundred — if not more — native tongues; but that literature is rarely inspired by clear objectives of survival and opposition to the dominant language. [441]

Since Ureña wrote those words, foreign champions of the native populations have done much to encourage efforts of natives to try to fashion tribal identities for the native speech, as if their situation were like that of the North American Indians in times past. But, as Ureña correctly says, apart from the interests of professional revolutionaries, native users of the native languages have rarely tried seriously to make them competitive, as literary vehicles, with the dominant languages, long since rooted in the native populations themselves.

Ureña then turns to the more likely possibility of cultivating distinctive mixtures of native and Hispanic languages.

> Should we create our own languages, offspring and successors to Castilian? A hundred years ago — a source of great fear to some, of insane hope for others — there existed the idea that we were unknowingly embarked on an effort to create native tongues. This mist has been dispelled by the unifying pressure of constant relations between the Hispanic peoples. The effort, supposing it were possible, would have required centuries of digging moat after moat between the language of Castile and the emergent languages of America, would have meant resigning ourselves with Franciscan heroism to an abject impoverished dialectical expression until there appeared the Dante that could give it wings and talons. Let us note, in passing, that the gaucho language of Rio de la Plata, the principal substance of that dissipated mist, does not possess sufficient diversity to attain even the stature of a dialect like that of León or Aragón; its light special tint does not materially distinguish it from Castilian, and *Martin Fierro* and *Fausto* are no more offshoots from the linguistic trunk than are the *coplas* of Andalucia or Murcia. [441]

But, what about a resurrection of the "literary culture" of the pre-Columbian poets of the great native civilizations? Why not a classical Mayan renaissance, to cherish what admittedly no longer had any inherent vitality of its own? That was Europe's experience with the Petrarchan-Erasman revival of ancient learning (including what Western scholars eventually resurrected of Sanskrit in modern India!); and it has apparently been the experience also of modem masters of secular Hebrew.

We should glance, for an answer, at the efforts of native language-culture specialists to "'contribute," as they say, "to the revelation of an alternative history within Native American traditions where the old positivist and

Vician terms could only see underdevelopment." Professor
Willard Gingerich, for example, is clearly persuaded that
pre-Columbian Mexican or Nahuatl literary culture matches,
in a parallel sense, the profoundest achievements of the
Western tradition. That is his thesis in a study titled
"Heidegger and the Aztecs: The Poetics of Knowing in
Pre-Hispanic Nahuatl Poetry," contributed to *Recovering the
Word: Essays on Native American Literature*, ed. by Brian
Swamm. and Arnold Krupat (Gingerich 1987, pp. 85-112).
"'The Nahuas were unique," he concludes, "in their pas-
sionate and centuries-long devotion to the awareness of the
poetic act as the foundation of human knowing." (109)
Even so, in identifying the literary/ linguistic sources on
which he bases that emphatic appraisal, he notes with
candor (110):

> Of course, there is no recorded "pre-Hispanic" poetry in
> America, as it was entirely contained within performance
> traditions without benefit of phonetic transcription. Except
> for the few surviving pictographic codices, of which none
> contains a visual text corresponding directly to the written
> songs which are the matter of my discussion, all extant
> Nahuatl literature comes to us in post-Conquest, colonial
> redactions. Since only Christian priests operated schools in
> early New Spain, the p-factor (priestly interpretation) must
> be assumed to be pervasive throughout all the written docu-
> ments. I follow, nevertheless, the time-honored if somewhat
> suspect practice of Nahuatl students in treating certain
> manuscripts from which the poems under discussion are
> taken, as substantially representative of the actual
> preConquest, orally transmitted stylistic and philosophical
> traditions. [John] Bierhorst's introductory essay (1985) to
> his edition of the *Cantares* manuscript adds a new reserva-
> tion concerning this practice.

The "somewhat suspect practice" which Gingerich
avowedly followed drew heavily, in his case, on John
Bierhorst.

> The translations of all *Cantares* and Romances excerpts . . .
> are my own. Unless otherwise noted, paleographs of the
> Nahuatl are taken directly from Bierhorst 1985; some of my
> phrases are also taken directly from Bierhorst's English
> versions. The Bierhorst volumes, the most authoritative
> transcription and translation of the *Cantares* manuscript
> now available, came into print only as I was completing the

present discussion, too late for me to make full use of its detailed language notes. (110)

Gingerich has left it to his readers to search out the "new reservation" Bierhorst has added on the admittedly suspect practice of Nahuatl students in taking the poems discussed as truly representative of the "actual pre-Conquest." But in the introduction to his *History and Mythology of the Aztecs: The Codex Chimalpopoca*, translated from the Nahuatl (1992), John Bierhorst himself helps to soften the force of the old *leyenda negra* by reminding his readers, as Gingerich has in the passage discussed above, of how much is due, in his field, to the labors of Spanish missionary scholars in preserving what would otherwise have been totally lost in the legacy of pre-Columbian Nahuatl oral literature and hieroglyphic or picture-writing.

In his opening paragraphs, Bierhorst reminds us that the notorious Spanish *auto-da-fé* of pre-Columbian manuscripts had been preceded by an equally thorough burning of such books that occurred a hundred years before the Spanish first appeared in the New World. That older *auto-da-fé* had been a solemn rite of the conquering Mexica who gave the Aztec empire its widest expansion. Writing of the decision "to bum the old pictographic histories," circa 1430, Bierhorst notes that the new picture histories that then replaced the old "presumably . . . exaggerated the deeds of the upstart Mexica . . . though we may only guess what changes appeared in the new histories or what earlier records, if any survived to contradict them." Then comes this pointedly positive piece of historical revisionism:

> A hundred years later the books were burned again, this time by Spanish missionaries . . . in the wake of the Conquest of 1521. . . . Once again, new histories rose out of the ashes. And it is this second wave of history writing, much of it preserved, that forms the basis for our remarkably detailed, if somewhat colored, knowledge of the rise of Aztec civilization. (1)

6. *A Glance Back at Winsor and Brasseur de Bourbourg on the* Codex Chimalpopoca

Bierhorst is at pains to admonish, in the same critical spirit, that "revisionist elements in the new histories are not always easy to isolate." In the rest of his introduction to his translations, he dwells on the "prime representatives" of these "fuller histories" which offer, as he says, "a rich sampling of the old Aztec oral literature, for which the pictorial codices must have served as prompt books." Discussing the manuscript tradition for the *Codex Chirnalpopoca* (pp. 10-14), Bierhorst updates for us the bibliographic labors of Justin Winsor on the same subject, as we find them reviewed in our *RNL* volume on the *Cultures of the Aztecs, Mayas, and Incas*, pp. 134-135. Winsor introduces his discussion with these words:

> Among the manuscripts which seem to have belonged to Ixtlilxochitl was the one known in our day under the designation given to it by Brasseur de Bourbourg, *Codex Chimalpopoca*, in honor of Faustino Chimalpopoca, a learned professor of Aztec, who assisted Brasseur in translating it. (See *APQ*, May, 1855, p. 326.) The anonymous author had set to himself the task of converting into the written native tongue a rendering of the ancient hieroglyphics, constituting, as Brasseur says, a complete and regular history of Mexico and Colhuacan. He describes it in his *Lettres à M. le duc de Valmy lettrc seconde*) — the first part (in Mexican) being a history of the Chichimecas; the second (in Spanish), by another hand, elucidating the antiquities — as the most rare and most precious of all the manuscripts which escaped destruction, elucidating what was obscure in Gomara and Torquemada.

The original of the passage just cited is to be found in vol. I of Winsor's great collaborative *History*. It is part of his long "Critical Essay on the Sources of Information" (pp. 153-172). The substance of Winsor's bibliographical notes, compiled in the late 1880s, merits comparison with the account in Bierhorst's updating of the materials over a century later in the previously-cited introduction to his 1992 English version of *The Codex Chimalpopoca*. We learn from Bierhorst, among other things, that the "present whereabouts" of the original manuscript are in doubt: "Apparently it has been lost since at least 1949." Students of Winsor will be pleased, however, to learn where they can best look to reconstruct the manuscript tradition down to his time.

We end where we started — noting once again that if contemporary scholars fail to take Winsor's bibliographical labors as their point of departure, they are doomed to waste much time and to draw conclusions that must forever isolate them from any genuinely comparative study of world literature acceptable to the masters of the great literary heritages of Asia and Africa, as well as of Europe and of the literatures of the Old World colonizers or conquerors in the Americas and Australia, as well as Asia and Africa.

EDITORIAL NOTE: ON PRINTING CONVENTIONS
Adopted for the *RNL* "Winsor" Volumes

It bears repeating that to make that Winsor legacy readily "legible" for modem readers, we have integrated the substance of the small-print footnotes of the original into the body of the text, and have brought together related passages which originally were widely separated. There has been minor editing to harmonize the sometimes varied materials brought together, and thereby facilitate reading; but each distinguishable unit of the whole is clearly marked at the start by superscript lower-case reference letters [a, b, c, d], etc. with source pages indicated in the corresponding endnotes. The reference letter ([a]) identifies the extended main text of each essay, as distinct from integrated materials, and it reappears as often as the main text is resumed, thereby clearly marking where an inserted passage ends. At the start of each article, however, the initial "drop cap" counts as a superscript[a].

A basic change introduced by our special editors has been the adoption of modem practice in the parenthetic references and lists of sources supplied. As in the first Winsor volume, the lists of "Works Cited" and of periodical/learned-society acronyms cover the range of references in all the individual articles, so that bibliographical repetition is kept to a minimum. Titles of books, articles, and periodicals are supplied in the text only where they are themselves the focus of discussion.

Winsor's Bibliographical Notes on the Aztec and Mayan Civilizations

By the close of Roman rule in Egypt [500 A. D.], the hieroglyphic system of writing had become absolutely a dead letter, and until the ... last century there was neither an Oriental nor a European who could either read or understand a hieroglyphic inscription.

E. A. Wallis Budge, Egyptian Language, 1910

No Mava Indian in 1886 had any notion of ancient Mayan history, civilization, or mythology.

Robert Wauchope, *Lost Tribes and Sunken Continents*, 1962

In the last century, following the discovery of the ruined Maya cities, almost none of the records could be read by Western scholars. . . . The situation was not much better than this when I was a student at Harvard in the 1950s.

Michael D. Coe, *Breaking the Maya Code*, 1992

The 1992 *RNL* issue on *Columbus, America, and the World* introduced our readers to the linguistic-literary scholarship of Justin Winsor with a book-length review article on "American Foundations of Columbus Scholarship" (pp. 157-226). Major subheadings emphasized its focus: "The Harvard/JustinWinsor Initiative in Cooperative "Age of

Discovery" Scholarship," "Winsor's 'Complete' Columbus," and "Winsor and Herbert Baxter Adams on 'The Perils of Historical Narrative'." An editorial introduction titled "The Irreplaceable Work of Justin Winsor (1831-1897)," projected eventual publication of a "Winsor" series of *RNL* issues on the literary-historical foundations of the "many nations of the New World that have already developed (or are now developing) independent national literatures of their own in languages shared with their European lands of origin."

During the next two years (1993-1994), readable texts were prepared of relevant selections from the first two volumes of Winsor's great masterpiece of cooperative scholarship, his *Narrative and Critical History of America* (1884-1889). The original text in four different sizes of type, a variety of lengthy footnotes and lengthier endnotes supported by additional footnotes, was redesigned so that notes and texts emerged as a substantially rewritten and new whole. The team effort to do that required a considerable expenditure of time and a heavy initial outlay of scarce funds. Meanwhile, during those same two years, *RNL* issues on *Hungarian Literature* and *Japan: A Literary Overview*, appeared.

Native American Antiquities and Linguistics (first of the projected "Winsor"*RNL* volumes) appeared in 1995 and attracted much attention from specialists in native American studies — most notably from Stephen Williams, recently retired Peabody Professor of American Archaeology and Ethnology at Harvard and Curator of North American Archaeology at its Peabody Museum. In response to receipt of the book, Williams wrote:

> I am reading through Winsor again. It is so much easier to follow in its new form, and every time one reads a condensed bit of knowledge one comes to it with other new perspectives and so much means so much more to me. For example, I have finally gotten my hands on David Warden. He really is completely unknown (despite Winsor) to all scholars of the History of American Archaeology. I had some students of mine work on a translation before I left Harvard. So many of my colleagues do not read any foreign languages at all — we anthropologists are so unlike good historians!

"Of course," Professor Stephens concluded, "there will be interest in the other two Winsor volumes as well."

That first volume reaffirmed our editorial decision that it would be the first of three, which, taken together, would "provide an indispensable scholarly support for later issues of *RNL* devoted to the many established, emergent, and neglected national literatures of our 'Greater America'." The volume consisted of bibliographical studies by just Winsor himself, though supported by a review article on "Winsor's *Aboriginal America* and the Perils of Empirical Archaeology." Surveying recent critical literature on the subject, that review article's major subheadings outline its contents: "The 'Other' Indians of American Prehistoric 'Dirt Archaeology'," "Major J. W. Powell's Crusade for a Language-Focused Indian Archaeology," "Lewis H. Morgan: Empirical Archaeology Coupled with the Perils of Ideology," "Old World Archaeology and Its New World Counterpart," and "Empirical Archaeology Today."

The issue in hand, on the *Cultures of the Aztecs, Mayas, and Incas* (1996), features Winsor's bibliographic studies on Ancient Mexico and Central America, supplemented by selections from Sir Clements R. Markham's "The Inca Civilization of Peru." The projected third volume, *Early Spanish, French, and English Encounters with the American Indians*, introduces narrative and critical, studies by George E. Ellis on "The Red Indian of North America in Contact with the French and English" and on "Las Casas, and the Relations of the Spaniards to the Indians"; but once again the major bibliographical contribution will be Winsor's.

1. Lessons of the Ancient World on Hieroglyphics and their Decipherment

In his masterful survey of the field of Aztec and Maya literary-linguistic culture down to his time, Winsor refers his readers to H. H. Bancroft's pages on the subject (iv. 543) for an epitome of the arguments advanced by García y Cubas to establish an historical link between ancient Egyptians and pre-Columbian Mexicans. Garcia's widely influential book of 1871 was titled *Ensayo de un Estudio Comparativo en tre las Piramides Egipcias y Mexicanas.* It was one of a long series of works on the so-called Egyptian theory which had been "mainly worked out" in the nineteenth century. Glancing beyond Bancroft, Winsor introduces.this bibliographical summary by William H. Tillinghast — one of his chief deputies at the Harvard

Library:

> An essay by A. Lenoir, comparing Central American monu-
> ments with those of Egypt, is appended to Dupaix's *Antiquités
> Méxicaines* (1805). Delafield's *Inquiry into the Origin of the
> Antiquities of America* (Cincinnati, 1839), traces it to the
> Cushites of Egypt, and cites Garcia y Cubas 1871. Brasseur
> (1864b) discusses the question, *S'il existe des sources de l'histoire
> primitive du Méxique dans les monuments égyptiens et de l'histoire
> primitive de l'ancien monde dans les monuments Américains?* in
> his ed. of Landa's *Relations des Chose de Yucatan* (1864).
> Buckle (*Hist. of Civilization*, I. ch. 2) believes the Mexican
> civilization to have been strictly analogous to that of India
> and Egypt. Tylor (*Early History of Mankind*, 98) compares the
> Egyptian hieroglyphics with those of the Aztecs. John T. C.
> Heaviside, *Amer. Antiquities, or the New World the Old, and the
> Old World the New* (1868), maintains the reverse theory of the
> Egyptians being migrated Americans. F. de Varnhagen works
> out his belief in *L'origine touranienne des américains
> tupis-caribes et dea anciens égyptiens montérie principalment par
> la philologie comparie; et notice d'une émigration en Amérique
> effectuèe à travers l'Atlantique plusieurs siécles avant notre ére*
> (1976). [Winsor I, 43]

There is, of course, a huge bibliography in many languages
on the history of efforts to decipher hieroglyphics or other
"coded" writing. Winsor is aware that his contemporaries
were, in this regard, going over old ground as if it were new;
and we can agree that the same is true of our own contemporaries working on decipherment of ancient American
hieroglyphics.

On the challenge of deciphering those hieroglyphics, John Lloyd Stephens had written in his *Incident of Travel
in Central America, Chiapas, and Yucatan* (1841): "For centuries the hieroglyphics of Egypt were inscrutable, and, though
not perhaps in our day, I feel persuaded that a key surer
than the Rosetta Stone will be discovered." Quoting those
words in his previously cited *Breaking the Maya Code*, Michael
Coe made them a point of departure for his not-too-brief
review of the history of the long resistance of Americanist
scholars to preparing themselves for the use of a native
American Indian Rosetta Stone, if they happened ever to
find one. Coe recalls that, while Spanish Christian missionaries studied the native Indian languages from the beginning, and had produced countless teaching- style dictionaries and grammars from the time of the conquest on, the

most learned modern "would-be decipherers of Maya hieroglyphic writing" consistently declined to do what the
great decipherers of Egyptian hieroglyphics, like Champo-
llion, had done, which was to discover at least approxi-
mately what the spoken language of the ancient Egyptians
might have been — settling quickly on the still vital Coptic
liturgical language of the Coptic Christian Church. Despite
all the diligent work of the missionaries, Coe acknowledges, modern linguistic scholars flatly declined to "im-
merse themselves in one or more of the Mayan tongues."
And he clarifies [54]:

> Incredible as it may seem, up until about two decades ago [c.
> 1972] the Maya script was the only decipherment for which
> a thorough grounding in the relevant language was not
> considered necessary — there are still a few "experts" on the
> subject, hidden away in the dusty recesses of anthropology
> departments, who have only the foggiest idea of Maya as a
> spoken language (and not much of Spanish, for that matter).
> We shall see the consequences of this ignorance in due time.

Coe's point is that, had they studied the spoken
languages of the living Mayas, those scholars would have
realized that a Mayan equivalent of the Rosetta Stone had
long ago surfaced.

2. Finding and Ignoring a Mayan/Aztec "Rosetta Stone"

In fact, not long after Stephens's prescient prophecy
of 1841, the celebrated French Americanist, Brasseur de
Bourbourg, had come across a Mayan Rosetta Stone in a
manuscript of the notorious Bishop Diego de Landa, reput-
edly one of the great destroyers of native American treasures. Brasseur found in Landa's *Relacion de las cosas de
Yucatan* (which Brasseur edited and published in 1864)
what has ever since been called his "A,B,C" of the Maya
script. And of this, Coe writes that, "with their characteristic obduracy, Mayanists spurned this precious document as
a true key to the decipherment for about one hundred
years; and this in spite of the fact that Bishop Landa
actually provided many more readings for signs than the
Rosetta Stone did for Egyptology." [260] Coe blames the
bad training of the Mayanists in comparative epigraphy.
Landa's famous "key" offered itself as a guarantee that the
deciphered hieroglyphs meant exactly what the old priests

said their transcriptions of the living Mayan into Spanish script meant. The original Rosetta Stone with parallel texts in Egyptian hieroglyphics, Copt demotic, and Greek, could serve as a linguistic key, Coe takes the trouble to explain, because one of its parallel texts, the Greek, stated, among other things, that the "inscription was the same in all three texts." [37]

One is reminded of the once famous "linguistic key" that used to appear regularly in the major European international trains. It took the form of notices in four languages — English, French, German, and Italian — on the inner window ledges warning passengers not to "lean out" of open windows. The key word in English, French, or German meant literally that leaning out was "not allowed" (Eng. = *forbidden*; French = *défendu*; German = *verboten*). The Italian warning, however, departed radically from that international norm: it said literally that it was "dangerous" (*pericoloso*) to stick one's head out the window (*sporgersi*) in a moving train. Needless to say, we get no such assurance of identical meanings in our four international train-warnings. They ultimately mean pretty much the same; but if we took the Italian pericoloso to mean "forbidden" we would be much mistaken about a very important aspect of Italian character.

Coe insists that, by building on Landa's insights, full decipherment of the Maya hieroglyphs has become possible. As the title of his book asserts, he and his peers have "found the key" that unlocks it all. The ancient Maya, he insists, could and did "write down anything they wanted to, in their own language." Of course, a possibility is there acknowledged that those Mayans might not have wished, actually, to write down very much. At any rate, while Winsor puts great stock in the achievement of the early Spanish transcribers and translators, he remains reserved to the very end on the prospects of genuine decipherment. What he says about the major sources of difficulty regarding Aztec picture-writing still applies in some measure also to the Mayan.

The Aztecs, Winsor notes, had advanced in their picture-writing to a point mingling figurative and symbolic phases of such writing; and the two "apparently varied in the order of reading, whether by lines or columns, forwards, upwards, or backwards." Understanding remained difficult because the same object held "different meanings in different connections," and still more because of the "personal element, or writer's style, as we should call it, which was impressed on his choice of objects and emblems." Color also altered meaning, all of which, Winsor concludes, "rendered interpretation by no means easy to the aborigines themselves, and we have statements that when native documents were referred to them it required sometimes long consultations to reach a common understanding."

Coe and his peers granted all of that with respect to Aztec picture-writing. But they claimed that they had thoroughly broken the more advanced Maya code. One needs to read Coe's book closely, to the very end, to be made aware of how divided major Mayan scholars remain on the subject. Coe complains that neither the archaeologists nor the anthropologists in the field have really welcomed his achievement. And they, he admonishes at the close, still control the refereed journals, the editorial boards of the major scholarly publishers, and of the funds that assign research grants. Moreover, in the lands of the major Mayan sites, like Guatemala, he charges, those academic leaders stand idly by while tyrannical governments systematically destroy the last remnants of the living Mayas. In Coe's words:

> The indigenous populations are being uprooted and demoralized by a systematic program of extermination carried out by a succession of military regimes. Creators of one of the most spectacular civilizations the world has even known, the Maya today have been reduced to what anthropologists condescend to call a 'folk culture,' with little or no voice in their own destinies. How many vacationing tourists who visit the glorious ruins of Yucatán are aware that Mexican law forbids the teaching in schools of the Yucatán Maya tongue — the tongue of the people who built these pyramids?"

Coe refers to those living Mayans as "Fourth World" people, to contrast them with the peoples of the "Third World" of emerging nations, whose eagerness to develop national literary languages has always been enthusiastically supported in western intellectual circles. And then he asks of the Latin American countries with large Mayan populations: "How many heads of state in those countries have any 'Indian' blood to speak of? And when has any Native American language been heard in the halls of the United

Nations? The answer is 'none' and 'never.' No imperial conquest has ever been so total, or a great people so shattered." [47]

But it seems that American champions of the lowly native populations around the sites of the great Mayan ruins in Guatemala are at last having a precious share of prime-time television broadcasts in the United States, through the medium of major U. S. Senate Intelligence Committee hearings on C.I.A. activity in Guatemala. Two American widows whose husbands were killed by government troops in Guatemala, probably with the collaborative tolerance or connivance of CIA agents in the field, told attentive senators and reporters that the killings of their husbands had been grossly misrepresented. It was officially claimed that the Guatemalan forces that did the killing were "fighting Cuban-inspired Communism — to keep it away from the Rio Grande." Against that, according to the *New York Times* (April 5, 1995), one of the widows gave sworn testimony that the so-called enemies being killed are "mostly Mayan Indians" who have "sought respect for their language and their lands." That often-repeated charge has lately resurfaced as a front-page story with pictures in the *Times* Sunday edition for March 24, 1996.

Had Michael D. Coe been called upon to tell what American Mayanists were saying about government violence against Mayans in Guatemala, the major newsmedia might have been able to show him identifying what tyrannical governments had done, or failed to do, in 1990, when the leading Russian Mayanist of the time, Yuri Valentinovich Knorosov, "had gone to Guatemala to receive an award." Coe identifies him as "the man who let us read the Maya glyphs." Accompanied by his young colleague Galina Yershova and her Guatemalan husband, Knorosov had arrived in Guatemala for the first time to stand at last "in the shadows of Maya pyramids." From the hands of Guatemala's President Cerezo, he received a gold medal. But there is more to tell. Not long after President Cerezo left office, Coe writes, a "sinister call" came to the Russians and their Guatemalan friends in Guatemala City. In Coe's words, it warned:

> Leave Guatemalan territory within seventy-two hours or be killed. Knorosov and his friends immediately went into hiding, then fled the country of the Maya — and of the

right-wing death squads who have been engaged in extirpat-
ing all remaining Maya culture, and the Maya themselves.
The man who had allowed the ancient Maya to speak with
their own voice was still unable to walk freely among the
cities in which they had lived. [275]

One needs to read only a few pages of Winsor on the
picture-writings of the Aztecs and Mayas to be reminded of
richer times in the history of serious scholarly research in
the field. The solid foundations laid at that time are carefully assessed for us in Winsor's masterful studies.

Wnsor takes for granted — if we may briefly
suminarize — that his readers are mostly of a scholarly bent.
All of them, he assumes, are generally aware that visual
records and reminders of important names, dates, and
events, etc., and means of conveying messages, were developed and used by the three most advanced native American
civilizations — the Aztecs, Mayas, and Incas — long before
the coming of Columbus. The Aztecs used pictorial representations in registering events or expressing ideas; the
Mayas clearly advanced to the use of phonetic picture-writing
to convey meaningful sounds, words, phrases, sentences.
In their cultural brilliance, the Incas apparently satisfied
themselves with the use of *quipus*, consisting of cords of
tightly-woven colored threads more or less elaborately
knotted to remind a learned elite of facts and happenings
of historical or at least dynastic importance. In none of the
three great civilizations, however, did the use of such
pictorial representations or knotted reminders much affect
the intrinsic development of the native tongues as instru-
ments of cultural expression.

The first article, on the writing of the Mayas and
Aztecs, is by Winsor. With his detailed bibliographical
notes carefully integrated into its text, it now serves us as
one of his most masterful pieces of scholarly writing. The
second article, on the Inca approach to keeping records, is
by Sir Clements E. Markham, with important bibliographical notes added by Winsor — all integrated to make up an
organically consistent whole. After two additional selections from Winsor, "Aztec Grandeur and Maya Glory — Fact
or Fiction?" and "A Geographical Survey of the Principal
Aztec and Maya Ruins," we close with Winsor's "Critical
Assessment of Sources on the Subjugated Peoples of 'New
Spain'," and Markham's "Bibliographical Spectrum on the

Historical Sources of Inca Civilization."

EDITORIAL NOTE: ON PRINTING CONVENTIONS
Adopted for the *RNL* "Winsor" Volumes

It bears repeating that to make that Winsor legacy readily "legible" for modern readers, we have integrated the substance of the small-print footnotes of the original into the body of the text, and have brought together related passages which originally were widely separated. There has been minor editing to harmonize the sometimes varied materials brought together, and thereby facilitate reading; but each distinguishable unit of the whole is clearly marked at the start by superscript lower-case reference letters ([a, b, c, d], etc.) with source pages indicated in the corresponding endnotes. The reference letter [a] identifies the extended main text of each essay, as distinct from integrated materials, and it reappears as often as the main text is resumed, thereby clearly marking where an inserted passage ends. At the start of each article, however, the initial "drop cap" counts as a superscript[a].

A basic change introduced by our special editors has been the adoption of modern practice in the parenthetic references and lists of sources supplied. As in Winsor's *Native American Antiquities and Linguistics*, The list of "Works Cited" and of periodical/learned-society acronyms cover the range of references in all the individual articles, so that bibliographical repetition is kept to a minimum. Titles of books, articles, and periodicals are supplied in the text only where they are themselves the focus of discussion.

Columbus and the Idea of America

Every people in the world has at one time or another laid claim to the discovery of America. In the United States, we hear mostly of Scandinavian or Irish "precursors" of Columbus, but elsewhere, as an eminent scholar has put it, "vigorously defended claims exist for the priority of the Chinese, Japanese, Polynesians, Phoenicians, Romans, Arabs, Turks, Hindoos, Basques, Welch, . . . French, Polish, Germans, Dutch, and Portuguese. . . . So many are the claims . . . that the question is less 'Who discovered America?' than 'Who didn't?'"

Even when it is agreed that Christopher Columbus was the "effective" discoverer, there are rival claims about his ethnic identity. Was he Spanish or Portuguese, or a Spanish, Portuguese, or Italian Jew whose intention in 1492 — so some supporters of the Jewish thesis have claimed — was to find a new-world haven for the Jews being expelled from Spain during that very year?

The reason for this great variety or claims is obvious. Long before America was discovered people had wanted such a land, had longed for a distant "brave new world" — as Shakespeare would later refer to it in his Tempest — which would lie before them like a "land of dreams, so various, so beautiful, so new," free from the enormous weight of all the heavy ages piled on the old worlds of Europe and Asia. Among the ancient Greeks, scientists and philosophers had speculated about the possibility of there being unknown lands in other parts of the earth's vast oceans. And, as any book that deals even superficially with the discovery of America is apt to remind us, it was the Roman playwright Lucius Annaus Seneca — a native of Spain (d. 65 A.D.) — who included in his tragedy of *Mædea* the prophetic lines:

> There will come a time, after many years have
>   lapsed,
> Cycles of time when Ocean will loosen the chains of
>   things
> And a vast land will be revealed,
> And Tiphys shall explore new worlds;
> Nor shall Thule remain ultimate on earth.

Tiphys was the pilot or helmsman of the legendary Argonauts of the ancient Greeks. He was credited with having sailed farthest north in the Atlantic — as far as Thule, which was probably what we now know as Iceland. There is a copy of Seneca's tragedies in the Columbian Library at Valladolid, Spain; and in the margin, next to the prophetic lines quoted (378-382), we find the following (written in Latin) in the hand of Columbus's son Ferdinand: "This prophecy was fulfilled by my father, Christopher Columbus, the admiral, in 1492."

1. America's Great Centenary Dates

The year 1492, needless to say, is the first of the great centenary dates in the history of the United States. Not many years ago, in 1976, "We the People" of the United States celebrated the 200th anniversary of our Declaration of Independence, followed, in 1987, with a celebration of the 200th birthday of the composition of our Federal Constitution. But, if we want a more precise calendar of great dates to commemorate, we need to remind ourselves that, as President Abraham Lincoln observed in his Inaugural Address of 1861,

> the Union of the American people is much older than its Constitution. It was formed, in fact, by the Articles of Association in 1774. It was matured and continued by the Declaration of Independence in 1776. It was further matured, and the faith of the then thirteen States expressly

plighted and engaged that it should be perpetual by the Articles of Confederation in 1778. And finally, in 1787, one of the declared objects of ordaining and establishing the Constitution was "to form a more perfect Union."

The bicentenary celebrations or commemorations of the four dates so carefully distinguished by President Lincoln — 1774, 1776, 1778, and 1787 — ran their course through the recent presidencies of Richard Nixon, Jimmy Carter, and Ronald Reagan. The last of those years, 1787, was of course the date of the true birth certificate of our political system, legitimizing us politically as the most constitutional-minded people in the world's history. The new government was actually organized in 1788 and its first President duly elected and inaugurated in 1789. All subsequent presidential elections have been scheduled for the year preceding inauguration; and so in the case of George Bush, it was not his election in 1988 but his inauguration in 1989 that represented an American bicentenary presidential event — "from George to George"!

And fast on the heels of the 200th birthday of our functioning republic came the year 1992. With that date, our minds had to be readied to go back not a mere 200 years but all of 500 years — half a millennium — to when it really all began for America. In the United States, a general consensus has emerged that the 12th day of the 10th month of each year is to be marked on the calendar as a distinctively Italian-American celebration. Yet for the quincentenary celebration, that consensus must be at least temporarily set aside, and the Italian-Americans must themselves take the lead in stressing the global significance of the day. It belongs, first of all, to the Americas as a whole, extending from the northernmost tip of the North American continent — where it almost touches the eastern extreme of the vast European/Asian landmass — down to the southernmost reaches of Tierra del Fuego, beyond the famous Strait of Magellan. But surely it belongs also to the lands of Europe which provided the men and means, including the nautical skills, that made the voyages of discovery possible; and to the lands of distant Asia, of India, China, and Japan, which those bold voyagers hoped to reach.

2. Columbus and the American Astronauts – Parallel Journeys!

It is altogether out of order to think of October 12th as some sort of ethnic Italian-American "birthday," particularly on the great centenary anniversaries. On that date, in 1492, Columbus, a native of Genoa ("proud Genoa, *Genova la Superba*") who had lived in Portugal and Spain, set foot on an island of the new world which he called San Salvador. The obvious parallel event and parallel date in our time is the American astronauts' landing on the moon of July 20, 1969. "This historic landing," said Professor G. L. Vincitorio, completing *The Record of 1969* as a continuation of James Truslow Adams's *The March of Democracy: A History of the United States* (1971),

> was compared to the discovery of the New World by Columbus. But, unlike the latter's departure from Palos, Spain, and his landfall at San Salvador, which were seen by few people, the dramatic events of 1969, from lift-off to splash-down, were in full public view. Perhaps as many as half a billion persons throughout the world followed the astronauts' 240,000-mile journey through space by means of television and radio.

We all know in general terms the history of our space and lunar explorations. Before the technology of our actual space flights was developed there had been literally centuries of scientific preparation. The trajectories for the orbital flights around the earth, and for the extra-orbital flights to the moon, had been worked out as far back as the days of Isaac Newton. Earlier than Newton, Galileo and Kepler had given imaginatively accurate accounts of the heavenly perspectives from the moon and the other earth-like planets. But we had to wait until World War II for a serious start to harnessing power sufficient to launch missiles into inertial orbit and extra-orbital flights through space. There was then the shock of the Soviet Union's successful launching of its sputnik or fellow-traveler, which evoked President John F. Kennedy's pledge of May 25, 1961, to land a man on the moon and return him safely to earth within a decade. In less than a decade, American technology had produced the Apollo spacecraft with its command, service, and lunar modules, which, after some practice runs, made it possible for Neil Armstrong and Edwin Aldrin to walk on the moon, while Michael Collins continued in orbit around the moon awaiting the return of the lunar module and re-engagement for the return flight to earth.

3. *Long Preparations for Columbus's Journey*

Columbus's landing on San Salvador on October 12, 1492 had an even longer scientific preparation, and there had been no visual anticipation (as there was in the case of the moon landing) of what the points of landing in the new world might be like. When our astronauts got close to the moon at Christmas time in 1968, they reported back their visual impression of what the telescope had long revealed: that of a "vast, lonely, forbidding-type existence — a great expanse of nothing that looks rather like clouds and clouds of pumice stone . . . not . . . a very inviting place to live and work." The first walk on the moon of the following year confirmed the impression. Hundreds of millions saw it on TV. But they also saw that there was no "new world" of "new peoples" on the moon, such as Columbus found when he first landed in our Western Hemisphere.

We have Columbus's words on much of what he found; and they are words that differ fundamentally from what our astronauts were moved to say in reporting back to us from the moon. In one eye-witness report Columbus noted that in pressing his explorations he had "taken some Indians by force from the first island" on which he landed, "in order that they might learn our language and communicate what they knew respecting the country, which plan succeeded excellently, and was a great advantage to us, for in a short time, either by gestures and signs or words, we were enabled to understand each other." Columbus adds that these interpreters, as we might say, continued to travel with him. "And though they have been with us a long time," we read in his report,

> they continue to entertain the idea that I have descended from heaven; and at our arrival in any new place, they publish this, crying out immediately with a loud voice to the others: "Come, come and look upon beings of a celestial race"; upon which both women and men, children and adults, young men and old, when they got rid of the fear they at first entertained, would come out in throngs, crowding the roads to see us, some bringing food, others drink, with astonishing affection and kindness.

Columbus reported that the island he called San Salvador was called by the natives Guanahani, meaning

Island of the Iguanas. On another island which he called *La Isla Española* — Hispaniola — because of its resemblance to Spain, he set up a trading post. Before he was done with his four crossings, between 1492 and 1504, Columbus had placed under the sovereignty of the Spanish rulers "more land," as he boasted, "than there is in Africa and Europe, and more than seventeen hundred islands, without counting Hispaniola." He was the first European to land on the continental Americas, as well as on the islands. Most of the names he supplied have survived though not, of course, for the continental landmasses, destined to be named after another Italian.

Columbus's dream had been, as he said, to "*buscar el levante por el poniente*" (to gain the East by going West), and, because he believed he had succeeded, he called the natives "Indians" — a name that has stuck, resulting in the paradox of their descendants' boastfully identifying themselves by that misnomer in claiming to be the original "Americans."

4. Culmination of a Great Age of Discovery

To put the meaning of October 12, 1492, in proper perspective for our time — the age of nuclear weapons and space explorations — it is important to remind ourselves of the fundamental differences between the great age of discovery inaugurated by the navigators of Europe, who ventured beyond the Mediterranean and the Atlantic seacoast to dare the perils of the open seas, and our own age of discovery inaugurated by a revolution in technology that has tended to depersonalize the adventure of its own achievements. In venturing upon the open seas, Portugal (the ancient Lusitania, a "nation of freebooters") had led the way, with its renowned Prince Henry the Navigator. Prince Henry had sought an Atlantic route to India by going South along the west coast of Africa and then east around the "dark" continent's southern extremity. He had died in 1460, but not before he had founded a naval observatory and a school of geography at Sagres, the extremest western promontory of Portugal, the country "where land ends and the sea begins," as the Portuguese poet Luis de Camoëns would put it in his great epic poem, *The Lusiads*. Prince Henry's school, it has been said, attracted "scholars, teachers, map-makers, and adventurous mariners" of all lands, who flocked there "like sea gulls around a lighthouse."

Christopher Columbus — we are told — landed in Portugal as a shipwrecked sailor in 1476, when he was perhaps 25 years old. His brother Bartolomeo had preceded him there, however, and was already prospering in Portugal as a "maker and publisher of maps recording Portuguese discoveries." It was in Portugal that Columbus established himself as a master of all the arts related to navigation and began to elaborate his design for reaching the far east by sailing westward. It was not a new idea, any more than the idea of a space flight to the moon was a new idea when the Soviets and Americans finally developed the means to turn the idea into an actuality. Columbus and his contemporaries were aware that Aristotle had thought it feasible to reach the far east by sailing westward from the Strait of Gibraltar and that the great Greek geographer Strabo had explained failures to accomplish the feat in these straightforward terms:

> Those who have returned from an attempt to circumnavigate the earth do not say that they have been prevented from continuing their voyage by any opposing continent, for the sea [to the West] remained perfectly open; they were prevented from continuing, rather, through want of resolution and scarcity of provision.

It was resolution primarily that Columbus brought to the task. But he sought also to make adequate provision for such a journey and, by appealing to the great governments of his day — by applying for large government grants, in the language of our time — he at last succeeded in getting all he needed. A large part of what he needed was, however, of a technological order. We must not imagine that it did not take great scientific and technological advances to make the westward crossings of the Atlantic possible. It is true that our astronauts who have walked on the moon were carried across great reaches of space on computer-controlled vehicles, and that such computer-control has started us off on an age of discovery that really strikes some of us as unheroic. Certainly our space-age science has forced on our pioneer-astronauts a tasteless, technical jargon that has tended to diminish their glory, even as compared with the voyages that opened up Australia two centuries ago.

Yet we must not imagine that the navigation plans developed in the days of Prince Henry and Columbus did not involve high technology as well as science and a large

measure of daring. Surely it took a great deal of all of that
to get the Portuguese around the southern tip of the vast
continent of Africa which they first put on the map. Africa
has proved to be no desolate moon, even though, after long
centuries of circumnavigation and exploration, the Portuguese have at last been forced out. What was it like to raise
great sails to the wind to round the South African "Cape of
Darkness" (later optimistically called the Cape of Good
Hope!) in 1497? The Portuguese navigators of the late 15th
century and early 16th century have, of course, had poetic
justice done to them in *The Lusiads* of Camoëns, of which
we have already spoken. Vasco da Gama (1469-1524) is
Camoëns' Ulysses or Aeneas in that poem. But even in
celebrating the great deeds of his hero, Camoëns, like
Virgil, foresaw the anxiety of events yet to come. In words
that remind us of some debates over the cost — if not the
hazards — of space exploration in our time, an old man is
made to say fearfully, in a famous couplet at the end of
Canto Four of The Lusiads:

> O curst be the man who first tied
> The flowing sheet to the tree!
> [*O maldito o primiero, que no mundo*
> *Nas ondas vela poz em secco lenho!*]

The poem celebrating the voyages of Vasco da Gama
and his Portuguese peers was the work of a man born in the
very dawning of the age of discovery, and it was completed
in 1572 over 400 years ago. But it was Columbus who had
already proved himself to be, without a peer, the greatest
navigator of that age. Why then has he not been compara-
bly celebrated in an epic poem? Perhaps because he did not
sail for his native Italy, under an Italian flag. It is a fact that
while it produced epic poets of the caliber of Ariosto and
Tasso, in the century following Columbus's great voyages,
Italy could not give him in prose or poetry anything even
remotely worthy of his achievement. Even Genoa, Portugal,
and Spain, which certainly have claims on his childhood,
young manhood, and maturity, have denied him epic celebration, for he was never really theirs in an epic sense. In
that sense, as an epic, heroic figure, Columbus plainly
belongs not to the old but to the new world. It is likely,
therefore, that fate will leave his ultimate celebration, in
scholarship and history, as well as in literature, and art, to
us!

5. *Giving Columbus His Due in Art and Literature*

Fortunately — here in the United States, at any rate — a solid foundation is already in place for giving Columbus his due. The five hundredth anniversary of the discovery is upon us, and we must look back across the centuries to put the milestones in perspective. Almost three whole centuries elapsed between the discovery of our American continent and the emergence on its shores of a new nation, claiming separate and equal status among the powers of the earth. But 1492 was the real national beginning. We need to celebrate it properly. And we can start by recalling that, when she gave her great navigators to the Spanish, Portuguese, and English, starting in the last decades of the fifteenth century, Italy was on the verge of economic, social and political ruin. The year 1492 is the year of the death of Lorenzo de'Medici *Il Magnifico*. Machiavelli was then 23 years old, and, within a year or two, he was to see Italy pillaged by the armies of France and Spain which eventually brought utter ruin to Columbus's birthplace, the great port of Genoa, just a few years before the terrible sack the Spanish inflicted on Rome in 1527, the year of Machiavelli's death.

In those days, money, capital, quickly fled from Italy and with it most of Italy's men of talent. Columbus himself was part of that flight of talent. The gainers were Portugal and Spain first, then the Netherlands, and finally England. From that flight, despite the national *risorgimento* of which the great Vittorio Alfieri was the poetic prophet, Italy has never fully recovered; and certainly there is no chance that it can ever do justice in art and literature to those who left its shores to contribute to the emergent grandeur of far-off nations like our own.

As already noted, there is a powerful temptation in the United States to let the Italian-Americans celebrate the day of America's discovery as an ethnic holiday. Columbus, it has been suggested, certainly qualifies as an expatriate Italian; or, rather, with greater accuracy, as an expatriate Genoese. Yet October 12th, it must be repeated, is not his but a new world's birthday. And the challenge, now, is for the new world as such, with the United States unavoidably in the lead, to celebrate the quincentenary of its discovery as it deserves to be celebrated, and as only Americans, North and South, can rightfully celebrate it.

6. 1892: The Columbus Circle Memorial

Back in 1892 — the four hundredth anniversary of the landing on San Salvador — Americans for the first time began to take the day seriously as an American national holiday. Johns Hopkins University, newly-founded as America's most prestigious school of higher learning, led in the academic celebrations, producing a volume titled *Columbus and His Discovery of America*, by Herbert B. Adams and Henry Wood, both professors at Johns Hopkins. In his address to the "officers and students" of his university on October 10, 1892, Professor Adams did not hesitate to say, among other things:

> The discovery of America has been called the greatest event in secular history. . . . What are all the conquests of antiquity, or the decisive battles and great inventions of mankind, compared with America, time's noblest offspring? The passage of Christopher Columbus across the Western sea, bearing the weight of Christendom and European civilization, opened the way for the greatest migrations in human history. . . . The discovery of America was the first crossing of Oceanus, that great and murmuring stream, that flowed around the Mediterranean world. Amid the grieving and travailing of human creation, men burst the confines of that outward sea and began to people new continents.

> One hundred years ago [1792] the discoverer of America was first publicly honored in this City of Baltimore. Today we recall and apply to him the spirit of our own Baltimore motto, which by some curious historic chance has come down to us in the language of Italy and of Columbus. *Fatti maschi, parole femmine*, manly deeds and womanly words, belong to the world-pilot of Genoa as well as to Lord Baltimore, the first great American apostle of tolerant opinion. The manliest deed in American history was the first great voyage of Columbus across an unknown, western sea.

The monument erected in Baltimore in 1792 to honor Columbus was "an obelisk, forty-four feet and four inches high, rising from a six and a half-foot square base," made of brick and mortar with a stuccoed or cemented surface that "has the appearance of grey sandstone." It was no work of art, in Professor Adams's view; but it was a beginning. A truly artistic monument, and certainly the "noblest statue of the noble Genoese pilot," was what the "Italians of the United States, Canada, Mexico, and Central

America" would present "to the people of this country" a hundred years later. That statue, he notes, now stands "at the west entrance to Central Park" in New York City on what we now call Columbus Circle, where it was "unveiled with appropriate ceremonies on October 12, 1892." Adams wrote: "It is of Carrara marble, and was modeled by Gaetano Russo, an Italian sculptor in Rome. It is one of the finest works of modern Italian art. The international monument, with its granite base, stands seventy-five feet high." In an appendix, we read further that the "cost of the memorial was $35,000," and that "the subscription was begun and carried through by Chevalier [Cavaliere] Barsotti, the proprietor of the Italian paper published in New York, *Il Progresso Italo-Americano*."

Professor Adams cannot, however, point in 1892 to a comparable Italian-American-supported *literary* tribute to Columbus's epic achievement. How would a Homer or Virgil, a Camoëns or Spenser, have celebrated that achievement had Columbus been one of their own? Professor Adams recalls how Dante's genius as a poet seemed to anticipate the task. When Dante wrote his *Divine Comedy* early in the 14th century, Columbus's voyage of discovery was physically still a long way off — more than one and a half centuries. But spiritually, it was something very close, something in the air. Dante sensed all around him in his Italy a spiritual longing to go out beyond the limits of the known world, and it inspired in him a piece of poetry that, even today, better expresses the daring of the discovery of America than any account in poetry or prose that has since been written about it.

7. Dante, Ulysses, and Columbus

In the 26th canto of the Inferno, Dante — guided by Virgil "meets Odysseus, the Grecian type of Columbus," as Professor Adams puts it, "the adventurous navigator who had sailed every sea." Odysseus, or Ulysses, as we prefer to call him, is indeed the wanderer, the traveler, the adventurer *par excellence*. His very name has come to mean a journey, with the proviso that it be an educative journey. Some years ago, here in America, we had a best-selling book called *A Doctor's Odyssey*. And the great novelist James Joyce called his vast account of a day's physical and spiritual journey through Dublin by the name *Ulysses*.

According to Dante, Ulysses is in hell for having been a chronic deceiver. Yet, if that is why he is in hell, we hardly take notice of his punishment as we hear him tell of his last adventure, undertaken long after the events represented in Homer's *Odyssey*. Where the ancient narratives left off, Ulysses had found his way back to his home in Ithaca — rejoining his wife Penelope, his son Telemachus, and his aged father. But, as Dante related, Ulysses simply could not stay put. He himself is made to say: "not fondness for a son, nor duty to an aged father, nor the love I owed Penelope which should have gladdened her, could conquer in me the passion I had to gain experience of the world."

"I put forth," he goes on to say, "on the open sea with but one boat." His ship is a small wooden one, and his crew is made up of old companions of the long journey from Troy. They sail westward across the Mediterranean, past Sardinia, with Spain at last on their right and Morocco on their left, heading for "that narrow outlet where Hercules set up his landmarks so that men should not pass beyond." But the daring of Ulysses takes him past the barriers of what we now call the Strait of Gibraltar. He names the cities, "Seville . . . on the right hand and Ceuta on the other," and out upon the Atlantic they boldy sail. His crew, like himself, were already "old and slow," and some of them wondered about risking such a voyage at such a time. To spur them on, Ulysses says with epic grandeur much of what Columbus would actually say under similar circumstances centuries later. As Dante reports the captain's plea:

> "O brothers," I said, "who through a hundred thousand perils have reached the west, do not choose to deny to this brief vigil of the senses that remains to us the experience, in the sun's track, of the unpeopled world. Take thought of the seed from which you spring. You were not born to live as brutes, but to follow virtue and knowledge." I made my companions so eager for the journey with these brief words that I could hardly have held them back. . . .

Ulysses and his men sail west and south and they arrive, most extraordinarily, within sight of what Columbus for a time believed himself to have found, the elevated earthly paradise which is, in the Bible, called the, Garden of Eden. They don't make it ashore. But that's another story. The important lines are the three beginning *"considerate la vostra semenza."* The temptation has been great in our time, and in America particularly, to live as though we were but beasts, with only sensuous, material appetites. Is that to be our destiny? Not if we keep in mind, as Dante says, who we are, our seed, our roots.

We have cited Dante's verses only as a reminder that, when the time comes to celebrate Columbus's achievement in literary art, the way has been prepared for us by Italy's universal poet. We have suggested obviously valid reasons why no Italian poet of the Age of Discovery — no Ariosto or Tasso — could effectively make the great "westward voyage" of Christopher Columbus an epic theme. Columbus's journey, we noted, was not "Italian" enough in substance to be celebrated heroically by native Italian poets. But neither was he sufficiently Spanish or Portuguese to receive his due from poets of those lands.

Shakespeare — who gave us the best examples in English of how history could be translated into high drama and literary art, and who made the fullest use of Italian stories and Greek and Roman heroes — for some reason failed to celebrate Columbus. The times and circumstances, he must have felt, were not ripe for it, even though, as his *Tempest* proves, he obviously had a powerful sense of the emerging ethnic complexities of what he called our brave new world.

. But perhaps, with Dante and Shakespeare as forerunners, some unknown American is destined to give Columbus his due in literature, when the times are ripe for it, which may be soon. And, as Shakespeare aptly put it in another context, we can hardly permit ourselves to ignore the fact that, in matters of high art, *ripeness is all*.

World Perspective on Shakespeare Translation

In the preface to their *Selective Bibliography of Shakepeare: Editions, Textual Studies, Commentary*, James G. McManaway and Jeanne A. Roberts apologized for restricting themselves to some 30 entries (out of more than 4,500) on Shakespeare translations and on books and articles about Shakespeare translation. "This is much to be regretted," they wrote, "for the reading, enjoyment, and theatrical production of Shakespeare is now worldwide." Within the two pages (out of 309) allotted for the purpose, they limited themselves to listing only "a few French and German translations" and to noting that "a very rich collection of translations is in the Shakespeare Library of the Birmingham English Reference Library" but they wisely also chose to list separately the sixteen articles that made up the 1956 issue (Vol. 92) of the Shakes-peare-Jahrbuch which surveyed the state of Shakespeare translation in general and particularly in Germany, Norway, Italy, Sweden, and France.[1] It is a pity that the bibliographers could not have made similar use of the first two annual volumes of *Shakespeare Translation* — published under the auspices of Seijo University in Tokyo — which had already appeared by

1975, for those volumes provided updated surveys of the state of Shakespeare translation in more than a dozen languages, including Japanese, of course, but also Spanish, Greek, Korean, Indian, Arabic, Polish, Hebrew, and Danish, as well as the major European languages.

Between 1974 and 1984, ten volumes of *Shakespeare Translation* had appeared — identified as an "Annual Publication on *Shakespeare Translation*" — edited by Toshikazu Oyama. The tenth volume, however, gave notice of the editor's death and indicated that publication would continue under the editorship of Yoshiko Kawachi of Japan's Kyoritsu Women's College. An eleventh volume in fact appeared in 1986 (published like the previous ten by Yoshiko Shoten, Ltd., Tokyo), but with a changed title. As the new editor explained in a preliminary announcement:

> The new title of our periodical, *Shakespeare Worldwide: Translation and Adaptation,* was agreed upon by everyone present at the special session on Shakespeare Translation during the Third World Shakespeare Congress held from 1 to 6 April 1986 at West Berlin.
>
> As chairperson, I would like to express my deepest gratitude to the editorial board and to all members and observers who traveled from distant countries to attend this session, offered valuable opinions and suggestions, and helped me to make this conference successful. [i]

It was only because of the two previous World Shakespeare Congresses that the one referred to "in that announcement took on the ambiguously suggestive designation of "Third World"; but there is a measure of propriety in that ambiguity. The "Second World" and "First World" nations — the major European states and the Soviet and American superpowers, as Charles de Gaulle and Mao-Tse-tung employed the terms — have had a long history of Shakespeare performance and criticism in their own languages. Translation of Shakespeare has also had a considerable development among the traditional neglected as well as the emergent national literatures of our time. But, for the extension of comparative studies in the manner indicated and advocated by the Council on National Literatures, it is essential for scholars and critics in the neglected and emergent literatures to do precisely the sort of thing that has been urged and done by the founders of *Shakespeare Translation* and their successors on the editorial board of

Shakespeare Worldwide.

In a special preface to the tenth volume, Professor Kawachi, designated as the new editor, recalled that the original decision to start publication had been taken back in 1971, when her predecessor, Toshikazu Oyama, "chaired the Investigative Committee on Shakespeare Translation at the First World Shakespeare Congress," which met in Vancouver, Canada, in August of that year. Besides its Japanese chairman, the committee had consisted of two Europeans—Hans W. Gabler of the University of Munich and Pierre Spriet of the University of Bordeaux — and two other Asians — Jagannath Chakravorty of Jadavpur University, Calcutta, and Toshiko Oyama of Tsuda College, Tokyo (the committee chairman's wife). Each committee member had prepared a preconvention "historical survey of Shakespeare translation in the country he represented and delineated briefly the present state of Shakespeare translation." The chairman's final report to the Congress, published in its proceedings, *Shakespeare 1971*, edited by Clifford Leech and J. M. R. Margeson (1972) stressed how the "wide differences" in linguistic and cultural backgrounds of the four committee members were reflected in their appraisals of the difficulties and limitations of adequate translation. In Oyama's words:

> Germany would be accredited with the oldest history in Shakespeare translation, having her own problem, however, which is that German translation has tended to become stereotyped, as a result of the cumulative efforts, French translations, from the nature of the language, cannot avoid the tendency to become longer than the original. India has a fairly long history of Shakespeare translation. However, the people of India are still in great need of standard translations in various dialects. Japan has no less serious problems. In the case of the Japanese translations, perhaps we might even say that "translation" is not the right word for the kind of work involved and the result thereof, the reason being that, because of the nature of the language, there is such a wide range of choice for the equivalent and the parallel to the original and the entire business is left to the free choice of the translator.

Although the committee on translation did not arrive at "any definite conclusion," its members agreed on several points defining a common ground for future discussion.

These were that "word- for-word translation is the most
appropriate style for the new Shakespeare translation,"
that Shakespeare translation "should be explored as a new
territory of comparative literature," that translation-prob-
lems could "contribute to new interpretations of
Shakespeare," that there would thereafter certainly be a
"much wider range of possibilities for international
co-operation in the field of Shakespeare translation than
has hitherto been supposed," and that the publication of an
annual review of "Shakespeare translation" — with that title
— ought to be started, "making the small pamphlet prepared by the committee for the 1971 Congress the first
issue of the series."[2]

As Toshikazu Oyama pointed out in an editorial
preface to the first volume (1974) the very idea of the
periodical was to give "all the people of the world" a direct
share in "making Shakespeare really global," even as Germany, a century before, had succeeded in making him truly
European. A case can be made for crediting Japanese
scholars of the caliber of Professor Oyama with having
assumed in the late twentieth century something very like
the responsibilities that German Shakespeare scholars had
assumed in the late nineteenth century, when they founded
their German Shakespeare Society in 1864 and inaugurated
publication of their prestigious *Shakespeare-Jahrbuch* (1865),
with which they succeeded in making England's great national poet first *unser* Shakespeare and then the Shakespeare
of all of Europe as well as of all the vast English-speaking
world.

Although he had an editorial board supporting him,
Professor Oyama worked virtually single-handedly to produce the first nine volumes of the series, with death over-
taking him in "the chrysanthemum season" of 1983, at the
age of sixty-five. He had already selected the articles to be
included in the tenth volume when he died, but other hands
had to see to its completion, providing tributes to his labors
by scholars of many lands.

The series received its first significant notice in a
major Shakespeare bibliographical survey in Vol. .59 of *The
Year's Work in English Studies, 1979,* where David Daniell
reviewed the first five issues and drew the conclusion that
"this entire series is already distinguished, and handsomely
produced; it is of great importance." The following year, in

their *ECCE Translator's Manual,* John J. Deeney and Simon
S. C. Chau noted that *Shakespeare Translation* is "the only
journal devoted to the discussion of the translation of
Shakespeare into other languages . . . with contributions
from all over the world."[3] *Shakespeare Quarterly* did not
review the series, but, as J. F. Andrews has pointed out,
"James McManaway was planning to do it at the time of his
death." Professor McManaway had encouraged the founding of the periodical and had called the editor's attention to
the ever-growing appropriateness of the lines of Cassius in
Julius Caesar (III. i. 111- 113):

> How many ages hence
> Shall this our lofty scene be acted o'er
> In states unborn and accents yet unknown![4]

It is fair to say that, while the series as a whole merits a
general assessment, as a contribution to global comparative literary studies, each issue has in fact been a book in its
own right, deserving a review of its own.[5]

1. The First Nine Volumes: Rapidly Expanding Horizons

Contributions from all over the world are indeed what we
find in Vol. 1 (1974) and Vol. 2 (1975), which clearly fulfil
the promise of Professor Oyama's report to the First World
Shakespeare Congress of 1971. In addition to the promised
surveys on the state of Shakespeare translation in Germany, India, France, and Japan, there are similarly-titled
surveys focused on Norway (Kristian Smidt), Korea (Jae-Nam
Kim), Spain (Estaban Pujals), the Soviet Union (Olga
Akhmanova and Velta Zadornova), Denmark (Thora Balslev
Blatt), and Greece (Panos Karagiorgos). There are articles
also on special problems of Shakespeare translation into
German (Wolfgang Riehle), on rendering the "double-
damned" Desdemona scene of *Othello* and the storm scene
of King Lear in the Hindi, Bengali, Gujarati, Marathi, and
Oriya vernaculars of India (Jagannath Chakrvorty), and
Hamlet's soliloquies into Spanish (Adele Alfonso Fast).
Besides these, there is also what has been called a "valuable
general essay" on "Some Problems of Shakespeare Translation" by the distinguished Finnish Shakespeare scholar H.
W. Donner.

A special preface to Vol. 3 (1976) reminds us that the
international Shakespeare Association projected at the

World Shakespeare Congress of 1971 had indeed been formed and had held its first Congress in 1976 in Washington D.C., as part of which there had been a Seminar on "Shakespeare in Translation," chaired by Werner Habicht (University of Bonn). In his special preface, Toshikazu Oyama thanks Professor Habicht for kindly permitting *Shakespeare Translation* "to include his chairman's report together with five articles in this volume which are based on and revised from papers prepared for the Washington seminar."

Professor Habicht's report on the 1976 seminar begins with a review of the purposes of *Shakespeare Translation* and of the contents of Vol. 1 and 2 and then provides an integrative overview of the substance of the 1976 seminar articles published in Vol. 3, together with a summary of the open-discussion that followed presentation of the seminar papers. The volume offers further explorations of problems of translation in the Scandinavian and Indian languages, as well as German and Polish, and a particularly interesting brief article by the nativeIsraeli Shakespeare scholar Avraham Oz, who was in 1976 completing a translation of *King Lear*, and whose translations of *The Merchant of Venice*, *As You Like It*, *Coriolanus*, and *Romeo and Juliet* had all already been staged by major Israeli theater companies. Titled "Divine Accidents Invoked: The Case of 'Bad' Puns in Translation," Avraham Oz's article begins with an observation that the sort of translation difficulty it discusses belongs to a category of "technical trivialities ... regularly confined to derogatory or condescending footnotes in more serious studies." To illustrate the difficulty, he singles out Romeo's punning on Mercutio's observation that "dreamers often lie" and the "persistent use of 'gentle' as a quibble on 'gentile' in *The Merchant of Venice*," contrasting how such puns are handled-when they are not altogether set aside-in German, Italian, French, Spanish, Portuguese, and Hebrew translations. By the time he gets to a discussion of his own approach to the difficulty 'in Hebrew, particularly with the gentle-gentile wordplay 'in *The Merchant*, the reader is apt to be fully satisfied with Professor Oz's conclusion that there can be no prescribing rules for "modifying the pun" in translation, as also with his hope that his brief essay "may serve as a starting point for a fruitful discussion of this usually neglected topic."

Toshikazu Oyama's special preface to Vol. 4 (1977) reports with regret that Hans W. Gabler, one of the five members of the original editorial board, had resigned; but it is also pleased to announce that Werner Habicht, whose report on the translation seminar presented at the 1976 ISA Congress had been published in Vol. 3, and the distinguished English Shakespearean Terence J. B. Spenser of the University of Birmingham, had joined the board. To the articles on the state of Shakespeare translation in Germany, Japan, India, the Scandinavian countries, Korea, Spain, the USSR, Poland, France, Greece, Israel, and several Arabic countries which had appeared in the first three volumes, the fourth volume added articles on "Translating Shakespeare's Sonnets into Romanian" (A. I. Deleanu), "Shakespeare in Portugal" (F. de Mello Moser), and "Translating the Classical Allusions in *Hamlet* into Chinese" (Simon S. C. Chau). Other articles discuss "A New German Shakespeare Translator: Wolfgang Swaczyma" (V. Shulz), "Greek Translations of Shakespeare's Plays" (P. Karagiorgos), the " 'To be or not to be' Soliloquy in Japan" (Hisae Niki), and, of a more general character, "A Translator's Dilemma" (Toshiko Oyama) and "The Philology of Translation" (O. Akhmanova and V. Zadornova)—the latter dwelling on the importance for Shakespeare translation of preparing new concordances, with the help of electronic computers that will approach Shakespeare's words as *global semantic units*, stressing his use of them to hold together the infinite variety of his poetic world.

Vol. 5 (1978) shocks us in its special preface with the news that both Toshiko Oyama and T. J. B. Spenser had died earlier that year. In her obituary notices, Hisae Niki observes that Mrs. Oyama was "one of the few Japanese women with an international standing," and that Professor Spenser, over and beyond his towering achievements as a Shakespeare scholar, bad charmed everyone during his visits to Japan "with his warmth and his lively sense of humour," while selflessly taking much time to give us "valued advice about *This Journal.* " Taking their places on the editorial board are Angela Mirenda (Virginia Polytechnic Institute) and the distinguished M. C. Bradbrook of Cambridge University, with whom many editors and contributors to *Shakespeare Translation* had studied. Vol. 5 adds Italian, Hungarian, and Hindi (India's official national language) to the list of "target-languages" surveyed, with articles on "Translating Shakespeare: An Italian View" (G. Melchiori), "Shakespeare's Sonnets in Hungary" (K. E. Kiss), and "Hindi Translations of Shakespeare. A Historical Survey" (11. K. Trivedi). The same issue offers an examination of six German versions of *Hamlet*, III, iv. 1-32 (R. Stamm), a review of recent Japanese Shakespeare translations and stage productions (Kazuko Hasebe), and what David Daniell has called a "charming essay" on the "problem of getting quotations across in another language" by the Soviet Shakespearean scholars Akmanova and Zadornova, with which they have apparently established themselves as regular contributors.

In Vol. 6 (1979), Milan Lukes's "Translator's Choice" adds Czech to the list of target-languages. Yoshiko Kawachi, destined to succeed Professor Oyama as chairman of the editorial board, makes her initial appearance as a contributor with an extensive bibliography of Japanese translations of Shakespeare, while Hisae Niki provides a very readable translation of the script for Akika Kurosawa's world famous film *Kumonosujo: A Japanese Macbeth.* Completing the volume are articles on "Rota's Greek Translation of *Hamlet*" (P. Karagiorgos), on "Fifty-odd Translations [in some 17 languages!] of Shakespeare's *As You Like It*. v. 1 " (C. Wittlin), and on "Translating Shakespeare in the Real World" (G. Boklund) — by which is meant "translating him for publication."

In Vol. 7 (1980), Finnish and Ukranian translations are examined 'in articles by M. Rissanen and W. T. Zyla. T. Anzai offers "personal reflections" on "Adapting *Much Ado* to Japan," while G. Bantock, who acknowledges that he "cannot understand the Japanese language," tries to make a case for university Shakespeare productions in Japan by a "professional

Shakespeare Theatre Company, consisting of Japanese actors and actresses performing exclusively in English," or perhaps in mixed English and Japanese. The volume also contains articles by Akhimanova and Zadornova ("Verbal and Non-Verbal Equivalence in Shakespeare Translation"), Yoshiko Kawachi ("Shake-speare and the Modem Writers-in Japan — Translation and Interpretation by Shoyo, Ogai and Soseki"), and Toshikazu Oyama ("Shakespeare's Thematic Characterization. An Essay by a Shakespearean

Translator"). The two Soviet Shakespeare scholars examine several Russian translations to stress the consequences of failing to distinguish adequately between the non-verbal or truly poetic meanings and the verbal or non-poetic meanings that can be read into Shakespeare's lines. Ms. Kawachi's study of Shakespeare's influence on Shoyo

Tsubouchi (1859-1935), Ogai Mori (1362-1922), and Soseki Natsume (1867-1916) — all three famous enough to be known by their first names — stresses how each made more or less direct use of Shakespeare in his efforts to "modernize Japanese literature." Although he was the first to supply a complete translation of Shakespeare's works, Shoyo, unlike Ogai and Soseki, never went to the West to study. Ogai spent much time as a youth in Germany, and Soseki, at a more advanced age, studied in England, where, in time, he made many literary friends, micluding the Shakespeare editor and critic William James Craig whom he later celebrated in a brief essay which has been called a "masterpiece of portraiture." Soseki eventually succeeded to Lafcadio Hearn's post at Tokyo University (Hearn had taken up Japanese citizenship and the name Yakumo Koizumi), starting his service with lectures on *King Lear* which proved to be "so popular among the students that the largest hall was nearly bursting with the audience." His subsequent lectures on the major plays established his reputation as a close interpreter of texts and an independent critic.

Professor Oyama's article in Vol. 7 anticipates what he says in that volume's special preface would be the kind of change of editorial emphasis he planned to introduce with Vol. 8, which was already in preparation. As Oyama explained it:

> Since the first publication of *Shakespeare Translation*, our editorial principle has always been to cover "the various fields of Shakespeare translation: theory and principle, practice and methodology of Shakespeare translation, historical survey of and research into Shakespeare translation." The present issue also follows the basic principle and includes as many articles as possible from every corner of the world. From the next issue, however, we would like to give a little more variety to the contents of our periodical, to enlarge the scope of our fields and to present the problems of Shakespeare translation in terms of general Shakespeare criticism, thus

hoping to contribute more to the whole trend of Shakespeare criticism.

In his contribution to Vol. 7, Oyama in fact goes far beyond the concerns of translation in the usual sense. Although he subtitles it "An Essay by a Shakespearean Translator," he makes virtually no use at all of the term *translation* or any of its cognates in the body of the essay. The author traces the development of Shakespeare's thematic characterization from *Richard III*, "a great work from his younger days," through three of the major tragedies, *Othello, King Lear,* and *Macbeth,* and into *The Tempest,* "a great work of his last days"; and the concern throughout is with words or expressions that serve at once to "personalize and depersonalize" the characters of a play. Oyama's point is that, while, on the one hand, "almost all the characters" in a play may be made to "repeat the same or slightly varied thematic key words, images and expressions in seemingly irrelevant ways" — thereby depersonalizing them — Shakespeare, on the other hand, makes it all occur in "the enchanted place" of his great stage, which "changes everything, making depersonalized characters more personalized, and thematic characterization more realistic." In *Richard III*, the recurring theme words include *scoff, taunt, bait, scorn, dally, flout, disdain*; in Othello they are *monster* and *monstrous*; in *Lear* it is Cordelia's early *nothing* that haunts all subsequent characterizations; in *Macbeth* it is the opposed terms *fair* and *foul, ill* and *good,* and *but nothing is but what is not*; while in *The Tempest,* it is the word *brave* that links Caliban with Miranda in characterizing the play's world as a whole. Professor Oyama leaves it for us to surmise what that sort of analysis had come to mean for him as a translator.

A preface to Vol. 8 (1981) recalls that, since 1971, when publication of *Shakespeare Translation* was first projected at the Vancouver World Shakespeare Congress, the International Shakespeare Association, also first conceived at that time, had already held its own "First" and "Second" world Shakespeare congresses, in Washington D.C. (1976) and Stratford- on-Avon (1981). Shakespeare translation papers delivered at the first had been published in Vol. 3 (1976); now, many of the papers delivered at the second were being presented in Vol. 8, introduced with a report by Yoshiko Kawachi, describing the event. Kawachi notes that the seminar on "Double Translation: To Language, To Stage" had had, in all, "fourteen participants from twelve countries: Norway, West Germany, Switzerland, England, France, Italy, Spain, Portugal, Brazil, India, Japan, and the United States," with Professor Kristian Smidt of Oslo serving as chairman. The seminar papers published include "Shakespeare in Norwegian" (K. Smidt), "Shakespeare Translation in Brazil" (B. H. C. de Mendonca), "Producing and Translating Shakespeare in Switzerland" (R. Stamm), "The Stage Translation of Shakespeare in Japan" (Y. Kawachl)" "The Ideal Stage Translation: A Portuguese View" (F. De Mello Moser), "Cultural Gaps in Japanese Shakespeare Translation" (H. Niki), "Translating Theatre" (L. Squarzina) and "The Function of a Complex Variable: Shakespeare at Stratford" (Muriel C. Bradbrook). The last two papers named stress the fact that the "specific action" of staging a Shakespeare play effectively, whether starting from an "original" or a "translation" text, is "absolutely not just a case of a literary understanding" (Squarzina), since, regardless of the literal text, the "natural instability of verbal structures is compounded by the cultural instabilities of all other languages that make up the functioning of that complex variable, the playin-performance" (Bradbrook).

There are, in addition, two articles on translating Shakespeare into Japanese, one by Soji Iwasaki, stressing the importance of symbolic design, the other by the very popular professor of English literature at Sophia University, Father Peter Milward, arguing that the goal of translating Shakespeare for Japanese students of English literature had best remain that of a "half-way house," facilitating their eventual mastery of the English text, since it is obvious, in his view, that "no translation is possible from the English of Shakespeare, particularly its more poetical passages, to any form of Japanese words." W. Nicholas Knight adds an article insisting that translators of Shakespeare into whatever language would do well to consult the law dictionaries of those languages to be sure they have got the native equivalents of Shakespeare's law terms right before venturing to use them. And there is, finally, an interview with a Tsuneari Fukuda, a well-known Japanese critic, dramatist, director, and translator, on "Translating Shakespeare for the Japanese Stage," which is published in

Japanese and "is not translated into English because," as Professor Oyama quite unconvincingly explains, "the topics of conversation are much more familiar to the Japanese" (though a brief introductory outline is indeed "given in English for the convenience of the reader").

Vol. 9, scheduled for 1982, appeared instead in 1983. As he says in this volume's preface, Professor Oyama had "been through a year of horrible illness," half the time in hospital, the other half away from "routine work for rehabilitation." But he hastens to add that "after the long gap of the horrendous ordeal" he is back at his desk looking forward to "our next issue . . . Vol. 10, which means ten years have already passed since the first publication of our periodical." Already in the planning stage, that volume, he concludes, is to be "a commemorative issue which will mark again the beginning of a new period for Shakespeare Translation."

Volume 9 contains articles on the "Ideal Translation" of Shakespeare for theater-use, by K. Smidt, on translating Shakespeare's literary use of plant names into Swedish, by Mats Rydén, on some further difficulties of the Japanese language for Shakespeare translation, by James Hisao Kodama, a sample script in English of a Noh version of *Hamlet,* by Kuniyoshi Munakata, and an extensive classified bibliography of "Books and Articles on Shakespeare Published in the People's Republic of China," by Chen Xionshang, largely limited to the years 1978-1981, in the introduction to which we read: "The All-China Shakespeare Society is going to be founded in 1983 so as to coordinate various local academic and theatrical efforts"; and also: "China and Japan share a similar time-honoured cultural tradition. Apart from extensive collaboration between our two nations in various other fields, I believe, as Orientals, Chinese and Japanese Shakespearean scholars will strengthen their friendly ties and combine to contribute more fruitfully to the world's Shakespeare industry."

But by far the most valuable contribution to Vol. 9 (1983) is "The Category of 'Personalization/Depersonalization' and the Translation Text," by Olga Akhmanova and Velta Zadornova. It is clearly written in response to Professor Oyama's *tour de force* on Shakespeare's thematic characterization published in Vol. 7; and it must have been highly gratifying to him to read the judgment of the two Soviet specialists in what might be called Shakespearean philology to the effect that Oyama's findings "are of the greatest significance as an important contribution to our studies in the field of verbal polyphony." Defining the scope of their comparative analysis, the two Soviet specialists write:

> Professor Oyama's article opens new vistas in the study of verbal polyphony. By examining the words "monster/monstrous" (*Othello*), "nothing" (*King Lear*), "brave" (*The Tempest*), and some others T. Oyama has shown how the semantic-stylistic "capacity" of a word is gradually revealed as the action develops. When used by different characters the word acquires "personalized" connotations and shades of meaning. When finally "depersonalized" it becomes the "leitmotif" of the "symphony" as a whole.
>
> Shakespeare wrote for the audience of the Globe, but now he is read and performed in many languages in every corner of the world. It remains to be seen how far Professor Oyama's theory of thematic characterization is revealed in the practice of Shakespearean translation.

The authors then examine what several major Russian translators have done with the words *brave, monster/monstrous* and *nothing*. Applying their "translation test" permits them to say that, "in some cases there are equivalents in the targetlanguage which without any conscious effort on the part of the translator can be regularly repeated to reproduce the original 'personalization/depersonalization' dialectics"; whereas in other cases complexities intervene: "The would-be Russian equivalent can be quite different both semantically and in terms of word-combination. "Still, "whatever the difficulties," they conclude, "the publication of Professor Oyama's seminal research is bound to alert translators to the new slant on the lexical-semantic composition of Shakespeare's plays."

2. Volumes Ten and Eleven: An End and A New Beginning

As already noted, Vol. 10 (1984) was the last issue of *Shakespeare Translation* prepared with Toshikazu Oyama as chairman of its editorial board. In addition to Yoshiko Kawachi's obituary notice, the volume includes prefatory tributes from Levi Fox, Director of the Shakespeare Birthplace Trust, Yoshiaki Fuhara, of Tsukuba University, S. Schoenbaum, Pre-president of the Shakespeare Associa-

tion of America, John Lawlor, Secretary General of the
International Association of University Professors of En-
glish, Kristian Smidt, of the University of Oslo, and Werner
Habicht, of Wurzburg University.

Professor Yoshiaki Fuhara observed that Oyama was
ever mindful "of the international community of
Shakespeare study," and that it was ever his hope "to bring
Shakespeare studies going on in many parts of the world,
including Japan, into still closer intercommunication "-to-
ward which end he played a "leading part . . . , his chief
editorship of *Shakespeare Translation* being a remarkable
aspect of it." John Lawlor noted that "Oyama was indeed a
tower of strength for English studies in Japan," and that the
"notable services which the Oyamas together gave to the
international study of Shakespeare were widely recognized
and applauded. . . ." But a truly fitting final tribute was
supplied by Professor Habicht, who wrote:

> Even in the German-language area, where for at least two
> centuries there has been no dearth of translations and of
> re-translations of Shakespearean drama, recent efforts at a
> systematic study of the problems involved owed consider-
> able impetus and encouragement to Professor Oyama's ini-
> tiative, by which, at the 1971 Shakespeare World Congress in
> Vancouver, he created a forum for a comparative study and
> discussion of translation problems and for re-channeling the
> results and possible solutions into the mainstream of criti-
> cism in English. The journal *Shakespeare Translation*, founded
> and edited in practical pursuance of these objectives, has
> indeed established itself not only as an important contribu-
> tion to Shakespeare studies but also as an excellent example
> of fruitful international and interlingual scholarly coopera-
> tion. May the continued existence and the efforts of this
> journal pay homage to Professor Toshikazu Oyama's memory.

Besides the introductory tributes, the tenth volume
includes a study by Janet Byron on problems of Albanian
Shakespeare translation, which brings to 26 the number of
national target- languages surveyed in the series, and articles on Schlegel's *Hamlet* (J. Wertheimer), two Portuguese
versions of *Hamlet* (B. H. C. de Mendonca), a new Chinese
version of *Measure for Measure* (Suo Tian Zhang), "Greek
Shake-speareana" (P. Karagiorgos), "Shakespeare in the
[Japanese] Classroom" (J. Matoba), and an assessment of
Terence Knapp's contributions to "Shakespeare Produc-

tion" as also, more generally, to "Shingeki (i.e. nontraditional theatre) in Japan,"' by S. Agnes Fleck.

With that, we turn to the eleventh volume, which is the first under the new title: *Shakespeare Worldwide: Tranlation and Adaptation.* The new editor's "Announcement," explaining the change of title, was cited earlier. The "editorial preface" of the founder, included in all issues under the original title, is reproduced here, and it is followed by a special "Preface to Vol. XI," provided by Professor Kawachi. The change in title, and the new format adopted, she explains, have had as their aim to extend "the coverage" offered. "In addition to our regular features about problems of translations," she writes, "we will discuss more thoroughly the contemporary stage adaptations, film adaptations, the ontology of play-texts and other pertinent topics." That the expanded coverage is designed to serve the broadest purposes of comparative literary studies on a global scale is made clear in her elaborating remarks:

> Part of the task of translators is to solve the problems posed by the differences in languages and cultures. If translations and adaptations are to become sources of information, their techniques must be analyzed and clarified. The study of translations and adaptations will help the development of new theories, new interpretations, and new criticisms. I believe "this little book" will be useful to that purpose.
>
> This volume is a special edition devoted to *Hamlet.* Readers will learn how this great tragedy, the so-called Mona Lisa of literature, was translated and staged in different countries. They will find the various - reflections of the reflection" mirrored through the different languages and cultures. [vii-viii)

In addition to seven articles on *Hamlet,* Vol. 10 includes "Shakespeare in Iceland," by Helgi Half-danarson, and a bibliographical listing, "Shakespeare in China 1992-1983," by Liu Houling. Houling's list is a miscellany of books, journal articles, and reviews, including translations and reviews of translations as well as editions and critical writings. It supplements the list by Chen Xiongshang in the ninth volume.

A new feature introduced by the new editor — a section "devoted to inquiries" and "open to free and impartial discussion," as Professor Kawachi writes, encouraging readers "to ask questions and to respond to, questions posed by readers" — is illustrated in Marvin Rosenberg's brief contribution, "Three Problems in *Hamlet*." [73-75] Although the problems have been much discussed by students of the textthe meaning of "fishmonger," "nunnery," and "country matters," as used by *Hamlet* — Rosenberg directs his inquiry to translators, asking how they have approached the "ambiguous meanings" in their languages.

In "Shakespeare Translation and Communication Across Cultures" by the familiar contributors from the Soviet Union Olga Akhmanova and Velta Zadornova, we are offered an examination of how translators in ten European languagesGerman, Swedish, French, Spanish, Italian, Russian, Polish, Czech, Serbo-Croat and Bulgarian — have in fact dealt with the difficulties presented by Hamlet's soliloquy (I. ii) "O that this too too solid flesh would melt." According to a "methodology" elaborated elsewhere, the authors first define what they call the poetic-semantic "fulcrums" of the soliloquy—"1) the destruction of the flesh and the impossibility of suicide; 2) the vileness of the world; 3) praise of Hamlet's father, also as a loving husband; 4) the wantonness of womankind, with special reference to Hamlet's mother" — and then they mark off the intervening "interludes," both of which, fulcrums and interludes, are to guide them in their analyses of the translations. Next, they proceed to "reduce" the many translations in several individual languages to a "single text," and then do the same with respect to translations in the "cognate languages" of the Germanic, Romance, and Slavic "families." Outlining the actual steps of their "philological approach" to "cross-cultural communication," they write:

> Contrastive analysis itself, both within one language and a group of languages, proceeds along the following lines. We begin by tracing the most significant *words* and *word-combinations* in the original and see how far they tally or "drift" apart. We cannot however reduce contrastive analysis to words only, without taking into account the "pivotal" *images* of the fulcrums. We should always bear in mind the dialectical unity and conflict of opposites: image and word.
>
> Although the division into several parts (or "fulcrums") is borne out by the "interludes," it is important to look at the text as a whole, to appreciate its "overall" cadence. Therefore the next step is to compare the phonotactics, *rhythm* and

prosody of the original and the translations, which in the case of poetic translation is of utmost importance. Attention to minutiae does not exclude interest in the general *lay-out* (style, manner of expression) of poetry in different languages. [88-89]

The actual "contrastive analysis," drawing on scores of translations, sets off the limits of what is possible and deepens one's understanding of the original text. The authors have indeed offered but a "glimpse of the enormous panorama of translation as cross-cultural communication," as they say at the close; but it is certainly a useful glimpse.

The articles on "*Hamlet* in Egypt" (Fatma Moussa-Mahmoud and Samir Awad), "*Hamlet* in Tamil" (Parasurama Ramamoorthi), "*Hamlet* in Korea" (Joo-Iiyon Kim) and "Hamlet in Japanese Dress: Two Contemporary Japanese Versions of *Hamlet*" (Adrian J. Pinnington), as well as the previously cited "Shakespeare in Iceland," which does not focus on *Hamlet*, all contribute to a broadening of our perception of the diversity of responses to Shakespeare around the world. The Iceland article extends to 27 the number of national languages treated at some length in the series. There is also a long introductory article by Rudoph Stamm, titled "A Challenge for Translators," and subtitled: "The Theatrical Physiognomy of Shakespearean Tragedy: A Brief Introduction with Special Reference to *Hamlet*." [1-23]

As its title suggests, the article by Professor Stamm is not really about problems of translating Shakespeare. It is a "challenge" to translators in the measure that it stresses the difficulties presented to the critical imagination by the text of *Hamlet*. The distinguished old professor rightly concludes, without references to translators' tasks, that the "mirror passages, reported scenes, impulse words, gestic implications and word scenery" he has examined are all very important "as theatrical signals linking action or speech and setting; and that their study, in the case of a play" like *Hamlet*, "can lead to an understanding of its three- dimensional form, its rhythm and its meaning not attainable through a merely literary or purely theatrical approach." [21]

A. J. Pinnington's piece on the currently very popular translation of *Hamlet* by Yushi Odashima — which is part

of his "monumental single-handed translation of the com-
plete dramatic works" of Shakespeare — and on "Kunishi
Munakat's imaginative re-working of the play into a Noh
performance," takes as its point of departure the "purist"
comment of Peter Milward, in an earlier issue of *Shakespeare
Translation*, that "translation of Shakespeare's plays into
Japanese is altogether impossible." He understands
Milward's concern to urge students of English literature in
Japan to get beyond translations to the original, and his
preference, on that account, for translations which are
really literal cribs, as opposed to versions with literary
pretensions of their own that tempt students to believe they
have the "real" Shakespeare when they are in fact most
removed from him. [51-52]

Pinnington argues, against such "puritanism," that
every modern production of a Shakespeare play is really a
re-working of the original, as each serious edition of the
text, to start with, "incorporates a myriad of textual and
typographical decisions and alterations aimed at rendering
the text more comprehensible to the modern student."
Similarly each new production is a re-working of the text, as
well as of the "details of delivery, costume, and staging"
that make the play come alive as no mere reading of the text
can. Pinnington stresses the successful efforts of the two
very different contemporary Japanese treatments of *Hamlet*
to give the play Japanese vitality, and his conclusion, on the
strength of his study, is that "Hamlet, whether in 'hakama'
or in jeans, is alive and well in Japan today. [70]

The piece on *Hamlet* in Korea is very brief. Joo-Hyon
Kim acknowledges that he has not been able to "figure out
exactly when Shakespeare was introduced to Korea," but
his impression is that the name of Shakespeare first appeared in a magazine in 1906. Prose and verse translations
of *Hamlet* appeared in 1921 and 1923, but they were "mostly
translated from the Japanese." Translations from the original began to appear after 1950. *Hamlet* has been the most
popular of the plays. As to the difficulties confronted by
translators, the author singles out *nunnery* in "get thee to a
nunnery," and silence in "the rest is silence"; but he acknowledges that, in addition to "these translation cruxes,
even the rendering of commonplace words and phrases
often requires further academic reconsiderations." Korean
translations of Hamlet, he concludes with an upbeat, "are

by no means satisfactory yet, but gradual improvements will be made." [47-49]

Quite different is the burden that the Tamil translator, and Tamil readers of translations of *Hamlet*, particularly, must bear, because of the Tamil literary heritage. Professor Ramamoorthi, who had previously written about Indian translators in *Shakespeare Translation*, speaks of "95 years" of *Hamlet* translation in Tamil, only to conclude that there is "something in the Indian sensibility which is against tragedy," [43] and, more pointedly: "The Tamil tradition could never consider Hamlet as part of their heritage. . . . No Tamil would accept the remarriage of Gertrude to Claudius. . . . We could only hope for better translations of *Hamlet* with the changing social scene in Tamil society." [44]

"*Hamlet* in Egypt" reminds us that, with respect to Shakespeare translation, it is not possible to separate Egypt distinctly from the rest of the nations of the Arab-speaking lands. Often translators, producers, or acting companies presenting Shakespeare plays in Egypt, are from Lebanon, or Syria, or Palestine, or Kuwait. Still, it is possible, in the case of *Hamlet*, to compile considerable factual material on performances, many of Arab females in the hero's role, and translations, the more important of which, for the first part of the century, are identified as those of Khalil Mutran (1916, but repeatedly printed into the 1970s) and Sami al-Jeredini (1922). Surpassing these are the more recent versions by Jabra Ibrahim Jabra (1960/1970) and Abdel Qadir al-Qut (1971). The latter is, from a scholarly standpoint, a landmark edition, with the translator indicating the original texts used and reflecting the best English language scholarship in his critical introduction and notes. With two good translations in hand, says the author, we have now to await "a good stage production of the play in Arabic." [34-3 5]

In Halgi Halfdanarson's article on Shakespeare in Icelandic, the emphasis is on the advantages the language and literary tradition of the sparsely populated island (which has no dialect traditions), offers the translator. Professor Halfdanarson has first-hand experience, having completed translations of nearly all the plays, continuing a tradition that began in the last quarter of the nineteenth century. Speaking of the many "definite advantages" the language "offers the translator," the author does not hesitate to say:

> The overwhelming advantage is its enormous vocabulary, epecially in the fields of poetry, history, and popular philosophy. . . . The people of Iceland have managed to preserve their language so well that they . . . find it just as easy to read the works of Snorri Sturluson, a 13th century poet and famous writer of historical sagas, as those of the country's greatest living novelist, Nobel prizewinner Halldor Laxness. Icelandic translators therefore have ready access to a tremendous wealth of vocabulary and style, and hardly ever need to fear sounding archaic even though they delve way back through the centuries. A bad translation into Icelandic is not the fault of the language, but of the translator. [82-83]

As in the previous two volumes, where the practice began, the eleventh volume supplies an appendix with the tables of contents of all the preceding volumes. Useful indices of names of persons and of Shakespeare's works cited had been introduced in Vol. 3 (with retrospective coverage of Vols. 1 & 2). Besides all of that, each volume identifies most of its contributors in some detail, with photographs.

3. Conclusion: A Caveat and a Modest Proposal

We mentioned earlier the one unfortunate consequence of the founding of *Shakespeare Translation*: its existence has in fact tempted editors of the proceedings of major Shakespeare congresses to virtually ignore all papers having to do with translation. One searches in vain through the published proceedings of the International Shakespeare Association congresses of 1976 and 1981, for instance, for so much as a passing notice that papers on Shakespeare translation delivered at them have had the distinction of being published in a separate journal. This rather detailed review of the contents of the ten volumes of *Shakespeare Translation* edited by Professor Oyama, and of the first volume of *Shakespeare Worldwide*, edited by Yoshiko Kawachi, is a form of compensation.

But what is really required is for the major Englishspeaking countries that treasure Shakespeare to start to sustain continued publication and wider dissemination of that specialized journal — which owed its origin to modern Japan's deeply felt appreciation of the influence of Shakespeare's genius on its own current creative and scholarly literary development. (A sense of the extent of that appreciation is the theme of the introductory essay of the *Japan* volume of the *Review of National Literatures* series.[6]) On another level, the Folger Shakespeare Library in Washington D.C. might do all Shakespearean scholars and comparatists generally a great service by establishing a Shake-speare-Translation room or section, not merely to shelve copies of translations from around the world, but also to serve as a research center for translators and scholars concerned with Shakespeare's global reputation and influence. The global approach to Shakespeare in the great multiplicity of the modern world's languages — established, neglected, and emergent[7] — can serve as a model, or even as a pilot program, for efforts to expand the horizons of comparative literary study by well-defined and manageable means. A select few of the many scholars and translators in many lands engaged in "cross-cultural" labors related to Shakespeare might be invited to join such a Folger-based translation center as "fellows" each year, helping to keep its holdings up-to-date and facilitating scholarly access to them. And the room might fittingly be called the Toshikazu Oyama Shakespeare Translation Memorial Library.

NOTES

1. James G. McManaway and Jeanne Addison Roberts, eds., *A Selective Bibliography of Shakespeare*, published for The Folger 'Shakespeare Library by the University Press of Virginia, Charlottesville, 1975, pp. v, 56-57.

2. Clifford Leech and J. M. R. Margeson, eds., *Shakespeare 1971: Proceedings of The World Shakespeare Congress, Vancouver, August 1971* (Toronto: University of Toronto Press, 1972), pp. 276, 278-279.

3. John J. Deeney and Simon S. C. Chau, eds., *ECCE Translator's Manual: An Annotated Bibliographical Handbook on English-Chinese Translation With Documentation and Organization Information* (Hong Kong: The Chinese University of Hong Kong, 1980), p. 202.

4. J. F. Andrews cited Professor McManaway's desire to give the series a review in *Shakespeare Quarterly* in a personal letter to the authors of this article. McManaway's letter encouraging publication of *Shakespeare Translation* appeared in Vol. 1. (See below in

text.)

5. The series was given due praise also in Anne Paolucci's "Shakespeare as a World Figure: Translation and Performance Around the World," in *William Shakespeare: His World * His Work * His Influence*, 3 Vols., J. F. Andrews, ed. (New York. Charles Scribner's Sons, 19-85), 111, 633-680.

6. John Gillespie, Sp. Ed., *Japan*, Vol. 16 *Review of National Literatures* (New York, Griffon House Publications for Council on National Literatures, 1989).

7. As part of the 1981 Shakespeare Summerfest in New York City, a series of bilingual "mini-readings/productions" were prepared, under the general title "Shakespeare and the World," with actors and scholars participating. Each presentation (on Saturdays, at the American Museum of Natural History, where the entire project was housed and continued for several weeks, from May through September of that year) featured a different national group and culture (Spanish, Italian, Russian, Japanese, German, Greek, Afro-American, French, Turkish, Yiddish, Armenian — the last three not yet represented in the roster of national languages placed in focus by *Shakespeare Translation*. (For a treatment of Shakespeare's impact on modern Armenian literature, see A. Paolucci, "Armenia's Literary Heritage: National Focus and Universal Receptiveness," *Armenia*, Vol 13 *Review of National Literatures* [New York: Griffon House Publications for Council on National Literatures, 1984], pp. 15-27.) In each of the "mini-productions" of the 1981 Shakespeare Surnmerfest, an introductory statement was followed by a variety of presentations, some with German and Italian arias inspired by Shakespeare, some with samplings from the target-language worked into the presentation, some with two sets of actors, and in the case of the AfroAmerican presentation, a "mini-production" (much compressed) of *Othello*. ["Shakespeare and the World" was prepared for Shakespeare Summerfest by Anne Paolucci, who served as its Director and also as one of the Assistant Directors of the parent project.]

Yugoslav Dialogues

The spider [boasts] of his native stock and great genius;
that he spins and spits wholly from him self . . . by feeding
on the insects and vermin of the age. As for us . . . we are
content, with the bee, to pretend to nothing of our own,
beyond our wings and our voice, that is to say, our flights
and our language. For the rest, whatever we have got, has
been by infinite labor and search, and ranging through
every corner of nature; the difference is, that, instead of
[the spider's] dirt and poison, we have rather chosen to
fill our hives with honey and wax, thus furnishing man-
kind with the two noblest of things, which are sweetness
and light."

Jonathan Swift, The Battle of the Books.

*Yugoslavia is today, by constitutional definition, what the United
States of America claimed to be at least until the Union victory in
the Civil War: a sovereign union of sovereign states. The Yugoslav
union consists of six independent republics and two autonomous
regions. It includes several national stocks and, even where
language is virtually the same, diverse national literary traditions. There is political unity, grudgingly accepted by some,
profoundly felt by others; and rich cultural diversity, ardently
cherished by all. The tension of "the one" and "the many" is
therefore strong for the political and cultural leaders of contem-*

porary Yugoslavia.

    To get a sense of that tension first hand, the editor of RNL *and its co-ordinator toured Yugoslavia in the days when this special issue was being conceived. They visited the six independent republics and two autonomous regions as well as the seat of the federal union in Belgrade, questioning scores of government officials, scholars, critics, and creative writers. Stressed throughout the visit was the fact that, while the difficulties of treating Yugoslavia's multi-national literature as a unit, in a single issue of our periodical, were great, in the end there would be a single issue – not six or eight issues – on the subject.*

    The following pages offer extracts of a journal of that visit – edited to isolate conversations and, as far as possible, dialogues that accurately represent the diversity of thought permeating Yugoslavia's literary milieu today. The journal entries were made daily, but from memory, so that there is nothing definitive about their syntax and diction; and it is probable that sayings ascribed to one person may in some instances have actually been said by another.

1. Belgrade

Monday, May 22. The Air France flight took us over Toulouse, Zurich, the Alps, and the Danube, visible far below us through openings in the clouds, to Belgrade.

    At the airport, our friend from the American Embassy, First Secretary for Cultural Affairs Edmund A. Bator, and his wife Martha, waved a greeting from an observation deck as we stepped out of the airport shuttle-bus, and then came down to meet us at Passport Control. Painters and plasterers were high up on scaffolds, smoking as they worked. Inspectors checked our papers perfunctorily, chatting among themselves with bureaucratic good humor.

    Beyond the control desk, the Bators introduced us to two women: Ljubica Lovric, Counselor in the Secretariat for Culture of the Republic of Serbia, and Danica Curcic, Counselor in the Federal Administration for International Scientific, Cultural, Educational and Technical Collaboration. As Anne Paolucci was the official guest, it was appropriate, no doubt, that lady officials be sent to receive her. While our bags were being placed in the Embassy car, they briefly reviewed with AP her month-long itinerary of visits to the six republics and two autonomous regions, no one of which could tolerably be slighted by an editor planning a special issue of *RNL* on Yugoslavia.

Protocol required that the Republic of Serbia, rather than the federal administration, be host for the first night. After lunch with the Bators at an outdoor suburban restaurant and a cocktail party at the home of Jerry James, Belgrade Representative of the Library of' Congress, we went as scheduled to the Hotel Metropole for dinner at eight. Puniga Pavlovic, Deputy Secretary of the Serbian Secretariat for Foreign Relations, was the host. The Yugoslav guests were Ljubica Lovric, whom we had already met; Milan Stambolic, editor of Nolit, one the oldest publishing houses of Belgrade; and Jovan Hristic, teacher, playwright, and critic.

Jovan Hristic talked in passing about his current play in repertory, about a woman and two men — her doctor and her husband. Before it is over, the woman dies, thus frustrating and yet resolving everything. HP noted that AP too had done a play about a woman and two men (performed off-Broadway in New York in 1971), all about death, but with no serious dying. As others crossed into the conversation, it was recalled that Martha Bator had played a part in AP's play when originally performed in Naples.

Hristic spoke appreciatively of Hegel. With sparkling eyes be cited a passage of the *Phenomenology*. The style, he hastened to add, was of course atrocious; but when we chided him for repeating that false platitude, he agreed that it was in fact the style of universal and permanent intelligibility. "In philosophy especially, writing that is facile for its own age often becomes hollow and stilted for every other." Italy's greatest modern philosopher, Giovanni Gentile, used to say that he learned how to write, as well as how to philosophize, from Hegel.

Hristic's eyes lit up again when we spoke of AP's study of Pirandello's *Liolà*. "It is Machiavelli's *Mandragola* modernized, " he said, before we had a chance to say it. We summed up AP's account of how Livy thoroughly Romanizes the story of the rape of Lucrece, how Machiavelli thoroughly de-Romanizes it to make it Italian, and how Pirandello makes it at once thoroughly Sicilian, modern, universal.

"I like Pirandello," said Hristic beaming, his mouth, eyes, and face all rounded. "How you want me — *come tu mi vuoi*, and . . . *se vi pare* — if you think so. That's the really new drama: when the woman tells how she tried to be what the mother wished her to be, but couldn't tell whether she was remembering or making it up!"

AP, we noted, had an Hegelian paper on the dissolution and multiple mirroring of 'personality' in modern drama, linking Shakespeare and Pirandello. George Herbert's words apply not less convincingly to Pirandello's Enrico IV than to Hamlet:

> O what a thing is man! how far from power,
> From settled peace and rest!
> He is some twenty several men at least
> Each several hour.

Pirandello writes, we agreed, as if he felt he had to do all over again what the original Greek dramatists had done to hold the complexity of character together. "He is a theatrical primitive." His characters are not finished products of the stage; they are not people masked with masks (*personae*) that give them unified identity, but rather the very masks themselves, suddenly unmasked, shown to be naked masks (*maschere nude*) masking nothing, but mirroring and re-mirroring the experience of unmasking.

"What makes it drama," Hristic said, "is not the content but the voice." We quickly asked if be knew Eliot's "Three Voices of Poetry.." He answered that be knew it well and had included it in his recent anthology of critical essays.

In generalized conversation, AP said she was looking for critics who could review the literary past of the South Slavs to indicate what the contemporary Yugoslavs have a right, even a duty, to cherish as a common heritage. Is the country's present unity merely a forced unity of political expediency? is there no vitally felt unity? Is there, from the past, no expressible sense of cultural oneness worth cherishing?

Hristic said there was, but that intellectuals, by and large, were reluctant to express it. "Not only here. Everywhere. In America too. The so-called cultured classes are either pretentiously cosmopolitan or abstractly individualist — which amounts to the same thing. Everybody's the same because everybody's different. But that's only the cultured classes. It's not so among the workers. " To illustrate, he told of a recent experience with cultural rootlessness and its popular antithesis:

"I was on one of our islands that used to be Italian, and I watched two Italian yachts sail into port. The owners, rowed in by their crews, came to have coffee on our hotel terrace. Their sailors were at the far end, having something too. Then, out of a little Fiat that drove up, came six or seven blue-collar Italian workers on a vacation, and they sat at a table near by. Before long the yacht owners started to talk "revolution," playfully singing *bandiera rossa* — the red flag — and toasting the glories of international communism. it was *aprés nous le déluge*. But something else, too. Everyone felt it. The Italian workers felt scandalized and denounced the millionaires. It was like black resentment of white radical-chic in your country, I suppose."

Communism, Hristic explained, seems to have a not-so-secret appeal to managerial-class capitalists these days. "Perhaps," he said provocatively, "that's because it knows bow to discipline workers, to make them work. The capitalist managers are obviously impressed; they'd like the support of such a force, at least till the deluge. And workers, I suppose, instinctively fear it, unless it comes with a patriotic appeal."

At the other end of the table, Milan Stambolic had surveyed the range of Nolit's publishing activities — titles, printings, percentage of translations, the number of non-Serbo-Croatian books, distribution. He reminded us that Yugoslavia had many more publishing houses than Americans, used to their big-distribution houses, are apt to expect. We reminded him of our many university presses.

After dinner, all except Ljubica Lovric returned to Edmund Bator's house to play, at Hristic's suggestion, "liar's dice," in which the most determined bluffer wins. The night ended with a chat about the "Black Africa" issue of *RNL*, where the editorial perspective was the opposite of what it would have to be for a Yugoslav issue—or so it seemed to one of our discussants. But soon enough a spokesman for "Black African" diversity rigorously challenged the very idea of "Black Africa."

Tuesday, May 23. Late in the morning, an Embassy car took us first to Edmund Bator's office and then to the Federal Administration for International Scientific, Cultural, Education and Technical Collaboration, for a meeting with its Deputy Director, Oto Deneš.

Dr. Deneš, attended by Danica Curcic (who had met us at the airport), sat us around a low table in the corner of his spacious office, which overlooks the junction of the Danube and Sava rivers. On the wall at our backs was a large map of Yugoslavia, with its six republics and portions of neighboring countries distinctly colored and outlined. On the wall opposite, over the Deputy Director General's desk, was a large portrait of Tito.

We were served — as we would be served again and again and again at such meetings — brandy, juice, and coffee. Behind dark glasses, which, because of a war injury, be must wear even indoors, Dr. Deneš joked pleasantly as be explained the function of his office, which was staffed "multi-nationally" with fixed "quotas" for the six republics and two autonomous regions. He stressed the multinational character of everything in Yugoslavia to anticipate (be said) the lesson we would learn in our crowded tour. AP remarked that her projected volume would of course respect the diversity while yet seeking to give it all at least an artistic organic unity.

Dr. Deneš pointed to the wall at our backs. "There's the map, showing what divides and what unites us. There are, as the textbooks say, three unifying forces or principles, which also divide. The mix is markedly different as you move from the northwest to the southeast; but everywhere Yugoslavia is a weave of the Mediterranean, Middle-European, and Slavic heritages."

"Venice, Vienna, Budapest," HP interjected. "But you have to add Istanbul, too!"

"Yes," said Deneš. "Yet there is a *Jugo*, a 'South' Slav core that holds it all together. Look here." He rose to point at the map: "We have seven neighbors — Austria, Hungary, Roumania on the north; Bulgaria on the east; Greece and Albania on the south and southwest; and Italy on the west. Our large cities gravitate toward the borders, toward foreign centers: Ljubljana, Zagreb, Belgrade, Skopje, Split, Rijeka."

"Even Titograd. Sarajevo is more central — though most Turkish."

"Moslem, not Turkish. We have three major religions: Orthodox, Catholic, Moslem; five literary languages: Slovenian, Serbian, Croatian, Macedonian, Albanian; Latin and Cyrillic alphabets; four major and several minor na-

tionalities; six republics: Slovenia, Croatia, Bosnia-Herze-
govina, Serbia, Macedonia, Montenegro; and two autonomous regions: Vojvodina and Kosovo-Metohija."

"What holds it all together — besides political force?"

"Political and economic motives are strong. Separation, for most of these parts, would mean not flourishing
independence but more or less repressive absorption by
one or another of our neighbors."

We suggested that Zagreb of the proud Croats, and
Belgrade of the expansive Serbs are, like ancient Athens
and Sparta, two foci of an ellipse, polarized to secure their
separate identities yet linked to sustain the unity of the
sweeping line traced around them. Who best celebrates a
common heritage for your rich variety? "Are there significant vectors in the past pointing toward a culturally unified
future for your Hungarians, Roumanians, Albanians, etc.,
as well as for your Slovenes, Croatians, Serbs, and
Macedonians?"

"Surely the literary work of our great romantic Vuk
Karadžic was genuinely Yugoslavian," Dr. Deneš said,
"rather than merely Serbian in scope. In Croatia, there
have been Ljudevit Gaj and Bishop Strossmayer." The
Deputy Director General reminded us, however, of the
current emphasis on cultural as well as economic and
administrative decentralization rather than centralization.
He pointed to the importance of identifying the cultural
characteristics of the components before looking to the
whole. "Each of our parts has grown, and is growing,
culturally in its distinctive way. They are in diverse stages of
growth. Serbia is the oldest, in cultural-ethnic terms;
Montenegro is the youngest, though some would say more
sophisticated. The Macedonians are in what we might call
the 'dictionary' stage. You will see for yourself when you
get to these centers. The diversity is very real. Decentralization is a real policy."

We noted that the height of centralizing efforts in a
federative system is usually reached when the central power
commits itself to "decentralization." In American history it
happened when Jefferson's states' rights party moved into
Washington and "federalized" states' rights. That kind of
thing always pulls the rug out from under the real
decentralizers. "That's the Belgrade tactic, isn't it?"

Dr. Deneš smiled behind his dark glasses. "In a

vacuum that might be so. But we are not in a vacuum. If foreign support is introduced, the scales can easily be tipped in favor of destructively factional decentralization. But we must move on. You are our guests today for lunch in the suburbs. We Yugoslavs, you know, have two custom-ary ways of killing visitors: by drowning them, with brandy, orange juice, and coffee; and by stuffing them with food. And here I am on the verge of introducing a third — I'm talking you to death." We protested that we treasured every word. . . .

By separate ways we went some 40 kilometers up the Danube to meet at the Vinogradi restaurant in Grocka. We drove with Edmond Bator; Martha would drive up with Richard Johnson, Deputy Chief of the Mission of the Ameri-can Embassy; our host Oto Deneš would come with the Director of the Administration for Development of Cul-tural Research (also President of the Cultural-Educational Council of Serbia), Stevan Majstorovic, Danica Curcic, and two officers from the U.S. affairs section at the Yugoslav Ministry of Foreign Affairs — Budimir Lonear and Risto Nikovski. A fourth car would bring up our friend Jovan Hristic and the poet-editor Ivan Lalic, to whom we bad been introduced in passing before dinner at the Metropole.

One of the Foreign Office officials, a large man who had lost a hand, was also an editor of *Kultura*, of which he showed us a back issue with an article by Herbert Marcuse and English summaries at the back. Late in the meal, in response to questions, AP explained the national orienta-tion of *RNL*. A discussion followed on the distinction between the deliberately cultivated cosmopolitanism of our time, with its smattering of superficialities and the genuine marks of universality in art. AP cited Rene Wellek's words, and Henri Peyre's and T. S. Eliot's. Genuine univer-sality is never deliberate; it results from writing honestly about what one knows thoroughly, rooted in real places. Hristic agreed and cited a proverb: "Art isn't something produced in the Pullman cars of an international express."

"Or in the international jets of the jet-setters—if you want to up-date it." The cosmopolitans in literature, writ-ing for international audiences, tend to feed culturally on themselves, someone observed, "like plants that hang in the air."

The editor of *Kultura* asked about the apparent

failure of America's so-called melting-pot. We noted that the original promise of American life did not require that its immigrant citizens reject their old-world heritages — on the contrary. George Washington projected a non-ethnic ideal for Americans when he said: "Citizens by birth or choice of a common country, that country has a right to concentrate your affections." We talked of the Blacks in the north, the tensions with the so- called white-ethnics in the cities, and, more recently, with the Jews, who dominate the teaching and administration of a New York City school system attended mostly by Black and Hispanic students. The elements of the American melting pot are falling back on their old backgrounds, it was observed, because the nation's ruling elite has abandoned itself to a rootless cosmopolitanism.

"It's like the deliberately cultivated internationalism of UNESCO, I suppose," said Oto Deneš. Its educational "aids" to developing countries are usually more of a hindrance than a help. The exemplary help of any one real country is much more serviceable.

The conversation took a pointedly political turn for a time and then evened off into anecdotes about plane travel, stealing souvenir ash trays, liar's dice, Turks, Serbs, commercial television, and heaven. . . .

Wednesday, May 24. After morning visits to the Yugoslav National Military-Historical Museum and the Modern Art Museum, we returned to Edmund Bator's office to meet with Ana Rasic who helps to administer the US/Yugoslavia Textbook Translation Program, which has produced some 100 books in editions ranging from 1,000 to 3,000 each.

The next stop was lunch with Sava Mrmak, at that time Director of Production for the new color TV Channel 2, as well as professor at the National Academy of Performing Arts. He had recently been to the U. S., was interested in American educational TV, and suggested that efforts be made to prepare AP's educational TV series (more than a score of half-hour interviews with editors of learned and literary journals, titled "Magazines in Focus") for showing in Yugoslavia.

Mr. Mrmak spoke in passing of the challenge of cultural life in Belgrade, with its rapid growth and even more rapid turnover of population. "After all, before the war it had 300,000 people; now it has swollen to 1,300,000. And most are essentially country people."

We noted that a developing people needs an intelligentsia that feels itself to be an essential part of the whole, like the head is for the body. The intelligentsia must be patient; it mustn't let itself lapse into sophisticated alienation. Mrmak concurred. He sensed, he said, a tendency toward such alienation among some of his advanced students at the academy, and it disturbed him. . . . Mrmak had recently done a 2-1/2 hour dramatization of *Crime and Punishment* for TV. His wife, who joined us halfway through the lunch, is a well known actress.

That night, we saw a comedy based on a serialized novel of the 1940s — a diary of a middle-class Madame Bovary-type wife whose soap-opera affairs and phantasies are for her the "gripping" reality upon which the unreal world events of that decade intrude from time to time, all viewed in retrospect. It was well done.

2. Novi Sad

Thursday, May 25. At 8:45, after breakfast, we set out by car, with Edmund Bator, for the principal city of the autonomous province of Vojvodina: Novi Sad. Just before crossing the Danube into the city we saw on a hilltop the old Austro-Hungarian fortress, Petrovaradin, built to ward off the Turks, now partially converted into a hotel — where we would spend the night.

In Novi Sad, our initial appointment was with Vukasin Drobac, Secretary of information, whose office was in a large modern public building. He met us in shirt sleeves, attended by Nicifor Teodorovic who hurriedly put on a jacket, and Jarmila Strubar, who was to serve as interpreter. Mr. Drobac looks like the American-Yugoslav actor Karl Malden; and that matter was discussed pleasantly over brandy, juice, and coffee. We arranged to meet for lunch at the Varadin Hotel. But first we would visit Novi Sad's cultural center and pride, the Matica Srpska Library and Publishing House.

The Matica Srpska's seat is an impressive Central-European style palazzo. We were received in a principal office by Dr. Bozidar Kovacek, Director of the library and professor of epic poetry at the University of Novi Sad; Miroslav Rankov, Deputy Director of the Matica Srpska

Publishing House; Bosko Petrovic, Secretary of the Matica Srpska and a leading writer of the region; and Aleksander Tisma, Editor of *Letopis*, a literary-cultural monthly, oldest of its kind in Serbia.

Our hosts led us at once into a gracious sitting room where (over brandy, juice, and coffee) AP was questioned about her cultural mission. She described the plan to issue an *RNL* volume on Yugoslavia. Then it was their turn to describe the Matica and define its mission, which they proceeded to do with great pride. In sum, it is a school, library, and publishing house, all under one roof.

The name Matica, we learned, means Queen Bee. A bee's hive or honeycomb is the Matica's emblem and appears on all its publications. It was founded in old Pest (since joined with neighboring Buda) in 1826. Its first corporate act was to assume responsibility for the continued publication of *Letopis*, which had been launched several years before by Konstantin Kaulici, a native of Novi Sad.

We asked whether there was any connection between the Queen Bee name of the institution and Jonathan Swift's fable of *The Battle of the Books*. Our hosts didn't know. We reminded them of the opposition of moderns and ancients, of spiders, who spit and spin out of themselves after feeding on the vermin of the age, and bees who go from flower to flower, filling their hives with gathered honey and wax, which provide sweetness and light.

AP suggested that, if researched, the idea might provide a point of departure for the Yugoslav issue. Our hosts brought out sample publications, and some old treasures of their bee-hive library. We noted the bee-hive emblem. Taking up AP's idea, someone observed that, while the Matica Srpska is the oldest "Queen Bee" of Yugoslavia, it is by no means the only one. There are "Queen Bees" in some of the other republics.

AP presented copies of the "Iran," "Black Africa," and "Hegel in Comparative Literature" issues of *RNL* to our hosts. One of them said he was an Hegelian, and our talk with him led from Hegel's aestbetics to a few words about the South-Slav sense of nationhood. He spoke of the 19th-century Illyrian movement that shaped the Serbian, Croatian, and Slovene literary languages; others spoke of the literary "founding fathers" of Yugoslav unity — from

Gundulic of Renaissance Dubrovnik ("Giovanni Gondola of Ragusa," we interjected smiling), through Bartel Kopitar and Karadžic and Gaj.

We mentioned Dante's *De Vulgari Eloquentia*, with its idea of an Italian language based on no one particular dialect, and pointed out the "imperial" artificiality of classical Latin, which reigned only superficially over the old Italic dialects, destined to survive it.

Hegel, it was noted, had explored very suggestively the nature of language as an expression of national character. His Russian disciple Belinsky was mentioned. The battle of the books — bees against spiders — is repeated, we agreed, whenever a national literary culture approaches maturity. Who is the true nationalist in 19th-century Russia, for instance? Is it the Slavophile, who clings blindly to Russian things, or the so-called Francophile, who insists that those who really want to give literary expression to the Russian spirit ought to do for their language and literature what the great French authors did for their language and literature?

"Exactly," someone answered. "It is one thing to imitate the thing and another to imitate the process. To imitate the originality of another, in the sense of process, is to be original oneself."

Attendants brought in several treasured manuscripts and incunabula for us to examine. Because of the wartime destruction of the national library at Belgrade, Novi Sad now had the largest collection of precious old books. . . .

That night our guide took us to the National Theater of Novi Sad for a folk play on peasant strengths and weaknesses, cunning, pathos, etc. — which included a long spoon-river-anthology sequence of monologues. It was fascinating, in its way. Afterward, we met the theater's Drama Director, Zoran Jovanovic, and a young woman completing her director's course at the Belgrade Theater Academy, whose doctoral thesis-production of Harold Pinter's *The Homecoming* would be staged at Novi Sad the following Monday. . . .

Friday, May 26. With our interpreter Jarmalar Stuhar, AP went for a morning visit to the Slovak publishing house Obzor and met with its chief editor and the literary critic Kimec. Reviewing the "main trends" in the Yugoslav literary tradition, Kimec briefly characterized the major authors who had most obviously contributed to at least the vision of a unified Yugoslav culture.

The next stop was the University, where Alexander Tisma, editor of the prestigious *Letopis*, awaited AP in the company of Dr. Aleksander Nejgebaurr, Head of the English Department at the University of Novi Sad. Of Russian origin, Dr. Nejgebauer speaks English (British) fluently. A question was raised about the kind of writing required for an issue of *RNL* on Yugoslavia addressed primarily to American and English-speaking scholars. "Obviously," he said, "it should not have the flavor of a specialized Slavic-studies magazine addressing itself to specialists in Slavic studies. I have admired the quality of your issues on *Iran* and *Black Africa*."

Dr. Nejgebauer named Bernard Johnson as one of the most competent English scholars in the field. He brought out a copy of *The Literary Review* (Winter, 1967-68, XI, 2), devoted to Yugoslavia, which offered an assortment of creative and critical writings. *Tri-Quarterly*'s issue on Eastern European literature was also at hand, as was an issue of the Croatian, *The Bridge*, in English.

AP had lunch with Dr. Nejgebauer at the Varadin Hotel (joined later by HP). Prodded, Nejgebauer spoke of aspects of Yugoslav literature that might profitably be explored for English-speaking comparatists. There is no doubt, be said, that the novels of Yugoslavia in the post-war period — whether focused on the pre-war decades, or the war itself, or on the "move to the city," or on national and social questions, or individual alienation — have a certain unity. A title for an article on the subject might well be, he went on, "The Novel and the Ethics of Survival." It would explore not only how the difficulties faced by Yugoslavs in every conceivable modern situation have been defined by the writers of novels, but also how some have been solved in the process. "At any rate," he specified, "such novels have been a source of inspiration in troubled times and have lit the way, through dark periods, toward solutions."

HP joined the luncheon dialogue, at this point. "So you think there is some literary sense of oneness emerging out of Tito's experiment with multinational political unity?" Dr. Nejgebauer answered that what had happened in Yugoslavia was "not an experiment." He leaned over the table, his eyes down. "What Tito did was no experiment. What was done was as deliberate, as direct and positive, as my sitting down to this meal to eat." His teeth peeked through his thin mouth as he smiled. "I am not eating experimentally but deliberately, just as I knew beforehand how I must eat if I am to eat. I have had no thought of avoiding poisons, of seeing or experimenting — as you say — to see whether eating this way or that will best serve my ends. I have sat down here to do precisely what I came to do and am doing. That is how it has been with Yugoslavia."

We returned to the theme of the novel and the ethics of survival. A battering necessity, be said, has forced the various nationalities to hang more and more together in order to survive, individually and collectively. "Expressing that need, our principal writers have sustained not only themselves, as human beings, but also a whole class of leaders and potential leaders."

We asked whether the "survival ethics" was really able to bridge the linguistic-nationality differences across the length and breadth of Yugoslavia. Dr. Nejgebauer responded by drawing on a large manila folder an outline of Yugoslavia, with a line running down the middle.

"From top to bottom," be said, "it is one continuous line of graduated, shaded differences of the same language. Within each distinguishable nation there are many shaded differences, as also across the borders separating the nations. But at any point along this central line, the dialects above and below are directly intelligible. Sometimes intelligibility has a great span, as through Serbia and Croatia; but there is always intelligibility, at least for a small span, around every point. The extremes, however, leaping from Slovenian to Macedonian, are not directly intelligible. That is why — for instance — in Macedonia, there is some dispute among the dictionary-makers and grammarians as to which dialect to make normative for the whole republic. Close to the Bulgarian border there is too great an identity of Macedonian with Bulgarian; at the other end the dialect is too close to Serbian. There are factions that prefer one to the other, for political as well as historical and cultural reasons. There are, of course, the Hungarian and Albanian minorities, which are not part of the main line of graded and shaded diversity."

"Does the ethics of survival," we asked, "extend

beyond your main line, to embrace the non-Slavic writers?"

"I think so," he answered.

We spoke of tragedy. AP summed up the Hegelian view, making applications to the theme of the ethics of survival. Dr. Nejgebauer said that he had a "theory" that great drama was possible only in collective societies. We suggested that the opposite would seem to have been the case historically, and that Hegel insisted that tragedy was possible only in periods of extreme individualism.

"Personality — the very possibility of *dramatic personae* — is absent in collective societies such as characterized the ancient East," said AP, "and there couldn't be any real tragedy in the Greek or Shakespearean sense. Hegel is emphatic on that point. The situation of Periclean Athens was Greece's height of individualism. So was the period in England from Spenser's birth to Shakespeare's death."

Nejgebauer rephrased his point. "Those were collective periods, because everyone at those times, in those places, shared the same social values."

"I suppose you would say," HP picked up, "that man was 'socialman' rather than 'alienated-man' in those days. That's Marx's concession to Hegel's ethics and politics, which he otherwise claims to have stood on its bead. But that is stretching the point — to characterize as 'collectivist' ages of such manifest individualism!"

We discussed the possibilities of social or public-mindedness that include rather than reject individualism. HP quickly reviewed, with literary applications, Walter Bagehot's idea of the "progress" of nations from forced unity, to felt unity, to a form of enforceable unity so deeply felt that the enforcing of it becomes, actually, self-forcing. Bagehot himself calls that last stage "government by discussion" and dwells on the fact that Shakespeare's England was a time, and place, of enforceable and felt national unity that bad flowered into government by discussion. That is the necessary milieu, not only for the emergence of tragic personality but also for comic self-assurance. "According to Hegel," AP said, "it is usually a moment of delicate balance. With time, either tragedy comes off the stage and is played out in real life, as in the case of Socrates — in which case society collapses in agony, conquered by foreigners or by self-division — or it learns to laugh at itself until the poetry of tragedy gives way to the prose of everyday life, where what counts is to muddle through, with a mixture of pathos and humor."

"That's what our ethics of survival is all about," Nejgebauer commented, smiling momentarily. "No. I would say that Yugoslavia has enforceable and felt unity and is approaching moderately the third stage, which you have distinguished as government by discussion." More humorously be added that be was developing still another theory about *Hamlet*. Hamlet and Claudius are very close.

Claudius was the old left, ready and eager to do what was needed to be done; Hamlet, in the same family, was the new left, alienated.

"A dropout," AP offered.

"Exactly," Nejgebauer   continued. "A dropout who doesn't see that anything worth doing can be done, but who has the same complaints. He cannot pretend to be on a path meaningful to him. But be is of the same family. The disoriented, yet forceful new left."

There is no censorship in Yugoslavia, he went on, except in the case of writings which are obviously subversive of the social order. Otherwise one is free to say and write what one pleases.

At the very moment that Dr. Nejgebauer said he had to leave, the desk attendant came to tell us that our driver had arrived with the car to take us back to Belgrade. As we went out together, we observed that Nejgebauer was the first distinctly Yugoslav "patriot" (as distinguished from Serbian, Macedonian, etc. patriots) we had so far talked to, one who actually held the view of Yugoslavia as a "commonwealth" or nation being formed as a state. He beamed in response that he had not always been such. He had been transformed, he said, by his visit to America. There he had sensed such a hostility to the things of Yugoslavia which he himself had tended to criticize that he reversed himself. He saw that he *was* those things that he criticized, and that he must defend and cherish them or be nothing himself.

We noted that, while Tito's political unity was holding, the most we could get out of some of the cultural leaders with whom we spoke was that there was a recognizable utility in the various nationalities hanging together; that separation would probably bring most of them into less favorable connections with other powers. He, we said, was the first one to *affirm* the cultural value of the enforceable, and now strongly felt unity achieved under Tito.

"I'm sure," he replied," that you will meet many others."

We parted and began the drive back to Belgrade. . .
.

Saturday, May 27. For the trip south to Priština, we had both a driver and a guide. Our itinerary included stops at the famous monasteries of Studenica and Sopocan — with an overnight stop at Sopocani — before visiting the chief city of the autonomous region of Kosovo-Metohija.

Our guide, Dušan Djokic, was a young painter (he showed us brochures of his two recent exhibits) and a student of architecture. He had been out of Yugoslavia only once, to Bulgaria. He had learned what he knew through books. On the way, he explained his theory of art. "Art for me is . . . that I must do what I must do. *Art pour l'art.*

"But you are also an architect. That can be quite utilitarian. . . ."

"Yes. My father was an architect. My grandfather, also. I too. But now I do drawings, paintings, engravings. Later, something else."

We spoke of the difference between the artificial and the fine in art, between the useful and the arresting. AP gave the example of the fork so beautifully made that it arrests the hungry man's eagerness to use it. Young Djoki stressed the importance of a creative breakdown of the traditional divisions between the arts — in response to an observation that some modern architects, pretending to emphasize "living space" as against arresting lines, have ended up, nevertheless, making buildings (like the Guggenheim Museum of Modern Art) which are really large pieces of sculpture.

"In modern sculpture," he said, "the reverse is true. The surface is no longer the important thing. It is the interior space that counts, that requires showing."

AP noted that the breakup of the body of sculpture, to get at the interior of what is *embodied* there, is really the work of painting. "Surely there are intermediate kinds of art forms; but that doesn't abolish the main distinctions, any more than the infinite gradations in the great chain of natural beings abolish the distinctions of the major species. The varieties strengthen the species, and it is so with the genres of art." Djokic agreed, adding that it works both ways—the strong genre, precisely because it is strong, over-laps the other genres.

"It is like the dialects, " AP added, "infinitely graded up and down the length of Yugoslavia, and Italy, and other countries."

We reached the monastery at Studenica. It was like the old stripped churches of Bologna and resembled in some ways St. Paul's Chapel at Columbia University. The Eastern Orthodox monks were at their daily chores. There is a fine crucifixion (pictured in the art books) and other things of interest.

We spent that night in Sopocani.

Sunday, May 28. It was a major religious holiday and the monastery church at Sopocani was crowded with the faith-ful. Communion cakes and wine were at hand; processions around the church, headed by an old bearded priest; much chanting, amidst the twitter of attentive birds, many of them perched on a ruined arch as a vantage point of good observation. We later examined the interior. Then on to the capital-city of Kosovo-Metohija. . . .

3. Pristina

We arrived at noon and went directly to our rooms at the Hotel Bozur. After lunch (prolonged through a heavy downpour), we walked through the distinctly Moslem city, the sounds and sights of which mounted in busyness as the sky cleared.

In the evening we met members of the Writers' Club in the hotel lobby, who escorted us to the basement enter-tainment room of the Club in an adjacent building. From there, our interpreter informed us, we would return to the hotel for dinner.

Our interpreter was Abdullah Karjadin, an Italo-phile. As a boy, he had spent much time with the Italian army in Yugoslavia and spoke rather fluent Italian. His English also had a trace of "army" usage about it. We had brandy, orange juice, and coffee in the company of the Secretary of the Club and its Cultural Director — Brahman Dedaj — and saw a TV newscast of President Nixon meeting with Soviet leaders in Moscow. Azem Shkreli, Director of the Theatre, joined us, and then we all went back to the hotel for supper.

The interpreter, who teaches English at the University, observed in passing that under Turkish domination the Albanians counted for nothing and that when the Turks were defeated, at much cost in blood to the Albanians, the new dominant people were about as bad. Another of our hosts put it this way: "For the Turks, we were slaves to be sold. Later, we were forbidden to write or speak our own language in public. There has been a rebirth, a *vita nuova*, since 1945. "

Monday, May 29. A scheduled visit to a newspaper publisher's establishment was by-passed because the place was under repair. Instead, we went directly to the book-publishing center — the Priština Publishing House. Fahredin Gunga, the Editor-in-Chief, is a thin, bony man with a patch on his cheek near his temple, a glassy, severe look in his eyes. He spoke slowly, almost through clenched teeth, with half-lidded eyes and furrowed brow, asking what he could do for us. AP spoke of the perspective of *RNL*. Kosovo-Albanian literature, he said, is part of Albanian literature. But surely, we said, it is also part of Yugoslav literature.

"Our literature," be said, "is one of the national literatures in Yugoslavia. "

"Are you saying you are just an important center for books and thoughts and feelings generated in Albania? Isn't there something distinctly Yugoslav about your own writings here?"

"There are over a million and a half Albanians in Yugoslavia. Why should we not publish on our own? But — why should we not rather," he said, "talk of *literary* matters?"

We stressed that *RNL*'s Yugoslav issue would have to treat the subject as a whole, dealing with Albanian literary matters as part of the Yugoslav experience, noticing perhaps how the Yugoslav arrangement enabled Albanian literary culture to flourish in Kosovo and how it differed from the situation in Albania. He agreed; but his concern — he insisted — was less with the "arrangements that make these things possible than with developing the possibilities, whatever the arrangements."

We then called on the President of the Writers' Club in his office. Our interpreter began to joke with him and that prompted us to observe that we could see, by his manner, that be was a natural leader-type — broad forehead, an almost axe-sharp nose, athlete's jaw, sharply cut mouth, slightly nasal speech, and clenched-fisted most of the time we spoke. He countered with a reading of our appearances.

We spoke of what might be said of the Albanian contribution in our Yugoslav issue. Perhaps the notion of a renaissance under the culturally pluralistic governance of the Yugoslav federal regime might be a good point of focus. Why not take up the "Queen Bee" emblem, already accepted by the Slav-nationalities? At first there was instinctive hesitation. AP explained the literary significance of the bee in Swift and Matthew Arnold. It might be an attractive gesture to accept the emblem!

We had lunch of local specialties, and then we were left to ourselves for the rest of the day and evening.

At a late supper, we recalled the principle of literary autonomy the editor of the Priština Publishing House had laid down for us: "Every nation of Yugoslavia has fought for, and therefore has been granted, the right to develop its nationality. The consequent literature of the Albanians in Yugoslavia is not inferior to that of the other regions."

That underscored for us the problem of our Yugoslav issue. It would have to point to the shaping of a national literature through the shaping of diverse national languages and a single national political consciousness. The boundaries within the Slavic tradition are the achievements of renaissance Dubrovnik at one end and the emerging national literary identity of Macedonia at the other: from Ivan Gundulic's epic *Osman*, in the literary tradition of Tasso and Ariosto, to the current work of Macedonian scholars to give their nation a distinctive language and grammar, the two extremes linked by the work of Kopitar for Slovenian, Karadžic and Gaj for Serbo-Croatian, Stross-mayer for Zagreb-centered South-Slav cultural unity, the Montenegrin Njegoš, the moderns Krleža and Andric, the whole maintained not only by Tito's politics but also by the "ethics of survival" Dr. Nejgebauer had spoken of — whicb links up with the literary and folk-epic tradition of the struggle against the Turks and with the Kosovo-Albanian post-war attitude.

4. Skopje

Tuesday, May 30. Our Priština Italophile-interpreter,

Abdullab Karjagdin, and the Director of the Cultural Commission, Brahman Dedaj, drove us to Macedonia's capital,
Skopje. After settling in at our hotel, we hurried off to meet
Cvetan Grozdanov, President of the Republic's Commission for Cultural Relations with Foreign Countries. He
introduced us to our gracious new guide, Alexandrina
Nonov. First we would have lunch in Nerezi, high on a hill,
overlooking Skopje, in a restaurant adjacent to the area's
most famous monastery church — St. Panteleimon — with its
"frescoes that you must see." From the hilltop we admired
a view of the city. "*Vedi nostra citta,*" we said, "*quanto ella
gira.* That's what Dante's guide says at the first sweeping
sight of the heavenly city."

"Ah," said our host, whose specialty — he told us —
was medieval art, "I have worked extensively on representations of the *cité celeste.*" He explained that the Psalms were
the inspiration of some of the finest representations. We
noted that St. Augustine had used the Psalm "By the Waters
of Babylon" as the basis for one of his most impressive
images of the opposition of the earthly and heavenly cities.
Our host said that there was much still to be said about the
theme of the *cité celeste* in the mosaics and frescoes of
Yugoslavia.

The meal was a banquet of some of the best cooking
we were to enjoy in our tour. It went on for at least two and
a half hours — witb the most pleasant kind of talk. At its end,
we learned that the monastery had already closed its doors
for the day.

"Too bad," said our host, "but never mind. Halfway
down this winding hill going back into the city, there is an
artist friend of mine you should meet. You'll enjoy that at
least as much as the monastery."

When we reached our destination — a lovely house
on one of the slopes near the city — our host went in to see
if his friend was home and not too busy for visitors. Both
emerged together, and the artist bobbled painfully toward
us to greet us. He bad spent some time in Italy and spoke
fluent Italian. His paintings were mostly abstract modern
icons — representations of geometric shapes rather than
human figures. One room was filled with small such icons
"made mostly for friends"; a second room had large pieces.
He explained that he made everytbing — backboards, frames,
moldings, mountings, etc.

We talked about the fresco restorations of St. Panteleimon. The painter grunted, indicating that we had done well not to bother with the church. "It is all ruined," he said. "All those restorers, so eager to clean things up! They mean well, no doubt, but they ruin everything. They don't know what being old means. On they come, in large groups, from everywhere — especially from American universities — and they scrub and clean and peel. But they don't understand that age isn't something superficial that accumulates on the surface and that you can peel off. I love old things," he went on. "But those people treat old treasures the way a modern beauty-parlor treats a vain old woman. She comes in old, and they work on her to peel it off and send her out looking young. But she is old, and what they really do is package her to look foolish. Like this can of processed fruit," be went on, picking up a can of fruit cocktail; "Here you are, the frescoes of St. Panteleimon, packaged and labelled. They should have left the oldness because, to take it away, they have been content to show us something unsubstantial, bare, altogether artificial."

We spoke of Henry Adams' similar view in *The Education*, where he contrasts the seductive fascination of "old" Rome with the artificial "grandeur" of restored Rome.

We spoke of much else, left late, outlining on the drive back a program for the next morning, with the understanding that we should leave Skopje after lunch for a three-hour drive to Ohrid, "pearl of Macedonia," on the lake of the same name.

Wednesday, May 31. The first morning stop was the Academy of Arts and Sciences, where we met its Vice-President, Professor H. Palenakovic. The Academy was in a handsome building, originally built and occupied by a rich Jewish family, long since appropriated to public use but still marked conspicuously with emblems of the faith of its builders. The Vice-President asked about our project. "Ah," he said, "a survey. Yes. Well, perhaps something on Macedonian folk art, *n'est pas?*" To the interpreter he said: "Whatever concrete thing they wish, you tell them we will be happy to do."

From there we went to a museum of modem art, and then we were driven to the Language Center, where we bad a most stimulating talk with the unpretentious people who had prepared the three-volume Macedonian dictionary (1961-66) and had, they said, millions of cards (word biographies) to serve them and other scholars in new enterprises.

We prodded our hosts — Blagojya Korubin, Todor Dimitrovski, Traiko Stamalov, Milica Koneska — to talk of their lexicographic labors, methods, achievements. The name of Samuel Johnson was introduced. AP noted how Johnson was the master Shakespearean of his day, well grounded in the King James version of the Bible, and saturated with the philosophic language of John Locke — all of which went into his witty dictionary, to shape English thought and style ever since. We spoke of the importance of Luther's translation of the Bible for the formation of the literary language of Germany; of Dante, Petrarch, Boccaccio for Italian; of the French rationalist philosophers for French. "But economic power and political power are important too." Florentine finance, we noted, certainly did much to make the language of Danta, Petrarch, and Boccaccio prevail throughout Italy, and the fleet that destroyed the Spanish Armada in 1588 certainly gave great authority to the language of the King James Bible and Shakespeare.

There was general agreement that the making of a national dictionary has to be a very open process. Someone noted the importance of tracing the relationship of the normative lexicon to particular dialects and the extent of that relationship, why one was preferred over another (even if the reasons are political rather than cultural).

What about the biographies of words and their meanings? the roots in folk-tradition, poets, prose writers, journalists, scientists, statesmen? We remarked that in the three articles on lexicography and language we had read in *The Macedonian Review*, this aspect was passed over. We had observed also that there was no illustrative introduction to the three-volume dictionary and no identification of sources for the prescribed usage.

One of our hosts explained at length that most of the entries were drawn from traditional usage, some from very current speech, some from written poetry, from prose, from scientific specialized sources. He said they almost regretted having compiled their dictionary as they had, without citing sources. We certainly would welcome an article on the subject — we said — describing what remained to be done, giving sample word-biographies and word histories: one, for instance, of a centrally important utilitarian word; another, of an emotionally charged literary word; another, of an abstract concept expressible in a single word; still another, of a typical scientific term. Such an article, with allusions to the practice of English, French, Italian, German, Russian, and other Yugoslav dictionary-makers, would be, we said, a work of permanent value.

Our hosts agreed. They had, they said, over a million cards of word-usage on file already and expected to have three million, before starting on a dictionary of the kind we were describing. The words, we suggested, should be submitted to poets, novelists, historians, scientists, etc., for *them* to choose examples of usage so that the result would be an analytical treasury of Macedonian culture. "Young people, creative writers, achievers, don't like this sort of work. But it can be the most permanent form for treasuring what is of real value."

There was general agreement on this too. We suggested that it is work truly worthy of a "Queen Bee." One cannot work at creative brilliance; one can only pray to the Muses and to Apollo. But to collect the best usage in one's language and pack it, with illustrations, into a great dictionary like the *O.E.D.* or the *American Century Encyclopedic Dictionary*, or the great French, Italian, German dictionaries — that can be done deliberately. Readers of *RNL*, we said, might smile to read that Macedonia now boasted of seventeen great novelists, ten masters of the epic, twenty great dramatists, etc.; but they would be truly impressed by an honest account of how, "with the busy-ness of bees, you have made a dictionary for this emerging, old literature."

We had lunch at the Writers' Club with the poet Bogomil Dzuzel (then Director of Poetry Evenings in Struga), the novelist Tome Momirovski, President of the local P.E.N. Club, and several other writers, critics, TV people, etc. We talked of playwrights — Pirandello, Arthur Miller, Albee, Pinter — and of the "three voices of poetry." Later, the discussion turned to A. C. Bradley's Shakespearean criticism and the Hegelian influence on his work.

AP observed that Hegel, like Aristotle, was able to write with great originality and profound insights about tragedy because be was a master not only of the art forms of Greek and Elizabethan tragedy, but also of the politics, of the social and family life, that made up so much of the content of tragedy. This led to a discussion, with continuing literary emphasis, of Yugoslav multinational politics and statecraft. The current issue of *The Macedonian Review*, someone observed, had a very interesting article on the sovereignty of the individual republics that make up the Yugoslav Federal Union. We had seen the article. HP said that its emphasis was wholesome but that the sovereignty of the Union needed to be stressed also, for the sake of intellectual honesty — which is a *sine qua non* for honest literature.

"The article doesn't mention sovereignty in characterizing the Yugoslav Union; but in characterizing the republics it notes that what is *alone* reserved to the Union is the determination of foreign policy, national defense, and the maintenance of the economic unity of the republics. Those are, of course, the ultimate characteristics of genuine sovereignty. When the tension between the one and the many becomes the theme of your imaginative prose and poetry, it will be wholesome for your literature, as it has been for all other serious literatures of the world."

Soon after lunch we were driven to Ohrid, down a road that skirts three artificial lakes to sweep through mountain gorges, to the natural lake celebrated as the "pearl of Macedonia." Our day in Ohrid was all vacation — strolls, talks with our lady guide and male driver, window-shopping along the main street. Ohrid is indeed a pearl!

Friday, June 2. Our plane for Belgrade — a small two-propeller model — took off at 6:05 A.M. A car awaited us at the airport and took us to the Bators. HP had lunch there (our hosts had arranged the day for us in their usual efficient way) with five Yugoslavs from the Institute for International Politics and Economics and the Political Science Department of Belgrade University, and four of Edmund Bator's colleagues from the Embassy staff. AP went instead to meet with the members of the Writers' Club. Our friends, the dramatist Hristic and the poet-critic Lalic, were there, and several women — more than usually came at such meetings. AP was asked about *RNL*; possible themes were mentioned; but almost all was said through the interpreter with what seemed to be exaggerated formality — as if no one except the interpreter was authorized to speak any language but Serbian. AP went later to lunch with Martha Bator. The stag-lunch for HP at the Bators' house continued until late in the afternoon. . . .

5. Dubrovnik

Saturday, June 3. Early in the morning, we flew to the Dalmatian coast. The Secretary of the Dubrovnik International Summer Festival, Ljubica Marinovic — "Buba" — met us at the airport and had us driven to the old Imperial Hotel, just outside the walled town. She talked, half-listened, took into account without ever suffering a serious interruption whatever in our responses needed to be taken into account. She left us at the Hotel to unpack and have breakfast, saying that she would be back at 10:45 to take us for a fast walk through the town.

It proved to be a delightful tour. At the end of it, Buba. left us in the central square saying: "A gentleman will call for you tonight at the hotel at seven. You'll like him. He's the painter Branko Kovacevic, and he will take you to dinner with the Director of the Dubrovnik Symphony Orchestra." She herself, she went on to explain, was busy with a large family wedding that evening.

Our host arrived promptly at seven. He took us for another kind of tour of the city, and eventually we were escorted to a private dinner club, where we were joined by our host's two grown daughters and his young wife — and also by the Director of the Orchestra (who left right after dinner to rehearse a visiting pianist for a Chopin concert). As Buba had told us, a great many palazzi, churches, fortress-type squares, courtyards of Dubrovnik are used as concert halls and theaters. "The whole city is a cultural festival."

After the music director left, the painter chose to speak with us in Italian and English, both of which he knew fluently. His daughters, who lived in Zagreb, bad come in for their father's "retrospective exhibition, " which would open in three days. We later went to see some of his paintings and noted how they reflected the openness of walled Dubrovnik, so markedly in contrast, say, with the tightfistedness of a city like Siena. His impressions of Dubrovnik were abstractionist, yet sensorily highly suggestive. We walked and talked — of life, love, marriage, and

death, and of cabbages and kings — long into the night.
Sitting with him in his favorite cafe, we were entertained by
his description of the weird impressions be experienced as
he approached New York City from Kennedy Airport
through the cemeteries and gas-tanks of Queens, his sense
of being lost in the downtown streets at night, the difficulties of getting from place to place, the longing to get out;
and yet bow pleasant his Gramercy Park lodgings had been.

We said goodbye in front of the Gambling Casino
opposite the hotel.

6. Sarajevo

Sunday, June 4. We rose early for a walk through the narrow,
hidden streets and alleys that circle Dubrovnik just inside
its walls. When we returned to the hotel at 9:15 A.M. our
driver — scbeduled to pick us up at 10 — was already there;
and so we set out at once up the Dalmatian coast.

The sights — off-shore islands and peninsulas — are
incredibly beautiful, especially seen from a speeding car on
hairpin turns. . . . Then, inland toward Metkovic and
Mostar. The region is a flat delta of marshlands — "good for
hunting," said the driver of our speeding Mercedes. An
hour later we reached Mostar, tracing the grassy banks of
its rapidly flowing river and crossing on foot the high arch
of its famous Turkish-built bridge, with its shiny foot-worn
stones, its ribs to give the feet a grip, its houses built out
upon the bridgeheads.

After lunch, we continued the long drive up to
Sarajevo and arrived at its Europa Hotel at 4:30 P.M. Our
new hosts, as appointed, called upon us there at 7 P.M.
There were four of them. Zdenko Radeljkovic, who spoke
first, had received an M.A. degree at Indiana University and
was completing a Ph.D. dissertation on Thoreau; with him
were Professor Svetozar Koljevic, who had published with
Oxford University Press an anthology of *Yugoslav Short
Stories* in English, a Secretary of the Sarajevo Writers'
Association, and a member of the Drama and Literature
Department of the University.

We had dinner at the Europa. Dr. Nejgebauer of
Novi Sad, we recalled, had urged us to see Svetozar Koljevic
and his brother Nikola in Sarajevo. Svetozar was somewhat
formal at first, but he soon loosened up, letting his talk
bristle with characteristic ironies. He spoke of the Yugoslav

epic tradition, reaching back — in the oral aspect of it — beyond the Dubrovnik renaissance and extending forward into the contemporary novel. We spoke of what we had learned from Dr. Deneš in Belgrade, from Dr. Nejgebauer and the people of Matica Srpska in Novi Sad, the Albanians of Priština, the dictionary-makers of Skopje, the painter of Dubrovnik, and our many guides and new-found literary friends. After dinner, we took a long walk through the streets of the old town, passed many mosques, turned down quaint streets, through the marketplace of Baš Caršije, around to the river side, and back to the hotel. . . .

Monday, June 5. After breakfast, accompanied by two assigned guides, we visited the Young Bosnia Museum, outside of which footprints mark the spot where a political assassin fired the shot that precipitated World War 1. We went through the Museum and then proceeded, by taxi, to the University. The halls and stairways of the building were packed with students. On the way tip to Svetozar Koljevic's office, Zdenko Radeljkovi remarked that, because of his irony, and because of a celebrated lecture he had recently given on a famous Baconian essay, Professor Koljevic was affectionately referred to by most of his students as "Jesting Pilate."

The window of his office looked out on an adjacent skyscraper, the towering "government building." We observed that the University was obviously conveniently located for students who like to mount anti-government protests. Our "Jesting Pilate" quickly countered with: "Rather, it is convenient to be close to the source of the money.

It was the beginning of examinations. Professor Koljevic telephoned to see who, among his colleagues, were free to join us. We met his brother Nikola and several others. HP, skimming through Svetozar's Introduction to the short story anthology, read aloud: "The experience of history, since medieval times, has followed one major pattern throughout the country, the pattern of realizing that to survive is to be prepared to die." We noted that it was a view we shared, and that our mutual friend in Novi Sad also shared.

Late that afternoon, Zdenko Radeljkovic drove us to the "Vrelo Bosne" springs, the source of Sarajevo's principal river. At a restaurant beside pools stocked with trout, we talked of our guide's dissertation on Thoreau — still in process — and of the difficulty of getting books through the Library of Congress.

He said it was a pity that Dubrovnik did not yet have a university. "After all, it has a genuine cultural history, with a medieval and renaissance legacy." It occurred to us that an article on the literary heritage of Dubrovnik, as a common legacy of all South Slavs, might go well in the projected *RNL* issue.

Later, we all met for supper in the old city — in a restaurant which had been the courtyard of an old Turkish hotel (Caravaniaraj). What had obviously once been a series of stalls and rooms had now become a series of little alcoves for dining. We had oriental spinach cakes (zelenica) and meat cakes for appetizers, turtle soup; grilled meats; and an oriental dessert (tufadjija). Eventually, we returned to the theme of the "ethics of survival" and went on to discuss the literature of servility and peace, freedom and war. HP spoke of the Western tradition, at least as old as Homer and Sophocles, and Herodotus, that victors in a war do not afterward celebrate the "righteousness" of their cause. The West, he suggested, had failed to live up to that tradition in the aftermath of World War II — at least on the side of the victors, who had abandoned themselves to self-righteousness in their victory. "It has been especially bad for literature."

But surely, it was urged, the Germans deserved to be thoroughly condemned in their total defeat! Victors, HP explained, cannot rightly be judges of the righteousness of their cause over the vanquished. Kill your enemies, if you wish, but don't lord your might over them as a righteous prerogative.

A heated discussion followed. "You are our guest," someone said, "otherwise we could say some sharp things."

"Well, when you visit us in America, we hope you will feel free to say what you think needs saying."

"We certainly shall, if possible."

"And we hope too that for literature's sake at least you will by then have come to value the Western tradition of respecting one's defeated enemy. *Noblesse oblige!*"

"Are you saying then," asked Svetozar, "that there are no real villains?"

"Not from the great epic and tragic literary perspectives. The great poets do not betray their characters, not even their wrathful Achilles, or Iagos, much less their Hectors or Antonys."

"Surely Iago is represented as a villain."

"A great actor would be ill-advised to play him as such. Demand me nothing, he says at the end. 'What you know, you know. From this time forth I never will speak a word.' "

At this point, the conversation took a humorous turn, under "Jesting Pilate's" skillful direction. Later, we all walked leisurely through the night-streets of Sarajevo — AP with Svetozar, HP with the others. At the hotel entrance, Svetozar caught up to say goodnight and goodbye, adding suddenly with good grace: "If I ever have to lose a war, I hope it is to you!"

7. Zagreb

Tuesday, June 6. We took a taxi to the airport for an early flight to the capital of Croatia. There we were met by a slender, handsome young lady with bright eyes, flashing smile, and short hair, who spoke fluent English with a British pronunciation: Vera Andrassy. She took us by taxi to the Palace Hotel in the center of town. On the street outside the Hotel, we were met by Dabney Chapman, Director of the USIS in Zagreb, who bad been waiting for us to extend an invitation to his house for dinner the following evening. Barbara White and Irving Kristol, who were on an inspection tour for USIS, would also be there.

Just before noon, Vera Andrassy took us to meet the Secretary General of the Writers' Association, the poet Slavko Mihalic, who is also the editor of *The Bridge*. With him were Saga Vereš, an editor of the *Encyclopedia* and a critic; a young novelist, Zvonimir Majdak, whose latest novel is entitled *Be Careful: I Don't Want to Lose my Virginity*; and Antun Šoljan, President of local P.E.N. A three-volume anthology of 20th-century Yugoslav literature, we learned, was in the making and ought to be of interest to us. We asked about the organization, the criteria for inclusion, how the various national literatures were to be represented, proportions of representation, etc. Each Republic would select entries for itself, no decisions would be worked out in advance about proportions. And everything was to be translated eventually for English, French, and Spanish editions.

We thought an article on the *method* for such an anthology — or even better, for the already existent *Encyclopedia of the Yugoslav People* (published in Zagreb) — would be a good companion piece for the projected article on the Macedonian dictionary. HP suggested that such anthologies and encyclopedias, gathering the best of all the nationalities and republics of Yugoslavia, were fitting tasks for a "Queen Bee." But, even though there was a Matica Hrvatska operating in Zagreb, the suggestion rang hollow. One of our hosts said cryptically that some things are not quite so simple as one might think.

Each republic is independent, on its own, our hosts stressed. We spoke of the concept of a sovereign union of sovereign states. A witty young theater director said finally that he, of course, cherished the Federal Union as indissoluble, but that it was hard for the moment to trace a literary aspect for it. AP emphasized that the diversity is absolutely essential, as the very substance; but somehow it must be possible to speak of Yugoslav literature as a whole . . . and . . . *RNL* meant to give expression to the possibility, at the very least.

"In other words, you are telling us, " he laughed, "that while we are working out our own internal squabbles you will be concentrating on effective cultural communication."

Someone else hastened to say that the Zagreb Encyclopedia had, in fact, precisely the vantage point we were urging.

We had a leisurely lunch in a spacious, tent-covered outdoor restaurant, and we all talked about everything under the sun: Sicily, North Africa, fish and fowl (Vera Andrassy sent back a fish offered us by the chef as "too big"), novels, plays, war, peace, dialects, the rich cultural legacy of Croatia, the willfulness of the Serbs, Dustin Hoffman, Zionism, *The Graduate*, *Little Big Man*, the American Civil War, Einstein, capital punishment.

Later that afternoon, we met with Vera Andrassy for a walk across town, past the great cathedral, up to the Mestrovic Museum. Not far from the Museum, we entered a small Catholic church (Sveti Stefan), which had a multi-colored roof similar to St. Stephen in Vienna. There were three Mestrovic works in it: a Virgin Mother and an infant perched on her Hindu-squat legs; that child grown to manhood, hanging with very short arms on a grotesquely (but arrestingly) long cross; and then that same crucified Christ again on his mother's lap, which he now overwhelms in the tortuous fashion of Michelangelo's late *pietàs*. It is an impressive sculptural triptych.

On our way to the Mestrovic Museum, we passed a TV crew filming the sequence of a "resistance" TV-ballet in the street. At the museum we were treated to a fine collection of splendid heads, mostly with the characteristic Mestrovic nose and fine large hands. The monumental pieces in the courtyard of what had been a Mestrovic residence were — taken together — simply overwhelming. They need to be isolated.

That evening we saw a Croatian version of *A Day in the Life of Joe Egg*. Afterward, we met the Director and then went to the apartment of our guide — our first time in a Yugoslav home — which has a sweeping view of the city from its suburban skyscraper balcony. We talked late into the night.

Wednesday, June 7. After breakfast, we were met by the novelist Zvonimir Maidah, substituting for Vera Andrassy. He accompanied us to the Zora Publishing House, which has its own printing establisbment, with great rolls of paper and huge pads of it in the yard. We waited in a conference room walled with translations of Irwin Shaw, Norman Mailer, Faulkner, etc., as well as of English, French, and Russian authors, until Augustin Stipcevic and his chief aide came in (with brandy, coffee, and juice). They explained that 40% of their books were translations from foreign languages and another 20% were translations from other Yugoslav languages. Salesmen canvass subscriptions from door to door. *Peyton Place* had been for long a bestseller, we were told.

Vera Andrassy arrived with several colleagues, and soon we were on our way to the Lexicographers Institute to meet the editors of the eigbt-volume *Encyclopedia of the Yugoslav People*. On the way, we talked about articles projected for *RNL*. We bad listed the names of Yugoslav, American, English, etc. scholars who might write for us. One of our hosts, singling out an English scholar on the list, said: "If you get *him* to write on 'Modern Yugoslav Poetry,' it will be all Serbian! He lived in Serbia; be always favors Serbia."

"These are merely suggestions at the moment," we said. "Perhaps we'll find someone else to write that article. Or, if we do use him, we'll make sure that — together with our special editor — we counterbalance the Serbian partiality of Professor ***." We spoke of the desirability of getting an article, perhaps on the *Encyclopedia*, that would stress the unifying cultural factors in the Yugoslav federation — the overlapping Mediterranean, Central European, and Slavic influences.

One of our hosts conceded that, south of Croatia, there was indeed everywhere the Slavic common denominator. "But the other two — the Mediterranean and Central European factors — are not really operative there, as they are indeed in Croatia and Slovenia."

"You people," we said to the young man who had made the distinction, "ought to be more generous with your treasures, then. So you have the Mediterranean and Central European things to perfection. Share them with your fellow Yugoslavs." The other replied, in the same vein: "Let them try to acquire them, if they can. They outnumber us. isn't that enough?"

At the Institute, with Dr. Vereš and the Deputy Editor of the *Encyclopedia* (whom we had met earlier), we discussed the method pursued in its preparation. There were general articles on each of the republics, with general reviews of the culture. But there were also separate articles on the languages, on the literatures as a whole, on periods of literature, all cross-referenced to articles on movements, genres, major works, and individual authors, all in alphabetical order, all signed. We talked of the important influence that major encyclopedia articles, written with definitive authority by great scholars, can have on an intellectual community. We mentioned the great articles on great subjects by great scholars — Maitland, Harnack, Croce, etc. — in the great editions of the *Encyclopedia Britannica*.

Later, at the hotel, we assembled with Irving Kristol, Barbara White, and Vera Andrassy for the drive to Mr. Chapman's house, for dinner. The Yugoslavs attending included Slavko Mihalic of the Writers' Club, Saga Vereš (whom we had just left), the novelist Zvonimir Majdak, an author of widely translated children's books, P.E.N. President Antun Soljun. . . .

Mihalić, a well-known Croatian poet, spoke with us in the garden, mostly in Italian, but also in German. He loves music, collects scores and records, and also paints. Of *RNL* he said that he knew exactly what we were after, and thought it proper, despite the distinctly pro-Croatian preferences he had expressed earlier. He praised the author of children's stories, to whom be introduced us, as an extraordinary satirist. We discussed Lewis Carroll, the letters he received from children all over the world, and before long we were matching quotations from great authors on the child's spirit as a motif of literature. . . . At table, in generalized conversations, we all spoke freely about . . . languages, loyalties, libraries, love, leisure (to list just the "l"s). . . .

Thursday, June 8. With Vera Andrassy, we walked from the Hotel to the Yugoslav Academy of Arts and Sciences which, though it is the center of Croatian cultural life, retains the general name. Slavko Mihalic, President of the Writers' Union, met us in doorway (he was just leaving the building) and turned back to point out some of the features of the elegant building. There was a statue of its founder, Archbishop Josip Juraj Strossmayer; there was a copy of his tomb, enlargements of the first writings in Croatian, etc., etc.

Strossmayer, said Mihalić, was really the main protagonist of the creation of a political union of the South Slavs. "He coined the name. In his conception, it was to have included the Bulgarians as well. And that almost materialized in 1948. . . . Moscow objected."

Mihalié then left us, with a gracious goodbye, and we went up the stairs, passing through several handsomely furnished great salons. An attendant asked us to wait in a comfortably appointed smaller room. Marjan Matkovic, Croatia's leading contemporary writer, had just returned to Zagreb that morning — we were told — especially to meet with us. He bad been quite ill, we learned.

Soon after, Matkovic made a vivacious entrance, sweeping in with several attendants, beaming, bubbling, talking incessantly, looking anything but ill. "Ah!" (through the translator) "tell them I'm pleased, very pleased, to meet them. Sorry to be late," etc., etc.

Though he seemed to interrupt us constantly, it was always after he had, in fact, understood what was being said; and he invariably responded first with purposive ambiguity and then with disarming directness. Few other parts of Yugoslavia, he said, had such a building, such an Academy, as this one, which the noble Strossmayer had left them. It is dedicated to the culture of the South Slavs, all South Slavs. Strossmayer was the first to define the concept. . . . The Archbishop was a great man — great, too, with the ladies. Many women claimed to have mothered his children. But the only child he proudly acknowledged was this Academy. "Not all one's children need to be two-legged!" Matkovic moved quickly to a window to indicate the large statue of Strossmayer in the park outside.

After having sung the Archbishop's praises, he talked, at our suggestion, of his own cultural master, the great Croatian author and scholar, Miroslav Krleža, aged founder of the eight-volume *Encyclopedia*, editor of many magazines, Yugoslavia's first modern poet, first modem playwright, essayist — tbe revolutionary who in fact "turned the Yugoslav intelligentsia to the left." Matkovic contrasted Krleža briefly with the one other Yugoslav contemporary writer of comparable fame, Ivo Andric. Though much good can be said of both, the advantage must go finally to Krleža, he concluded. "Andric became a Serb for dubious reasons," Matkovic had written an article on the top three or four Yugoslav writers for *The Atlantic Monthly*. Krleža and Andric were of course included. The editors protested: "Why not Djilas?" He had answered: "If you had asked a German critic of comparable stature (comparing small things to great) to write about the three or four leading modern German writers, would you chide him for having left out Goebbels?"

The conversation turned, in time, to a discussion of the permanence of the Yugoslav political union. "Nothing," he said, "is indissoluble. But Yugoslavia's unity today is a reality." We asked what literary expression there was of the value of such unity. . . .

Later, as we rose to leave, we noted (pursuing his vein of humor) that be still talked like a bold partisan though he was obviously part of the establishment, enjoying its most gratifying prerogatives. But we also, finally, asked about his health. "They say you have been ill. Yet, you seem to be hale and hearty."

"There are external signs and internal signs. And they are often contradictory." With that, he circled our shoulders affectionately with his arms and walked with us out of the room.

Next on our schedule was AP's departure by train for the capital of Slovenia, Ljubljana, and HP's flight back to Belgrade for supper at the Writers' Club and — the following morning— a talk at the Institute for International Politics and Economics. The topic was to be "The Kissinger-Nixon Foreign Policy."

8. Ljubljana

Friday, June 9. AP had noted, on her arrival here the night before, that the women-hosts in this capital of Slovenia were not in the least passive, that they were in fact treated with gracious respect by their male intellectual peers and with gracious deference by their bureaucratic peers. There was the novelist and President of P.E.N., Mira Mihelic — who spoke English quite well; a short-story writer, Gitica Jakopin; and Nada Kraigher, novelist, economist, and agent for co-pyright permissions in the Yugoslav Authors' Agency.

AP also met the novelist Potrc, who is with the Mladinska Knjiga Publishing House — a book company which issues classics, fine arts volumes, children's stories, McGraw Hill reprints, volumes in German, French, English, etc., as well as in other Yugoslav languages. "Right here," he commented, "we have thirty-two separate publishing houses. More than in New York City!" Almost 4,000 titles had been published since 1945. There is a Slovene Classical Authors series, which spans 150 years. Ninety finely-bound volumes have already been issued, each with a 27,000 printing sold mostly by subscription.

There was also Primoz Kozak — playwrigbt-critic — wbo had been a member of Paul Engel's Writers' Workshop at the University of Iowa, and Bogdan Pogacni — leading journalist and long-time Paris correspondent of *Delo*. Pogacni, who listened appreciatively to his female cultural colleagues, stressed particularly that Slovenes cherish all aspects of their past with a kind of prolonged, civilizing romanticism. "We have a tradition of books and reading, and look to our classical and popular folk-poetry for our essential being. Even our partisan brigades, during the war, chose their names from famous Slovene writers and poets."

All of these people were at supper with AP at the Slovene Writers' Club when HP was driven in from the Ljubljana airport by a large-eyed, red-haired, beaming young woman — recently appointed administrative secretary of the Ljubljana Writers' Association. At the table, where HP and Bogdan Poganic vied with one another in singing the praises of forceful, cultured women as one of the surest signs, perhaps, of genuine civilization, the differences between Slovenes, Croatians, and Serbs came to be discussed in terms of women. But finally, someone cited Tennyson impatiently:

> As the husband is, the wife is:
> Thou are mated with a clown,
> And the grossness of his nature
> Will have weight to drag thee down.

Saturday, June 10. Nada Kraigher called on us early in the morning to drive us to Lake Bled, which is for the northern tip of Yugoslavia what Lake Ohrid is for the southern tip. But first we stopped at the National and University Library of Ljubljana, just behind the University. Here again we met a forceful woman, the Director Radojka Vrancic, with her top aide, a gentleman who, like Nada Kraigher, spoke rather fluent Italian, as well as English. Their building, they said, was handsome but not sufficiently utilitarian. Too hard to heat. Nada Kraigher left us as we started a brief tour. We lingered over an exhibition of early manuscripts, incunabula, first editions, letters of leading Slovene poets, etc. Among the handwritten entries in the library catalog was one for an American Indian grammar of the 19th century made by a Slovene.

Our guide returned, and we set out for Bled in her little East German car. We spent the rest of the morning enjoying the spectacular view of the beautiful mountain lake from the terrace of an old fortress.

At the resort Golf Hotel, we ran into Irving Kristol and Barbara White of the USIS inspection team once again. In the afternoon, we talked at length with Nada Kraigher about her war-time adventures as a partisan and as a refugee in Italy, her travels to India, her economic theories about the future of Yugoslavia as well as of the U.S.A. and

U.S.S.R. We drove back to Ljubljana quite late. . . .

Sunday, June 11. The journalist Bogdan Pogacni picked us
up very early with his son — "Bogey Jr." — for a long drive
out to one of Ljubljana's popular folk-festivals. Young
Bogey, who spoke English rather well, explained that he
had changed his university major three times, not wanting
to commit himself prematurely to any one particular career. For the moment, he was interested in public relations,
though be imagined that his interest was really more theo-
retical than practical.

"The art of selling itself has to be sold," his father
observed. And in this connection, we spoke of Aristotle's
Rhetoric and of its literary as well as practical application.

The conversation touched many subjects — poetry,
journalism, Hegel, Marx, freedom, etc, Father and son
joked at one another's expense.

We reached the site of the festival. All was old,
traditional — except, of course, for the TV cameras and
crews. We ate the specialties of the festival, talked with the
organizers, and chatted with the TV people, watched many
of the costumed group — performances, then—in the afternoon — started back and had a very informal, leisurely
supper at a roadside restaurant.

Later, we went slightly out of the direct way back to
visit the birthplace of the celebrated Slovenian poet, Jurcic.
His *Weltschmerz*, our companions noted, was that of Foscolo's
Ortis rather than Goethe's Werther.

Back in Ljubljana, we stopped to call on a painter
who had been with Tito during the "resistance." The famous portrait of Tito, which is seen everywhere, was his
work. His most recent fine-art photovolume was a retrospective collection of prints for Tito on his 80th birthday.

The painter led us through his apartment and several studios circling an interior court. He had all the
equipment, large and small, necessary to make and frame
all his paintings, engravings, etc.

Bogdan Pogacni returned to the Hotel with us for
our bags, and then he drove us to the airport for the flight
back to Belgrade. Our farewells were touchingly memorable. In Belgrade, we spent the night alone in the Bators'
house, since our hosts had gone off for the weekend to
Dubrovnik, to celebrate their 20th wedding anniversary.

9. Titograd and Cetinje

Monday, June 12. Barbara White was on the plane we took in the afternoon for the flight to industrial Titograd, capital of Montenegro (Crna Gora: Black Mountain). At our destination, Svetolik Roganovic, President of the Commission for Cultural Relations in Montenegro (a large, moustached man), and Sveten Perovic, Secretary of the Writers' Union of Montenegro (slender and bearded), met us and drove us to the Titograd Hotel in the center of town.

We met again at 7 P.M. to be driven to the Deputies' Club for dinner with members of the Writers' Union. Several present, including Miss White, were rather fluent in Italian, so the talk was in three languages, with three-way interpretive translations. Montenegro has, of course, a Serbo-Croatian language, someone said; but it has also a distinctive national history and national literature. The first Serbian kings in the 12th century, came from Montenegro. The old capital, Cetinje, had never been ruled by the Turks. After AP, in response to questioning, explained what her idea was for an *RNL* issue on "The Multinational Literature of Yugoslavia," someone observed, through an interpreter, that it would be better to speak of the national literatures, rather than of one multi-national literature, of Yugoslavia.

We went over the familiar ground, noting that Yugoslavia is a unifed reality and that, as we perceived it, many writers and critics throughout its length and breadth, past and present, attached great value to a union of South Slavs. We alluded to Archbishop Strossmayer's contribution to the concept. Immediately, someone interjected that the term owed its construction and currency to the great Montenegrin poet, bishop, and ruler, Peter II — known as Njegoš. "Njegoš came *before* Strossmayer!"

"Good," we said. "So you have indeed a tradition of great writers who value and love the unity of the Yugoslavs."

"That goes without saying," someone insisted, with a debator's finality.

There was some vehement talk about the expression of love of unity and of diversity in the writings of great Yugoslav personalities. "Love builds, love generates, creates. Love can build a genuine Yugoslav literature, making one out of many, without excessive pushing, so long as there are writers of ability who are not ashamed to say — in

all your independent republics and autonomous regions —
that they value Yugoslav unity dearer than life."

"You sound," someone said, "like marriage counsel-
lors!" The talk turned to the idea of the one and the many
in the ancient Indian philosophers and the Greeks. "Of
course," an earnest fellow at the end of the table interjected
firmly, "it is a problem to express the many-ness of the
Yugoslav national literatures, and their oneness, simultaneously. But that is the essence of all reality, is it not?
Reality is simultaneously one and many. if either component is taken one-sidedly, the reality is lost. It slips out of
our intellectual grasp."

"But there is a productive side to it, too. Love
doesn't analyze, doesn't merely understand; it builds, makes,
creates."

"You are saying," the same earnest fellow replied,
"that writers who, in their love of beauty, seize simultaneously on the one and the many can make the great
Yugoslav literature of tomorrow."

We agreed. But another of our hosts reminded us
that Yugoslavia's diversity is different from America's,
where the ideal has long been to integrate the diversity
almost, one might say, on a personal basis. "You have been
a federation of states, but not of different nationalities."

It used to seem, we noted, that American society
would melt out differences in its so-called melting pot, but
that was a temporary misconception. From the beginning,
and increasingly now, the genuine ideal has been to treasure and cultivate the almost infinite cultural, ethnic, racial, and religious variety of the American people — quite as
your cultural leaders call for now. Americans derive — like
the honey and wax of the bee-hive — from every conceivable
background. No one obliges them to prefer Whitman to
Leopardi, or Shakespeare to Dante, or Milton to Virgil, or
whoever. "What is required is simply that we not push our
preferences to the point of dissolving our political union as
Americans." We quoted George Washington's statement of
the unifying ideal, which has no special ethnic, racial, or
cultural bias: "Citizens by birth or choice of a common
country, that country has a right to concentrate your affections."

Olga Perovic, editor of the magazine *Prakse* or *Pratica*,
said much in defense of the prerogatives of the indepen-

dent republics. There was a dispute about exactly what the latest Constitution specified, and a copy was sent for and read. A champion of the sovereignty of the parts read with emphasis the words which clearly affirmed the sovereignty of the republics. We pressed for more, and pointed out that the Federation was also sovereign and that the parts were parts of a whole that was not itself a part.

Who, we asked, are the writers who best represent the Montenegrin contribution to the diversity of Yugoslav literature? There was lively discussion. Finally, the earnest fellow at the end of the table said, with a kind of compelling authority: "The best Montenegrin literature is the literature of humanity and heroism, which is to say, the literature of freedom." He then explained how a hero-poet of his people had expressed it: "Heroism and humanity: you have heroism when you fight to root out the evil in others; you have humanity when you fight or struggle to root out the evil in yourself.

As to the writer who best represents the spirit of Montenegro — the same earnest fellow, after a while, said that it was no doubt the bishop-poet-ruler Njegoš, whose residence and museum we were scheduled to visit the following day.

Tuesday, June 13. Svetolik Roganovic and Svetan Perovic called on us for the morning drive up to the old capital, Cetinje, and down again to Kotor Bay, Bar, and the resort community of the converted monastery of St. Stefan.

The road to Cetinje took us through the bleakest stony regions of the Black Mountain (Crna Cora) Republic. Here was the place where 3,000 Montenegrins confronted 32,000 Turks; and there, another such place, where the odds were even worse. "In these mountains," said our bearded host, "freedom survived because nobody thought it worthwhile to track it down into such a retreat. Soon you will see wastes comparable to those on the moon! It is not really necessary for your astronauts to have gone so far!"

Cetinje is in an elevated bowl, cool because it is high, but sheltered from the winds. During the reign of Montenegro's one royal family, it bad been a splendid little capital. We passed a street of mansions that had been embassies of the major European powers and now served as museums, schools, etc.

We visited the old monarchic palace. Our guide was an Australian woman who bad married a gentleman of Cetinje. She showed us all there was to see, pointing things out with her little finger, her eyes sparkling as she shared an historical confidence. From there, she accompanied us to the monastery-museum which bad been the residence of the gigantic (six-foot, seven-inch) poet-bishop-ruler Peter II — Njegoš. She introduced us to a scholar who was preparing a book on Njegoš, and left us with him.

We toured the impressive building, lingering in the bishop's library. There was a statue of the Romantic poet Vuk Karadžic, who had sought refuge there when he was forbidden to publish in his native land, when it was occupied by the Turks. There were copies in many languages of Njegoš's *The Mountain Wreath*, and a statue representing the blind seer of the poem. From there we were taken across the town to a great shed, to see the great Mestrovic statue of Njegoš, which had been ready for almost a decade and which in less than ten days (we were told) would be raised to its permanent site on an elaborately levelled and reinforced mountain top. There was a rusty lock on the door of the shed, and while our guide struggled to open it, one of the party noted that, in compensation for making the huge statue, Mestrovic had asked only that he be given a large local cheese and a piece of the smoked ham (*prosciutto*) for which the region is famous.

As one might expect, it is a monumental piece. Njegoš is seated, with a large book in his lap, his legs crossed in the usual Mestrovic manner, his left band thoughtfully poised at the left temple, his right hand clenched at his heart, his brow furrowed, mouth taut, like a Montenegrin fighter. A stylized eagle is carved above his head, completing the back of his great chair. . . .

On, to the moonlike wastelands. At one point, our driver informed us that he had made the same tour with the same car with Adlai Stevenson as the Republic's guest, several years earlier. We stopped at a rustic wayside restaurant and had some of the famous smoked ham and cheese, and some local wine.

All this while we bad been climbing, but finally we snaked our way ribbon-like over the top and started the long descent toward Kotor Bay.

After walled Kotor, we went on to Bar, which faces

Italy's Bari — and is groomed to become an important port, joined to Belgrade by a major railroad line — and then across the causeway to the island-peninsula of St. Stefan, the whole of which is a vast hotel complex. . . . We started up the road back to Titograd by way of the neck of the great lake that Montenegro shares with Albania.

Wednesday, June 14. Our guides and companions for the day were the publisher-critic who had sat at the head of the table for the first night's dinner, Milorad Stojovic, and an instructor in English — a heavy man with longish hair, who is also a linguist. They would take us first to see the house-museum of Montenegro's most famous modern hero-poet, and then in the afternoon, up a famous mountain gorge to an old monastery.

Our guide Stojovic, chief scholarly authority on the hero-poet's life and works, bad supervised the transformation of his house into a museum and a school, according to the poet's will. At the dedication the year before, the daughter of American architect Frank Lloyd Wright, wife of the poet's grandson, had been the guest of honor. The museum-school and the mountain-top ruins of an Illyrian town, site of the poet's grave, dominate a vast rolling plain. As we looked through the museum, we spoke with our guide about the heroism and humanity theme which he said characterizes the best Montenegrin poetry.

Shortly after 4:30 P.M. — as we had agreed at the end of our morning excursion — we set out again and soon reached the banks of the river that had cut Crna Gora's celebrated gorge, the largest canyon (it is said) in all of Europe, second in the world only to Colorado's. "There it is," said our linguist-translator. "You will see it cut deeper and deeper as we go along. You must see it to . . . to know what it means to be a Montenegrin!"

What impressed us most, initially, were the grand lines of the railroad being cut parallel to the river, in an endless series of ledges, bridges, and tunnels, to link Titograd to Belgrade. (We had already seen the completed link between Titograd and Bar.) Whether it would bring economic prosperity to the area remained in doubt; but there was no doubt about the inherent spiritual value of the sheer work of cutting into the massive rock of the mountains along the heights of a river gorge.

We stopped at a famous turn that enables one to look back upon a most impressive sight. "It never gives the same impression twice; it is always new, always personal." We were reminded of Leslie Stephen's worshipful accounts of climbing in the Swiss Alps. . . .

Beside the old monastery — celebrated in the guide books for its fresco of a raven feeding a saint — was a rustic café where we had something to eat and talked for several hours. We were asked about the much-publicized racial tensions. Is the mixture of peoples — "you have them from all parts of the world, don't you?" — too much? We said that the United States was indeed at a point of feverish crisis, destined either to collapse from internal dissension or to flower into an American equivalent of England's grand Elizabethan age.

"Yes," said Stojovic, through the translator, "you are at a great turning point. Everything to gain, everything to lose. But your writers, at least the ones that reach us, don't give us a true sense of it, certainly not with literary force. It is full of tragic potential and also, as you say, of epic grandeur." He went on: "Political union is a necessity. That is the attitude of many of us here who cherish the union of South Slavs."

"You in Yugoslavia," said AP, "are in a very good position to show the validity of such a notion of the state. it is the traditional ideal of ordered freedom, of unity that preserves diversity — which is what Yugoslavia apparently seeks for itself. If you want to read the most impressive expression of it in recent times, you should take up the works of Walter Bagehot, the great economist, but also a great literary critic and perhaps the finest prose writer in English of the 19th century. You should read his *English Constitution*, his *Physics and Politics*, and perhaps more important, his literary essays, which are full of the spirit of his ideal of 'government by discussion,' founded on a politics of enforceable, felt unity."

Our hosts graciously joined us in drawing Yugoslav as well as American literary applications. As the gorge fell under deep shadows, we started back for Titograd.

Thursday, June 15. The next morning, we were met by Svetolik Roganovic, Svetan Perovic, Jelena Radulovic, and Slavko Lehic, for a drive and boat ride to Montenegro's great lake that links it with Albania. It proved to be a splendid outing, with much pleasant talk, refreshing lake air, and excellent food and drink at a lodge overlooking the lake. That evening we flew back to Belgrade.

10. Belgrade Farewell

Friday, June 16. We met again with Dr. Oto Deneš to sum up the tour. "Have you gained a perspective for your projected issue on our literature?" AP outlined some of the possible topics that had emerged in the course of the one-month visit. With the lines of a smile peeking out around his eyes, behind his dark-tinted glasses, Deneš emphasized that be had not in any way wanted to direct the course of our inquiry, or to suggest any restrictions. We chatted about the various responses in the various republics and autonomous regions — noting, however, the constants as well as the variables. Deneš's initial comments were mostly restrictive, qualifying — "Well, that is not precisely so," "Yes, but . . ." — and then suddenly, he interrupted himself. "I began by saying no restrictions, and here I have already suggested half a dozen!" We promised, in return, not to mind any of them . . . but, with discretion!

We observed that his comment on the three unifying influences present in varying proportions everywhere — Mediterranean, Central European, Slavic — had served us in good stead to clinch many an argument. "Straight out of the textbooks," he replied. Still, he had to acknowledge that brief words from him counted for volumes from others. We noted that, as he could see, we had not been fed or drunk to death; and, as for the third way of killing guests in Yugoslavia — talking — we had, apparently, more than held our own.

AP presented him with four recent issues of *RNL*. There would be several others before the Yugoslav issue would join the pile. His own book, dealing with the bearing of cultural, popular, and political influence on the conduct of foreign relations, would be out within the year. He would send AP a copy, he said. The forces he is analyzing define people in terms of soccer and basketball, popular music and films — define very powerfully and very differently from literature. We replied that, with its emphasis on nationhood, *RNL* might help to make literature once again an effective competitor. Deneš suggested that perhaps only in America could such a magazine venture be so much as contemplated, much less accomplished. "It requires a certain . . . detachment — though that is not the best term — that is virtually impossible in most places. I have looked through your 'Black Africa' issue since you left; I am very interested in the African nationality questions. You are doing a great thing, bringing the literary legacy of your diverse people together in this way. A great mosaic!"

We spoke about the symbol of the Matica or Queen Bee, about Strossmayer and the great Montenegrin poet-bishop-ruler, Njegoš. Edmund Bator reminded Deneš that he was invited to a garden party at the Bator home the following evening. Before we left, one of Deneš's young assistants gave us an English offprint of an article he had written on pre-Greek and Homeric echoes in the oral epic poetry of the Yugoslavs. . . .

Saturday, June 17. Almost all the Yugoslavs we had met in Belgrade, and several others (in addition to most of the Embassy people and visiting USIS inspectors), attended the Bators' garden party. Oto Deneš came over at once to say that HP's talk on the Kissinger-Nixon foreign policy at the Institute had, in a long-delayed reaction, been finally "well-received."

"It was — how shall I put it — impudent, perhaps, but delightfully exciting. You have made many friends, or if not friends, admirers." Reviewing the report of the delayed reaction, for our literary friends, Deneš brought on a discussion of the literary expression of America's domestic trials and apparent collapse as a foreign relations leader.

"When are you going to give us great literary works on the real dilemma of your Negro problem — works on the psychology of slavery?"

"Do you mean works like the Greek tragedies that teach us how, to be a free person, a man must assume full responsibility for all that he does, or suffers to be done to him? But surely that is your legacy of Marxism and humanity, as well as ours. Slavery, oppression, analyzed down to the smallest springs of action, must be deemed voluntary on the part of the victim, or freedom loses its meaning."

One of the Yugoslavs spoke of the Turkish domination and its trial of the character of its victims. What about — an American asked — the oppression of your Albanian minority? "One day," someone warned, "don't be surprised if one of those socially-abused Albanian kids throws a bomb into a crowd."

A Yugoslav poet frowned. "Do you think your so-called 'fair' treatment now can really compensate for inveterate grievances?"

We recalled the American Christian missionary lady, who — on hearing that an Arab ruler's son was studying at Columbia University — urged his professor (whom she knew) to plead with the young man to do something about the plight of Christians in his country when be took the throne. According to the professor (a great classicist, who had advised Woodrow Wilson on middle-east matters), the Arab replied that be was determined to put an end to all such oppression of Christians in his country once and for all — by annihilating them as recalcitrants! When the goal is a society without grievances, without biases, without dissent, the only sure remedy that inevitably suggests itself is surgery — leaving only us *happy few*. The civilized task is not to solve the major conflicts but to endure them, to temper precisely the urge to find Marxist economic or Hitlerite racial "final solutions." For a moment, several minds and voices seemed to be in accord on this painful subject.

We talked about doctoral dissertations and then about plays and poetry and the study of languages, and eventually about cooking.

Much later, our friends the playwright Jovan Hristic and the poet-critic Ivan Lalic became a focus of conversational interest. HP spoke critically of the fame of certain European novelists in America — novelists who wrote for American publishers and the radical-chic reviewers. Hristic asked about Alberto Moravia and Carlo Levi. And when he had heard enough, he said: "So. You don't like Levi, and I can see why. But tell me. I have been afraid to ask you. What do you think of Malaparte?" HP said that he was an honest writer, as compared to others. "Good," said Hristic, "because I like him very much. I was afraid what you might say." Malaparte changes sides, he went on. But that's what a real Italian must do, isn't it? Geographically, historically, Italy has to waver, in every war — musn't she? First on one side, then on the other, usually in the wrong order. "Malaparte expresses that fate. Levi does not. He is consistently on one side, and therefore not true to the real Italian spirit. You agree?"

Lalic talked about poetry. He asked who we most deeply preferred. "I mean, beyond the greats, beyond Homer, Virgil, Dante, Shakespeare, etc. Who talks directly to your hearts with his song?"

AP said Leopardi. HP said, "And the English Leopardi, James Thomson, who is also an English Dante. One day, when England is resigned to its loss of political greatness — the greatness that gave her Spenser, Shakespeare, Milton — the great atheist pessimist Thomson will rise to take a place in relation to Shakespeare like that of Heine in relation to Goethe, Leopardi to Dante."

Lalic said: "I don't think Heine is a great poet. Leopardi, yes. He will stand beside Dante, as Italy's dark second. Always has. But not Heine . . . not even Goethe himself . . . . They are not great."

"Well, if you do not think Goethe is great, then obviously you can't accept a comparable position, like Leopardi's, for Heine. But Heine is great."

"He is so many thing," AP interjected. "Jew, Christian, atheist, German, wanderer — who better than he expresses the anguish of all of us? Surely he has the music of the best poetry flooding his heart. Think of *Der Tod*. Do you know it?"

"I know it," said Lalic, "with the melody of Brabms in my ears." And suddenly all three — AP, HP, and Lalic — began to sing it together, straight through to the end, while Hristic beamed. "Yes," said Lalic, "that is great."

"Brahms has given us the perfect literary reading," said HP, "but the music is already all there. All the agony of his sick bed is there."

"Like Leopardi," said Lalic. "I like Leopardi better."

HP recited verses of Leopardi in Italian — the lines from "Night Song of the Wandering Shepherd" — *poi di tanto adoprar . . .* — and Lalic gave the closing line of "L'infinito" — *m'è dolce naufragar in questo mare*. Hristic repeated the line in Italian and then in English. "'I feel so wonderful to drown, to be shipwrecked and die in this infinite sea.' I love that.'"

"But our poet of the *City of Dreadful Night* is better." HP persisted. "He knew Heine and Leopardi and Dante better than any of us. His translations are masterful. And his night of pessimism is complete, without compromise. He has sat with Matthew Arnold in the Grand Chartreuse beside the dead Christ, and he will not move until Christ is risen; and he knows, or thinks he knows, that Christ will never rise. And if Christ be not risen, then we are the most foolish of men and our teaching is most vain."

"He is not risen," said Hristic, beaming darkly, "and he will *never* rise!"

"And you rejoice in it," said HP with mock reproof. "But not our James Thomson. It is, for him, not *dolce*, like Leopardi's shipwreck, but *dreadful night*, night of the Melancolia that transcends all wit. The mighty winged woman of Albrecht Dürer. To rejoice, one must be able to sing finally with Bach's St. Matthew: *Er ist nicht hier; er ist auferstanden!* But Hristic simply repeated: "He is not risen. And he will never rise!"

With Lalic, we discussed how well some of the great composers read the German lyrics. Some seemingly inferior lyrics are seen to be musically great. Lalic thought that Schubert, who sometimes did very well, often showed poor taste in poetry, even for an entire song cycle. We noted that some of the great poets — Goethe, for instance — didn't much like music that matched the excellence of the poetry, competing with it as the focus of interest. That was his response to Beethoven's *Erlkönig*. Brahms was fine, said Lalic. Schumann perhaps the best. We talked of Mozart, and the manifest beauty of the lyrics once we have heard Mozart's musical reading of them. We sang together fragments of the 'statue's *Don Giovanni* aria, *Il catalogo*, *Batti, batti*, and — finally — *Così fan tutte*.

It was a memorable ending to our tour.

The next morning, after farewells with Martha and Edmund Bator, we boarded the plane for New York.